LIVY

BOOK VI

T0381584

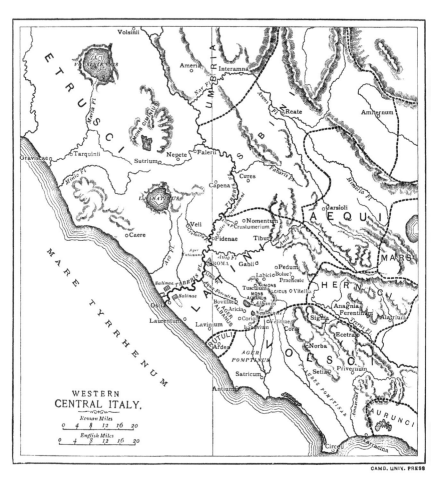

WESTERN
CENTRAL ITALY.

Roman Miles
0   4   8   12   16   20

English Miles
0   4   8   12   16   20

*available for download from www.cambridge.org/9781107659780

LIVY

BOOK VI

EDITED BY

F. H. MARSHALL, M.A.

CAMBRIDGE
AT THE UNIVERSITY PRESS
1934

CAMBRIDGE
UNIVERSITY PRESS

University Printing House, Cambridge CB2 8BS, United Kingdom

Published in the United States of America by Cambridge University Press, New York

Cambridge University Press is part of the University of Cambridge.

It furthers the University's mission by disseminating knowledge in the pursuit of education, learning and research at the highest international levels of excellence.

www.cambridge.org
Information on this title: www.cambridge.org/9781107659780

First edition 1903
Reprinted 1908, 1934
First published 1903
First paperback edition 2014

A catalogue record for this publication is available from the British Library

ISBN 978-1-107-65978-0 Paperback

PREFACE.

THE text of this edition of the Sixth Book of Livy is based upon that of Madvig and Ussing (2nd edition), and is printed from the stereotype plates of Mr Stephenson's book, previously published by the Cambridge University Press; to Mr Stephenson, therefore, the English abstracts in the text are due. Certain alterations have been made, chiefly in a conservative direction, several words bracketed by Madvig being retained. Points of interest with regard to the text are discussed in the Appendix.

I have not thought it necessary in a school edition to acknowledge all the sources from which I have derived assistance in preparing the introduction and notes. A few books, however, must be specially mentioned. I have freely consulted the editions of Weissenborn-Müller and Luter-bacher; for points of syntax I have found Riemann's *La Langue et la Grammaire de Tite-Live*, Dräger's *Historische Syntax*, and Roby's *Latin Grammar* of the greatest service; for questions relating to history and antiquities I have made considerable use of Schwegler's *Römische Geschichte* (as far as it treats the period covered by this book), Mommsen's

Roman History, Römische Forschungen, and *Römisches Staatsrecht,* as well as of the various dictionaries and manuals of Antiquities ; Pais's *Storia di Roma* has proved occasionally suggestive, but, as I have remarked elsewhere, must be used with the greatest caution. In writing the introduction I frequently consulted Weissenborn's introduction to his edition of Livy. Warde Fowler's *The Roman Festivals* and Greenidge's *Roman Public Life* should also be mentioned. I may add that it has been one of my chief aims to explain and illustrate with care points of historical and archæological interest connected with the book.

The maps are based on those given in Conway's edition of Book II., but considerable alterations have been made to suit the requirements of the present book.

Finally I have to express my warmest thanks to Mr P. Giles of Emmanuel College for his great kindness in reading through the whole of the introduction and notes in proof, and for contributing many valuable suggestions.

F. H. MARSHALL.

LONDON,
August, 1903.

CONTENTS.

		PAGE
MAP OF WESTERN CENTRAL ITALY	.	*To face title-page*
PREFACE		v
INTRODUCTION		
§ 1. *Life and work of Livy*		ix
§ 2. *Livy as historian*		xi
§ 3. *Livy as writer and stylist* . . .		xvi
§ 4. *The history of the period* . . .		xix
MAP OF ROME		*To follow* xxxiv
TEXT		1
NOTES		61
APPENDIX ON THE TEXT		155
EDITIONS AND EDITORS		161
INDEX I (ENGLISH)		164
INDEX II (LATIN)		167

INTRODUCTION.

§ 1. LIFE AND WORK OF LIVY.

VERY little definite information as to Livy's life has come down to us, and what we do know must be pieced together from various sources. Titus Livius (for he apparently had no *cognomen*) was born in 59 or 57 B.C. at Patavium, the modern Padua. The place was one of considerable importance at that time, and carried on an extensive trade with Rome. We are informed that Patavium was noted for the strict morality of its inhabitants, for the Younger Pliny (*Ep.* 1. 14), in writing of a lady named Serrana, says: *nosti loci mores; Serrana tamen Patavinis quoque severitatis exemplum est.* There can be little doubt that the immorality which prevailed at Rome appeared to Livy even darker than it was, when contrasted with the simplicity of manners which characterised his native town; and this may to some extent account for the high moral tone which pervades the history throughout. Livy seems to have kept almost entirely aloof from the stormy politics of the time in which he lived; he preferred, as he says in his Preface, to turn away his eyes from the miseries of the dying Republic and to fix them upon all that was good and great in the past history of the nation. His sympathies, however, were plainly with the aristocratic party and the senate. This we might have inferred from the whole of the extant portions of his work, in which he regards with disapproval all that savours of a revolutionary spirit; but we have also the express evidence of Tacitus to show that he openly praised the Pompeians (*Ann.* 4. 34): *Titus Livius, eloquentiae ac fidei praeclarus in primis, Cn. Pompeium*

*tantis laudibus tulit, ut Pompeianum eum Augustus appellaret;
neque id amicitiae eorum offecit.* He probably lived a large
part of his life in Rome (for there is much to show that he knew
the city well), busily engaged on his mighty work, but towards
the close returned to his native Patavium once more, where, as
Jerome tells us, he died in 17 A.D.

Livy's history extended from the earliest times down to the
death of Drusus, the younger son of the Empress Livia, which
took place in 9 B.C. There were no fewer than 142 books, 35 of
which have come down to us, the rest having been lost in the
Middle Ages. Summaries (Periochae) of the contents of the
books, drawn up about the fourth century, offer a very in-
adequate substitute for the lost parts of the work (cf. the
Periocha placed at the end of the text of this book). After the
death of Augustus in 14 A.D. it is only natural that Livy should
have desired to carry his history on to that date, in which case
the books would probably have reached the round number
of 150; but if this were his purpose, it was frustrated by death.

To determine the dates of the composition of the various
parts of the history the evidence of the books themselves must
be relied on. They were certainly published in sections, each
of which was probably distinguished by a certain unity of
subject. The opening words of the present book seem to
suggest that books I—V were published together, and that
book VI is the beginning of a fresh section of the work; it
must be borne in mind that the division into decads is arbitrary
and of comparatively late date. From various indications it
may be concluded that the first nine books were written between
27 and 20 B.C. Thus in I. 19. 3 Octavianus is called by his title
of Augustus, which was not conferred upon him till 27 B.C. In
the same passage reference is made to the closing of the temple
of Janus for the third time in Roman history. Now we know
that the temple of Janus was closed for the fourth time in 25 B.C.,
so the conclusion is that the first book was written between 27
and 25 B.C. In IX. 18, where Livy is discussing the chances
Rome would have had in a conflict with Alexander the Great,
he alludes incidentally to the rivalry between Rome and Parthia,
and talks of certain *levissimi ex Graecis, qui Parthorum quoque*

contra nomen Romanum gloriae favent. Is it likely that he
would have refrained from alluding to the restoration (in 20 B.C.)
of the standards captured by the Parthians at Carrhae, if he had
been writing at a time subsequent to that date? We are therefore justified in concluding that book VI was written between
27 and 20 B.C.

§ 2. LIVY AS HISTORIAN.

Before we pass to the consideration of some of the most
prominent characteristics of Livy as a historian, it will be well
to take a glance at the conception of historical writing which
prevailed in the Roman world at, or shortly after, the period
in which he lived. It was very different from that of our
day. We hear little or nothing about the sifting of sources,
the evidence of archaeology, or the scientific method of research, but much, on the contrary, about the relations of history
to rhetoric and poetry, and of the opportunities it affords for
the display of style. Take for example the words of Cicero
(*De leg.* I. 2. 5): *potes autem tu profecto satis facere in ea*
(sc. *historia*), *quippe cum sit opus, ut tibi quidem videri solet,
unum hoc oratorium maxime;* or again those of Quintilian
(10. 1. 31), which, it may be safely assumed, express an opinion
that had prevailed in Livy's day also: *historia quoque alere
oratorem quodam uberi iucundoque suco potest...est enim
proxima poetis et quodam modo carmen solutum.* Finally,
there is the evidence of Livy himself (Pref. § 2): *novi semper
scriptores aut in rebus certius aliquid allaturos se aut scribendi
arte rudem vetustatem superaturos credunt.* With this view of
the character of history, as the Romans conceived it, before us,
we are in a better position to appreciate some of the more
striking features of Livy's method of historical writing.

Livy's authorities and his use of them. In this book (c. 1)
something is said about the sources from which the historian of
early Rome could draw his information. Most characteristically
Livy remarks (§ 2) that the only faithful guardians of the memory
of past actions are literary documents, and that these for the
most part perished in the burning of Rome by the Gauls.

Observe that he regards as of little account for the historian
that vast source of information which has enabled us to learn
so much about even Assyria and Egypt, as well as of the early
history of Greece and Rome—the evidence of the monuments.
A thorough search must have revealed much that was valuable
even for the history of Rome before the burning of the city by the
Gauls, but Livy is content to say that practically everything of
value perished in that conflagration. Nor does he appear to have
made much use of archaeological evidence after 390 B.C.; laws
and treaties engraved on stone and bronze, inscriptions set up in
private houses, lists of magistrates, so invaluable for chronology,
all these are practically neglected. Even on those rare occasions
when Livy mentions an inscription or a monument in support
of his statements too much reliance must not be placed on his
accuracy. Thus there is grave reason to doubt the genuineness
of the inscription said to have been placed beneath the statue
dedicated by T. Quinctius Cincinnatus in the temple of Jupiter
on the Capitol (c. 29. 10). On the other hand we are enabled to
correct Livy by means of an *elogium* of Camillus, i.e. an inscription, no doubt set up by some member of the *gens Furia*,
on which were recorded that hero's principal exploits (*C. I. L.* 1.
p. 285). The inscription says. *Etruscis ad Sutrium devictis,
Aequis et Volscis subactis, tertium triumphavit* (this bears out the
account given by Livy in cc. 2—4 under the year 389 B.C.), and
then goes on: *quart(um) se(vere in) Velitern(os animadvertit).*
The last statement must refer to Camillus' 4th consular tribunate
in 386 B.C., but there is no mention of the series of victories
over Volscians, Latins, Hernicans, and Etruscans described by
Livy in cc. 6—10. This confirms what would on other grounds
be probable, viz. that Livy has simply related the same campaigns
twice over. Everything seems to show that Livy was not anxious
to investigate personally the ground of many of his statements;
even the *libri lintei* in the temple of Iuno Moneta (cf. 4. 7. 12)
do not appear to have been consulted by him at first hand.

We may next enquire what historians Livy consulted in
writing book VI. It is indeed impossible to be quite sure what
authority Livy is in the main following at any particular time;
he only mentions one by name, viz. Claudius (c. 42. 5). Q.

Claudius Quadrigarius began his history with the Gallic war of 390 B.C., so that it is very probable that Livy made pretty extensive use of his work for the period covered by the present book; but if he used Claudius as the main authority for the wars of these years, it is certain that he consulted other annalists from time to time, with the result that the same event is sometimes given twice over. In relating the events connected with the Licinio-Sextian rogations he would be sure to draw largely on Licinius Macer. Other authorities he may have used are Valerius Antias and Q. Aelius Tubero. Now all these annalists wrote some 300 years or more after the events which this book professes to describe, so that at best they were very unsatisfactory guides to follow. But besides this, there is good reason to believe that Valerius Antias (cf. 36. 38. 7) and Licinius Macer (cf. 7. 9. 5) were sometimes guilty of deliberate falsification. Of the earlier authorities, Q. Fabius Pictor (about the time of the 2nd Punic War), who wrote in Greek, and L. Calpurnius Piso (cons. 133 B.C.), Livy probably made but little use, and perhaps his references to them are taken from the later annalists. He did not therefore always use the best authorities available; let us now look at his methods of criticising those he did use.

There are one or two instances in the present book. In c. 12. 2 Livy is struck by the constant recurrence of the Volscian wars, and indeed he may well be so. He then hazards a series of conjectures in explanation, none of which can be considered very plausible. It never seems to occur to him that the same campaign may have got repeated again and again in slightly varied form, or that trivial border forays may have been magnified into great wars. In c. 20. 4 he remarks that he can find among the authorities no very definite acts of treason laid to the charge of Manlius. This surely might have aroused his suspicions as to the correctness of some of the details of the story. However, he lightly passes by the difficulty with the remark that there *were* doubtless good grounds for the condemnation. Similarly in c. 20. 12 he mentions that the authorities differ as to the form of trial which Manlius underwent, but he makes no effort to get at the exact truth. One more instance of Livy's want of critical faculty may be mentioned; in c. 42. 5

and 6 he says that the majority of the authorities are against Claudius with regard to the date of the battle fought with the Gauls on the river Anio, and he at once decides to follow the majority, without apparently taking quality into consideration. Yet even so he makes a mistake. After stating that the majority put the date of the battle at least ten years later, in VII. 9 and 10 he gives an account of the fight under the year 361 B.C., or only six years later than the date assigned by Claudius. Other instances of carelessness, particularly in respect of constitutional details, will be pointed out in the notes.

All this, however, merely indicates that Livy shared the views of his age with regard to history, and that he did not consider that deep and searching criticism was necessary. It is far more instructive to turn to the positive side, and to look at the merits which stand forth so conspicuously in Livy as a historian.

His candour. First and foremost comes his candour, his earnest desire to be fair. It is very important not to confound want of criticism with want of truth, for Livy, though constantly erring from a neglect of historical research, never, so far as we can judge, deliberately violates the truth. His example in this respect was rendered the more valuable by the fact that many of his predecessors in the field of history had been by no means equally scrupulous. The candour of Livy was, together with his eloquence, the quality which particularly impressed his Roman readers. Quintilian writes of him : *nec indignetur sibi Herodotus aequari Titum Livium, cum in narrando mirae iucunditatis* clarissimique candoris (this refers, probably, to both purity of style and straightforwardness of character), *tum in contionibus supra quam enarrari potest eloquentem* (10. 1. 101). In the judgment of the elder Seneca (*Suas.* 6. 22) he is *natura candidissimus omnium magnorum ingeniorum aestimator.* Tacitus (*Ann.* 4. 34) remarks that he is *eloquentiae ac* fidei *praeclarus in primis.* Some evidence in support of these judgments can be found in the present book. There is, for example, no mistaking the fact that Livy's sympathies are in the main with the patricians and against the plebeians ; yet this does not blind his eyes to the fact that the miseries of the plebs are real and that the patricians are overbearing and oppressive (cf.

c. 34. 1, where the *vis patrum* is spoken of, and c. 32. 3, an
exposure of patrician malpractices at the elections). Again, the
fairness of the writer, who thoroughly detests Manlius' conduct,
is shown unmistakably by the way in which he mentions the
points in his favour, viz. the absence of any positive act of
treason and the glorious array of noble deeds done in behalf of
his country. Even the passages cited above as showing Livy's
lack of criticism are sometimes evidence of his desire for truth ;
he wants to know *why* the Volscians never failed to raise an
army, he does not conceal the fact that accounts as to the trial of
Manlius differ, and that the battle with the Gauls cannot with
certainty be assigned to a particular date.

His moral earnestness. Livy's emphatic opinion is that the
chief purpose of history is a moral one. This he indicates with
great clearness in his preface (§ 10) : *hoc illud est praecipue in
cognitione rerum salubre ac frugiferum omnis te exempli docu-
menta in inlustri posita monumento intueri; inde tibi tuaeque
reipublicae quod imitere capias, inde foedum inceptu, foedum
exitu, quod vites.* Nor is it altogether certain that this view of
Livy as to the main function of history was a wrong one. It is
indeed not unfortunate for us that he had this aim before him,
the aim of drawing noble lessons from the noble lives of the
heroes of the Republic, rather than that of proving that a large
part of the so-called history of Rome was nothing but a
fabrication.

The present book is not wanting in instances of this moral
earnestness. In the downfall of Manlius he sees the downfall
of immoderate ambition, which blots out the memory of many
past services to the state : *illud notandum videtur, ut sciant
homines, quae et quanta decora foeda cupiditas regni non
ingrata solum, sed invisa etiam reddiderit.* Very striking is the
way in which he brings out the moral strength of the Roman
plebs, which prevents it breaking the law in order to rescue its
favourite Manlius after the dictator's judgment : *sed invicta sibi
quaedam patientissima iusti imperii civitas fecerat, nec adversus
dictatoriam vim aut tribuni plebis aut ipsa plebs attollere oculos
aut hiscere audebant.* Note too the way in which he dwells
lovingly upon the character of Rome's great heroes, how loath

he is to believe anything which would sully the fair fame of Camillus (c. 38. 10); he feels that all that is great in Rome has been built up by the stern virtues of her famous men.

His reverence for religion. Closely allied to Livy's moral earnestness is his reverence for the Roman religion. His Stoic belief in the power of fate does not shake his confidence in the influence of the gods; and this is no light thing, especially when it is remembered that he lived in an age when scepticism was the fashion. '*Credo rem Antiatem diuturniorem manere dis cordi fuisse*' he writes in c. 9. 3. His victorious general Cossus cries out to the troops with all the fervour of a Crusader '*veniat in mentem unicuique deos esse, qui Romanum adiuvent, deos, qui secundis avibus in proelium miserint.*' Throughout this book the part played by *religio* in early Roman history is strongly accentuated, and the speech of Appius (c. 41. 4 ff.) gives us some idea of the Roman reverence for the *auspicia* before the time when they were degraded to the position of political instruments by men who had long since abandoned all belief in the reality of the gods.

§ 3. LIVY AS WRITER AND STYLIST.

Just as Livy's life was passed under both the old and the new forms of government, the Republic and the Empire, so his language may be said to hover between two styles of Latinity. It occupies a middle position between the golden Latin of Cicero and Caesar and the silver Latin of Tacitus and the Younger Pliny. Livy's Latin does not indeed diverge to a very great extent from that of Cicero; but the lapse from the latter's high ideal of purity comes out every now and again in a certain freedom of construction which prose writers had not before permitted themselves, in the use of new words, in the adoption of poetical turns of expression, from all which it can be seen that Livy is leading the way to what is known as silver Latinity. As conspicuous examples of this tendency may be mentioned the use of *non dubito* with the acc. and inf., of the subjunctive to express frequency of action or occurrence, of *fretus* with the dative, and the giving of an adjectival meaning to adverbs, this last being, perhaps, an imitation of a Greek construction. Yet these small points and others like them detract but little from the conspicuous merits of Livy's language ; they cannot obscure its richness, its clearness, its variety, which avoids monotony even where the material is most unpromising, and its glowing beauty, whenever the subject is one calculated to arouse animation. Particular instances of construction or phrase peculiar to Livy are commented upon in the notes as they occur, but it may be useful to illustrate certain features of his style by examples brought together from book VI.

Richness and fulness. These qualities are alluded to by Quintilian (10. 1. 32) in the words '*illa Livi lactea ubertas*' and are contrasted with the *brevitas* of Sallust. The present book furnishes ample illustration of this feature of Livy's style, not merely in such phrases as *opere ac labore* (c. 1. 6), *luctum lacrimasque* (c. 3. 4), *neque nego neque infitias eo* (c. 40. 4), etc., but more particularly in passages of vivid narration, such as the entire story of Manlius or the picture of peaceful life at Tusculum (c. 25), where the historian gives full play to his great descriptive powers. Such fulness is at times apt to degenerate into tautology and verbosity, defects which ancient critics were not slow to note in Livy's style. Quintilian (8. 3. 53) speaks of the μακρολογία of Livy, and cites in illustration a passage which shows that words unnecessary to the sense should not always be expunged as glosses: *vitanda* μακρολογία, *id est longior quam oportet sermo ; ut apud T. Livium, Legati non impetrata pace retro domum, unde venerant, abierunt* (cf. in this book c. 6. 5 : *quod non prohibitos tantum modo voluntarios dicerent militare, ubi vellent*). These occasional defects served to give point to the sweeping criticism of the Emperor Caligula : *ut verbosum in historia negligentemque* (sc. *Livium*) *carpebat* (Suet. *Cal.* 34).

Leaning towards rhetoric. That Livy was interested in rhetoric we know from other sources besides the internal evidence of his history. Thus the elder Seneca records the following criticism : *Livius de oratoribus qui verba antiqua et sordida consectantur et orationis obscuritatem severitatem putant, aiebat, Miltiadem rhetorem eleganter dixisse* ἐπὶ τὸ λεξικὸν μαίνονται (*Controv.* IX. 25. 26). With this may be compared his advice to his son as quoted by Quintilian (10. 1. 39): *fuit igitur brevitas illa tutissima quae est apud Livium in epistola ad filium scripta, 'legendos Demosthenem atque Ciceronem, tum ita, ut quisque esset Demostheni et Ciceroni simillimus.'* Some indeed have thought that Livy was a professional teacher of rhetoric, and it has been mentioned above (§ 2) that his *eloquentia* was particularly noticed by Roman writers.

Book VI affords abundant instances of this special feature of Livy's style. Wherever an opportunity offers, he loves to insert a stirring speech. These speeches are sometimes of considerable length, such as those of Manlius (c. 18. 5 ff.) and App. Claudius (cc. 40. 41), but more often they are short, and spoken under the influence of strong emotion (cf. c. 6. 12, c. 7. 3, c. 12. 8 etc.). Very noticeable is the way in which Livy changes suddenly from the indirect to the direct (cf. c. 6. 12, c. 15. 9 etc.); he appears to feel himself under restraint so long as he uses the indirect, but finds relief by breaking out into the more rhetorical direct. Occasional exaggeration in the course of the narrative, such as c. 2. 13: *septuagesimo anno,* c. 33. 1: *consenuerant,* may be attributed to the oratorical instinct. Nevertheless, the history owes much of its charm to this characteristic, which enables Livy to avoid dulness and monotony, even when recounting an interminable succession of seemingly purposeless wars.

Poetical colouring. The introduction into prose of words and phrases of a poetical nature is characteristic of what is known as silver Latinity. Here Livy begins a practice afterwards carried to a greater pitch by Tacitus. It seems almost certain that Livy was acquainted with Virgil and that he had access to the *Aeneid* before its formal publication, so many are the examples of a striking similarity of phrase between the historian and the poet. The poetical colouring in Livy becomes most pronounced when he is thoroughly animated, as, for example, when he is describing some battle scene. A good instance occurs in c. 12. 8–10, where, in the course of a few lines, we find *obnixos...stabili gradu, micent gladii, haerere iam aciem collato pede,* and *terrorem equestrem*; but the whole passage has a poetical ring about it.

The following are some of the poetical words and phrases

which are found in the present book: c. 2. 11, *moles* = trouble, a sense which constantly recurs; cf. Verg. *Aen.* 1. 33, *tantae molis erat Romanam condere gentem*—c. 3. 1, *terror ingens* ingruerat—c. 7. 3, *obversus*—c. 10. 8, *adhaerentem lateri;* cf. Verg. *Aen.* 4. 73, *haeret lateri letalis harundo*—c. 23. 5, *rapere* = *raptim capere*—c. 24. 5, *subiectus in equum;* cf. Verg. *Aen.* 12. 288—c. 24. 10, *summo certamine animi;* cf. Verg. *Aen.* 5. 197, *certamine summo*—c. 30. 5, *caedunt caedunturque;* cf. Verg. *Aen.* 10. 756—c. 39. 7, *dictatorium fulmen;* cf. Verg. *Aen.* 6. 842. These instances will suffice to show that Livy would probably have agreed with Quintilian in thinking that history was 'very closely allied to poetry, and was a kind of poem untrammelled by metre.'

These remarks on Livy's style may be closed with the mention of a well-known criticism of C. Asinius Pollio, an older contemporary of Livy. It is quoted by Quintilian (1. 5. 56: cf. also 8. 1. 3): *Pollio reprehendit in Livio Patavinitatem.* There has been much discussion as to what this *Patavinitas* really was, but from what has been said above it may be gathered that Livy departed in many ways from the strict standard of Latin prose to which Pollio was accustomed. His introduction of new words and his occasionally poetical diction probably offended so fastidious a critic, and it is possible that some of the peculiarities of Livy's style had their origin in his provincial up-bringing, though we, of course, cannot detect this in the way that Pollio could.

§ 4. THE HISTORY OF THE PERIOD.

(*a*) *Its general characteristics.* The period of history embraced in book VI lies, according to Livy's chronology, between the years 389 and 367 B.C. It falls naturally into two main sections, viz. the foreign relations and the inner history of the city. These two divisions will be treated separately and in greater detail later on; an attempt will be made here to indicate the importance of this period, viewed in its relation to the general course of Roman history.

The invasion of the Gauls took place just at the time when

Rome seemed to be emerging successfully from her life-and-death struggle with the surrounding peoples, the Etruscans on the North, the Aequi on the East, and the Volscians on the South. The burning of the city was a grievous, but by no means a crushing blow, and one of the great features of interest in this book is the triumphant way in which Rome rises again from what seemed at first to be her ruin. At last she succeeds in securing herself thoroughly against her two most formidable neighbours, the Etruscans and the Volscians. Now too comes the first decided break with the Latins and the Hernicans, who make common cause with the Volscians, and thus are foreshadowed the supremacy of Rome over her former allies and the dissolution of the Latin League (338 B.C.). A turning point in the history of the city has been reached; henceforward the Romans will carry their arms against new foes, beginning with the Italians, until finally they become masters of the world. Herein then lies the key to the interest of the wars recorded in this book. Regard them as an interminable series of struggles, leading to no tangible result, and they seem dull and monotonous; but once take a broader view, and see in them the first step towards Rome's great conquests, and they will appear in a very different light. We can now see clearly that these wars, the fruits of which were secured from time to time by the foundation of colonies, were the prelude to that peace near at home, without which she could never have gained supremacy over the rest of Italy, and afterwards over the world.

In a similar way substantial progress marks the internal history also. There are two great causes of discontent among the plebeians, viz. economic distress and political inequality. While the former is brought into most vivid relief by the story of Manlius, the latter is strongly emphasized by the struggles leading to the laws of Licinius and Sextius. It is true that the measures introduced for the relief of the small landowner are unsatisfactory, and calculated to give a temporary respite only, not to effect a cure. All through the history of the Republic the same economic difficulties are constantly arising, and in the end contribute largely to its downfall. On the other hand the battle for political equality is fought once for all and won by the plebeians. With the close of this book an old order of things has passed away. The noble clans have been compelled to surrender their exclusive claim to the chief magistracy, with the result that the Roman state is henceforward really one, no longer twofold. The new nobility which arises is drawn equally from patrician and plebeian ranks, and consists of men who have by personal merit won for themselves the highest office in the state.

(*b*) *External relations.* It is not necessary to show at any great length that the details of the wars recorded in this book are quite untrustworthy[1]. One or two pieces of evidence will suffice. In c. 3 we find an account of a brilliant victory gained by Camillus over the Etruscans in 389 B.C.; three years later (c. 10) a no less brilliant victory is won by the same Camillus at the same place. Now it was seen above (p. x) that the silence of the 'elogium' of Camillus as to this second campaign confirms our otherwise very reasonable suspicions as to its ever having taken place at all. The series of victories over the Volscians is not less open to doubt. We are told in c. 2. 13 that Camillus brought the Volscians to surrender after a seventy years' war; yet three years after (c. 8) they are again in arms and afford Camillus another triumph. Once more in c. 24 M. Furius Camillus, in spite of the rashness of his colleague L. Furius, completely routs the Volscians for the third time. These victories cannot be regarded as historically trustworthy. It may be that some member of the *gens Furia* deliberately inserted victories into the annals for the further glorification of the heroic M. Furius; it may be, as Prof. Pais suggests, that there has been much confusion between the exploits of M. Furius and those of his son L. Furius; or again, Livy may have repeated the same events inadvertently in the course of consulting several annalists. Yet though the details are un-

---

[1] A minute analysis of the history comprised in book VI will be found in Prof. Ettore Pais's *Storia d' Italia dai tempi più antichi sino alle guerre puniche*, vol. I. pt 2, ch. 6; the conclusions arrived at, however, are of a very sceptical character and should be received with much caution.

trustworthy, a clear view of the progress of the Roman arms abroad can be obtained from these chapters. These external relations of the city may be discussed under three heads, as they concern respectively (1) the Etruscans, (2) the Volscians, and (3) the Latins and Hernicans.

(1) **The Etruscans.** By the capture of Veii (V. 21) the immediate danger which threatened Rome from the North was removed, but though the district bordering on the N. bank of the Tiber was now in Roman possession, there was always a way open to their Etruscan enemies, so long as the Ciminian Forest, the natural boundary between Northern and Southern Etruria, remained unsecured. The tightening of the grip of Rome upon Southern Etruria is recorded in the present book. The terrible Gallic disaster had naturally inspired those Etruscans who had been conquered with the hope of recovering their independence. But their effort was crushed (c. 3), and the permanent character of the Roman success is clearly indicated by the establishment of four new tribes in the conquered territory, one of these being located in the district surrounding the *Lacus Sabatinus* and the others, in all probability, in the neighbourhood of Veii and Falerii (c. 4. 4 and c. 5. 8). But the work of settlement could not be regarded as complete till the two towns of Sutrium and Nepete, 'the gates of Etruria,' which commanded the passes between the North and the South, were occupied by Latin colonies. The alliance with these towns had proved unsatisfactory (cc. 3, 9, and 10), and we are not surprised to find Livy recording the foundation of a colony at Nepete in 383 B.C. (c. 21. 4), while Velleius Paterculus (I. 14), though not agreeing with Livy as to dates, mentions the foundation of another colony at Sutrium about this time. These steps may be regarded as indicating the complete reduction of S. Etruria, a task in which the Romans were no doubt considerably assisted by the pressure which was being put upon the Etruscan seaports by Dionysius I., the tyrant of Syracuse, who during this period sacked the temple of Pyrgi, the arsenal of Caere (Diod. 15. 14).

(2) **The Volscians.** In spite of the confused nature of the accounts of the Volscian wars given by Livy, it may yet be clearly discerned that the Romans were making substantial

progress towards the final conquest of these foes. The Volscian territory extended S. of Latium along the coast up to the river Liris, while on the E. it was bounded by the mountainous country of the Hernicans and Marsians. The most reliable evidence of Rome's progress is to be sought in the foundation of Latin colonies, which are pushed forward into the heart of the Volscian territory. Fighting goes on between the Romans and the Volscians almost uninterruptedly for thirteen years (389—377 B.C.), and in spite of the aid given to the Volscians by several of the Latin colonies the balance of success lies with the Romans. Here again the details of the wonderful victories gained by Camillus may be set aside ; we must be content to see in Livy's account a picture of the general course of the war. In 385 B.C. Satricum, which commanded the coast district near Antium, was colonised (c. 16. 6) and notwithstanding the conflagration recorded in c. 33, it seems to have remained a Latin stronghold. In 379 B.C. (c. 30. 9) the Romans are found strengthening their position at Setia, a fortress protecting the Pomptine district, while the surrender of Antium two years later marks an important step in advance (c. 33). Henceforward the Volscians never appear really dangerous, and Rome passes on beyond their borders to engage a new enemy, the Samnites.

(3) **The Latins and the Hernicans.** The league renewed between the Romans and the Latins in 493 B.C. and that concluded between the former and the Hernicans in 486 B.C. were based ostensibly upon a condition of equality between the contracting parties. But as time went on the control of foreign relations (such a statement as that in 8. 2. 13 notwithstanding) and the chief military command probably fell into the hands of the Romans exclusively ; and though the Latins were granted a share in the colonies founded by the League in conquered territory, they could not fail to see that they obtained no adequate return for the assistance granted to Rome against her enemies. The first open expression on the part of the Latins of a discontent which must long have existed secretly, occurs in this book of Livy. The chief cause of this spirit of revolt was undoubtedly the belief that Rome had become seriously weakened by the Gallic invasion and could now be defied with impunity.

A second cause (or possibly result) of disaffection was the closing
of the Latin League about 385 B.C.[1] Henceforward new colonies
did not become members of the Latin League ; in other words
they were bound directly to Rome and had no relations with
the other Latin cities. Satricum (c. 16. 6) seems to have been
the last colony admitted to the full rights of the League. Rome
was henceforth determined to concentrate all power directly in
her own hands.

The city had only just freed herself from the Gallic invasion,
when the attitude of the Latins and Hernicans began to occasion
serious alarm (c. 2. 3). The curious story (see Plut. *Cam.* 33) of
the demand made by the Latins that the Roman maidens should
be given to them in marriage and of its frustration by the wit of
the serving girl Philotis (or Tutela), though of course quite unhistorical, is yet an indication of the existence of a general belief
that the allies took advantage of Rome's hour of weakness. It
is true that at first the ruling bodies in the Latin cities did not
venture to proceed to overt acts of hostility, but the spirit of
discontent revealed by the help given to the Antiates by Latin
volunteers (c. 6. 4) was bound sooner or later to force the
governments into open warfare. In 383 B.C. the Latin city of
Lanuvium rose in rebellion, and the colonies of Circeii and
Velitrae joined in bearing arms against Rome (c. 21. 2). The
example set by these places was followed by Praeneste (c. 22),
which was not subdued until after it had occasioned considerable
alarm in Rome (cc. 28, 29). The attitude of Tusculum also was
so unsatisfactory that the Romans thought it advisable to compel
its citizens to receive the *civitas sine suffragio* (see c. 26. 8 n.), thus
depriving the town of the right to exercise any independence in
external affairs. Though these sporadic attempts at rebellion
on the part of the Latins were overpowered without great
difficulty, it was evident that the existing state of things could
not last much longer. Either Rome or Latium must be supreme,
and there was little doubt as to which side would gain the
victory in the approaching struggle.

[1] This closing of the Latin League is inferred from the absence of
colonies, known to be founded after this date, from the list of federal
cities given by Dionysius (v. 61).

(c) Internal History.

(1) **Rome after the retreat of the Gauls.** The misery at Rome after the retreat of the Gauls must have been terrible. It is hardly surprising that the sight of the city lying in ruins should have led to the proposal to emigrate to Veii.   The situation at this moment is graphically described by Plutarch (*Cam.* 31) : δεομένων (sc. τῶν πολλῶν) μὴ σφᾶς ὥσπερ ἐκ ναυαγίου γυμνοὺς καὶ ἀπόρους σωθέντας προσβιάζεσθαι τὰ λείψανα τῆς διεφθαρμένης συμπηγνύναι πόλεως, ἑτέρας ἑτοίμης παρούσης.   Livy seems purposely to avoid dwelling upon the utter desolation which prevailed everywhere, and delights rather to describe the speed and energy with which the Romans rebuilt their city, and the reverence for the gods which was their first care (c. 1. 9).   But the effects of the devastation must have been felt for many years after, and indeed they can be traced in the internal history of Rome throughout the sixth book.

Although the Gallic invasion must have affected all classes, it fell with peculiar severity upon the poor.   Their farms no doubt had been burnt to the ground, their lands ravaged, their flocks and herds driven off, and all their agricultural implements destroyed.   And now they were called upon to give their services in rebuilding the city and to contribute to the expenses of such public works as the facing of the Capitol with hewn stone (c. 4. 6) and the erection of a city wall (c. 32. 1, 2).   Absolute ruin was before them, unless they could borrow money for the repair and restocking of their homesteads ; but this was a desperate remedy and one calculated to intensify the economic troubles, which to a greater or less degree had always been present at Rome since the establishment of the Republic.

(2) **The question of the ager publicus.** It was the custom of the Romans to deprive their vanquished enemies of a large portion of their territory.   Of the land thus won the part suitable for agriculture ought, according to the recognized system, to have been divided among the citizens in small allotments ; the less fertile districts, especially the uplands, were retained in ownership by the state and let out for the grazing of cattle at a fee (*scriptura*) proportioned to the number of animals

sent out to pasture. Now had this system been carried out strictly, the result should have been fairly satisfactory ; but the temptation to turn their monopoly of government to their own advantage proved too strong for the patricians. A tacit agreement seems to have been arrived at between them and the richer plebeians, whereby as little arable land as possible was distributed in allotments. The state in theory retained the ownership (*dominium*), but the rich were allowed to settle on (*occupare*) the land and to draw large revenues from it by means of their command of capital and, consequently, of labour. A small percentage of the profits was due to the state by way of rent, but even this payment was frequently evaded. The rich also monopolised the pasture lands with their flocks and their herds, with the result that the small landowner, who stood in greatest need of help, found himself thrust out at every point.

This position of affairs enables us to understand the reasons for the agrarian agitations which meet us constantly in this book and which culminate in the great Licinio-Sextian rogations. We find that the tribunes first tried to rouse the people to put forward a demand for the distribution of the *ager Pomptinus*, the district lying to the S. of the Alban Mount, which, after being rescued from the hands of the Volscians, had evidently been taken in occupation by rich patricians. At first the prospect of lands without any adequate means of stocking them caused but little enthusiasm among the plebeians ; but as the all-important task of rebuilding Rome grew lighter, they supported the proposal with greater readiness (c. 5. 1 ff. and c. 6. 1). In 385 B.C. the Senate attempted to assuage the popular discontent by a grant of land at Satricum in this district, but the meagre character of the distribution defeated the object with a view to which it was made (c. 16. 6, 7). Two years later there was another attempt to win over the plebeians by the division of the whole of the *ager Pomptinus* into allotments (c. 21. 4) ; the colonies of Sutrium, Nepete, and Setia, though doubtless planted primarily for military purposes, may also have served as a temporary check to the prevailing discontent. But it was a change in the entire system which was required, and an effort, ultimately unsuccessful it is true, was made in this direction by the legislation of Licinius and Sextius. Their measures will be discussed further on; meanwhile another great cause of plebeian agitation must be touched on.

(3) **The question of debt.** This was, as we have seen, very closely bound up with the agrarian question. The man who owned but little land and had but a small amount of capital was exposed to constant risk. A single bad harvest or the raid of an enemy might leave him helpless; he might at any time be summoned to join the army, and in his absence his property would suffer for want of attention. The only resource of the ruined farmer was to borrow money from the richer citizens, whether patrician or plebeian. But the law of debt in ancient society was of extreme severity. Thus Athens at the time of Solon had passed through a crisis owing to the cruel use made by creditors of their advantage over debtors; cf. Plut. *Solon* 13: χρέα λαμβάνοντες ἐπὶ τοῖς σώμασιν, ἀγώγιμοι τοῖς δανείζουσιν ἦσαν, οἱ μὲν αὐτοῦ δουλεύοντες, οἱ δὲ ἐπὶ τῇ ξένῃ πιπρασκόμενοι. So too at Rome the person of the debtor was at this time regarded as the ultimate security for the debt, with the result that, if the loan were not repaid by a fixed date and if the debtor's property did not cover its value, the creditor could seize him and make him work off the debt by personal labour. At Athens the power of the creditor over the debtor's person was abolished by the Solonian legislation; at Rome it was considerably restricted by the Poetilian law of 326 B.C., but was not finally abolished till the time of Julius Caesar. Another hardship was the exorbitant rate of interest charged. In this connection may be quoted a passage from Tac. *Ann.* 6. 16: *sane vetus urbi fenebre malum et seditionum discordiarumque creberrima causa, eoque cohibebatur antiquis quoque et minus corruptis moribus. nam primum duodecim tabulis sanctum, ne quis unciario fenore amplius exerceret, cum antea ex libidine locupletium agitaretur; dein rogatione tribunicia ad semuncias redactum, postremo vetita versura.* The limit placed on usury by the law of the Twelve Tables (probably 10 per cent. on the year of 12 months) had no doubt been disregarded in the confusion following the Gallic invasion, and thus the relations between debtor and creditor, at all times liable to give rise to a critical situation,

speedily brought on a sharp conflict. Money had to be borrowed to meet the expenses of rebuilding and restocking, and the succession of wars with the surrounding peoples not only brought an additional burden in the form of an increased war tax, but also prevented the proper working of the farms; cf. c. 11. 9 : *et erat aeris alieni magna vis re damnosissima etiam divitibus, aedificando, contracta.* The miseries of this time are vividly illustrated by Livy, as his wont is, by the picture of the centurion handed over by judicial sentence to the mercy of his creditor, after all attempts to stem the overwhelming tide of usury had been made in vain ; they are further impressed upon us by the whole story of Manlius, which entirely hinges upon the harsh operation of the law of debt. The delay in the appointment of censors (cc. 27, 31) increased the confusion which prevailed with regard to property, and led to the utter demoralisation described in c. 34. If we cannot consider the details given by Livy as trustworthy, there is no doubt that he has succeeded in what was evidently his main purpose—in impressing upon his readers the reality of the economic distress prevalent in Rome after the burning of the city.

(4) **The story of M. Manlius.** Ἅμα δὲ τούτοις πραττομένοις κατὰ τὴν Ἰταλίαν ἐν τῇ Ῥώμῃ Μάρκος Μάνλιος ἐπιβαλόμενος τυραννίδι καὶ κρατηθεὶς ἀνῃρέθη. Such is the brief sentence with which Diodorus (15. 35. 3) dismisses the episode of M. Manlius, out of which Livy has made so brilliant a story. As we read the latter's account, teeming as it does with incident, we cannot help wondering how much or how little can be regarded as based on solid fact. Prof. Mommsen (*Röm. Forsch.* 2, pp. 179 ff.) has examined the whole story of Manlius at length, and what is in the main an outline of the conclusions he has arrived at may here be given.

First and foremost a large part of the account has arisen from a desire to connect the seditious M. Manlius of this story with the legendary saviour of the Capitol. Hence the details of the trial, at which the memories aroused by the sight of the Capitol play so important a part, may be put aside as fabulous. The *cognomen* Capitolinus was evidently due to the fact that Manlius lived upon the Capitol, and had nothing whatever to do with the saving of the citadel, for we find that the name Capitolinus was borne by the Sestii and Quinctii, other families who also had their dwelling upon the Capitol. But the false interpretation of the *cognomen* gave a splendid opportunity for dilating upon the military exploits of the hero, and this is done in the minutest detail in Livy's account (c. 20. 7 ff.). Again, Manlius is represented as the bitter opponent of the successful aristocratic general M. Furius Camillus. It is obvious that the story gains much in picturesqueness by the contrast between the fortunes of the two preservers of Rome from the Gauls, one of whom is loaded with honours by the government, while the other is driven by neglect into the arms of the plebeians. It is probably due to this striving after effect that Manlius' story is made to extend over two years (385 and 384 B.C.), in order that his end may be placed in a year when Camillus is consular tribune. Prof. Pais (*op. cit.* vol. I, pt. 2, pp. 98 ff.) thinks that the later quarrels between the *gentes* of the Furii and Manlii are anticipated in the present rivalry between Camillus and Manlius. There are great discrepancies between the various accounts of the trial and death of Manlius. Livy himself admits that two versions were current (c. 20. 12). That which represents the trial as having taken place before *duumviri perduellionis* would seem to be the more ancient ; but can we be sure that there was any trial at all? Dio Cassius (in Zonaras 7. 24) gives a curiously mixed account. He says that Manlius attempted to seize the Capitol, but was captured by treachery. Thus far he is more or less in agreement with Diodorus ; but he subsequently adds the formal trial and execution after the manner of Livy. This confusion on the part of the authorities rather inclines one to the belief that the simple sentence of Diodorus is most likely to contain the truth, and that out of the rising of a Manlius in the interest of the debtors and out of his violent death the Livian story has arisen through family traditions and the ingenuity of annalists.

What value then has the story of Manlius for us? It impresses upon our minds a fact of the greatest importance for the proper understanding of the inner history of Rome, viz.

the terrible inequality existing between the rich and the poor, and the misery brought about by the systematic borrowing to which the poor were driven. Manlius is the champion of the poor farmer, who finds it impossible to make a living in the face of innumerable difficulties, and who is in the end at the mercy of the large landowner. Prof. Mommsen thinks that the picture of Manlius, the debtors' champion, is borrowed from the disturbances which arose in consequence of the prevalence of debt after the Social War ; that his death is the counterpart of that of the praetor Asellio, who in 89 B.C. was murdered by enraged creditors for administering the law in favour of debtors. Prof. Pais, on the other hand, thinks that the material for Livy's description has been drawn from the agitations of the 3rd century B.C. But after all the essential part of the story may well be true for the period following the Gallic invasion, when distress must have been widespread and the harsh character of the law of debt must have been felt more keenly than ever. This is the fact that is brought before us in Livy's brilliant narrative, which may be considered to have a value very similar to that of the numerous speeches inserted by the historian, the chief function of which is to represent more or less accurately the feelings produced by a particular situation. We can well believe that at this period a patrician came forward, at first as the genuine champion of the wrongs of the plebeians ; that the temptation to turn the existing discontent to his own advantage proved too strong for him, and that in the end he perished in an attempt to establish a tyranny.

(5) **The Laws of Licinius and Sextius.** Some of the criticisms which have been brought against the account of the great internal conflicts, as narrated at the end of book VI, may first be considered. As in the case of the details of the various wars and of the story of Manlius, so here also most of the incidents which serve merely to enliven the narrative may be put aside as unhistorical. The tale of the sisters Fabiae makes an excellent introduction to the events which follow, but bears upon the face of it the stamp of a late and untrustworthy origin. The discrepancies between the different accounts relating to

the intermission of the curule magistracies confirm the suspicions which are naturally aroused by the intrinsic improbability of such a state of affairs, at least for any considerable time. Livy (c. 35. 10) makes the *solitudo magistratuum* last for five years; Dio Cassius (*ap.* Zon. 7. 24) puts it down as of four years' duration; while, according to Diodorus (15. 75), it was only for one year. Here again Diodorus' account would seem much the most reasonable. With the traditional part assigned to Camillus in these struggles Livy himself is not altogether satisfied (c. 38. 9), and a certain amount of scepticism as to the prominent position given to that hero does not necessarily shake our faith in the essential parts of the narrative. The various speeches of Licinius and Sextius and that of App. Claudius Crassus are clearly to be received in the spirit in which they are given to us, that is to say, they are not intended for accurate reports of speeches actually made, but are designed to illustrate the feelings which animated the respective parties in the struggle.

But not merely the comparatively unimportant details have met with criticism. The actual legislation attributed to Licinius and Sextius has been called in question[1]. It will be well first to give their proposals as we find them in Livy (c. 35). They were (*a*) *de aere alieno* : that the interest already paid should be deducted from the original debt, and that the remainder should be paid off in three instalments. This simply amounted to the abolition of interest on loans. (*b*) *de modo agrorum* : that no person should occupy more than 500 *iugera* of the *ager publicus.* (*c*) That the election of consular tribunes should cease, and that one at least of the two consuls should be a plebeian. Another proposal was added subsequently, viz. (*d*) that the keepers of the Sibylline Books should in future be ten instead of two in number, and that of these half should be patricians, half plebeians (c. 37. 12). The most serious criticism has been directed against the law which imposed a limit upon the occupation of the *ager publicus.* The well-known land law of Tib. Gracchus (133 B.C.) was identical in

---

[1] See Niese in *Hermes* XXIII. pp. 410 ff., and Pais *op. cit.* pp. 138 ff.

character with this one, and Appian (*Bellum Civile* I. 7) says that the law of Gracchus was the revival of an earlier one, which according to Plutarch (*Tib. Gracch.* 8) only remained in force for a short time. It is contended that this law referred to by Appian must be the one attributed to Licinius and Sextius, but nevertheless cannot possibly have been passed as far back as 367 B.C.; in all probability it should be dated at about 180 B.C. Another argument is that the Licinian law clearly supposes that a considerable number of persons occupied more than 500 *iugera* each; such a supposition would be utterly irreconcilable with the extent of Roman territory at the earlier date, and points to a time when Rome was practically mistress of the whole of Italy. If once the genuineness of the agrarian law is made doubtful, the other laws must inevitably be viewed with considerable suspicion. Prof. Pais thinks that the consulship may have been opened to the plebs about 367 B.C., but that the provision for the relief of debtors and the admission of plebeians to share the custody of the Sibylline Books are both to be referred to a considerably later date.

Though it cannot be denied that there is no slight weight in the above arguments, it may yet be fairly maintained that they only point to an exaggeration of the provisions of the agrarian law of 367 B.C. and do not entirely invalidate it. We have seen above (p. xxiii.) that there must have been widespread distress after the Gallic invasion and that there were repeated agitations to secure the distribution of land; cf. c. 5. 4: *nobiles homines in possessionem agri publici grassari, nec, nisi, antequam omnia praecipiant, divisus sit, locum ibi plebi fore.* We have seen too (§ 4 b) that Rome, in the years covered by the narrative of this book, gained substantial additions to her territory. It may therefore have very well been that a law was passed to restrict the amount of land that could be occupied by any individual, not indeed to 500 *iugera*—the number may easily have been altered under the influence of the later law— but to a degree which better accords with the extent of the Roman territory at this time[1]. It is to be noted that Livy

[1] Perhaps the maximum was 100 *iugera*, the amount given by the writer of the *de viris inlustribus*, 20.

makes no mention of a provision for the compulsory employment of a certain percentage of free labourers ; that was a
measure called for by later economic conditions only. But
such a clause would almost certainly have been inserted by
him among the Licinio-Sextian laws, had they been simply
transferred from the 2nd century B.C. to the 4th. With regard
to the first law it is intrinsically probable that some measure
was passed at this time for the relief of the suffering debtors,
and the proposal to remit interest on loans was not an extravagant one in view of the special hardships prevailing. The
throwing open of the consulship to the plebeians about this
period may be regarded as certain ; for this we have the
authority of Fabius Pictor (*ap.* Aul. Gell. 5. 4) : *qua propter
tum primum ex plebe alter consul factus est, duo et vicesimo
anno postquam Romam Galli ceperunt.* The stipulation that
one consul must be a plebeian was, however, not infrequently
disregarded on subsequent occasions. There is no adequate
reason for discrediting the statement that the college for the
custody of the Sibylline Books was now made accessible to
plebeian candidates. It was connected with the cult of Apollo,
and, though of great importance for the development of the
Roman religion, would be considered less exclusively patrician
than those colleges of priests which were concerned with deities
of a peculiarly Roman character.

Some estimate of the importance of the Licinio-Sextian laws
may now be made. As has been often pointed out, they
indicate a combination of the richer and poorer plebeians for
the purpose of wringing from the patricians advantages which
could only be gained by a united effort. Many plebeians were
well enough off materially, and no doubt exercised their advantage over debtors to the full as cruelly as any of the
patricians did. But the consular tribunate did not give them
the outward distinctions, such as the *ius imaginum,* which
were the object of their ambition, and was, moreover, very
hard to win in the face of patrician intrigue ; cf. c. 32. 3, and
c. 34. 3 : *adeo ergo obnoxios summiserant animos, non infimi
solum, sed principes etiam plebis, ut non modo ad tribunatum
militum inter patricios petendum... sed ne ad plebeios quidem*

magistratus capessendos ullo viro acri experientique animus esset. This wealthy class of plebeians is represented by Licinius and Sextius themselves, and the story of the condemnation of Licinius for the contravention of his own land law is perfectly true, if it is regarded as a revelation of their real aims and interests (7. 16. 9). So too Livy represents the poorer plebeians as wishing to carry through the laws relating to debt and the occupation of the *ager publicus* without the one concerning the consulship (c. 39. 2) ; they had no practical interest in the high offices of state. But this combination of all ranks among the plebeians proved of great advantage to Rome, for on the one hand political unity was assured by the creation of a new nobility drawn from both patricians and plebeians, while on the other a temporary relief at least was gained for the poorer farmers. The breaking down of patrician monopoly in the control of religion was begun by the opening of a sacred college to plebeians, an event of even more importance in its promise for the future than in the immediate advantage derived. Livy has given us in his graphic account of the Licinio-Sextian laws and the strife connected with them an epitome of the inner life of Rome at this time, and though what he has written may not be perfectly trustworthy in its details, it is yet in a broad sense truly historical.

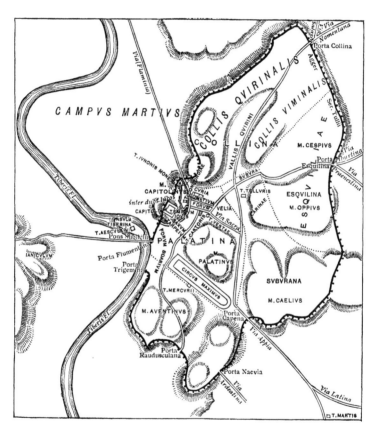

EARLY REPUBLICAN ROME

TITI LIVII

AB URBE CONDITA

LIBER VI.

B.C. 390. *Short preface in which Livy points out that with the rebuild-* 1 *ing of the city the records become more trustworthy.* *Q. Fabius is impeached for a violation of the* ius *gentium (cf.* v. 35, 36).

QUAE ab condita urbe Roma ad captam eandem urbem
5 Romani sub regibus primum, consulibus deinde ac dictatoribus decemvirisque ac tribunis consularibus gessere, foris
bella, domi seditiones, quinque libris exposui, res cum 2
vetustate nimia obscuras, velut quae magno ex intervallo
loci vix cernuntur, tum quod parvae et rarae per eadem
10 tempora litterae fuere, una custodia fidelis memoriae rerum
gestarum, et quod, etiamsi quae in commentariis pontificum
aliisque publicis privatisque erant monumentis, incensa urbe
pleraeque interiere. clariora deinceps certioraque ab se- 3
cunda origine velut ab stirpibus laetius feraciusque renatae
15 urbis gesta domi militiaeque exponentur. ceterum primo, 4
quo adminiculo erecta erat, eodem innixa, M. Furio
principe, stetit, neque eum abdicare se dictatura nisi anno
circumacto passi sunt. comitia in insequentem annum 5
tribunos habere, quorum in magistratu capta urbs esset,

6 non placuit; res ad interregnum rediit. cum civitas in
opere ac labore assiduo reficiendae urbis teneretur, interim
Q. Fabio, simul primum magistratu abiit, ab Cn. Marcio
tribuno plebis dicta dies est, quod legatus in Gallos, ad
7 quos missus erat orator, contra ius gentium pugnasset; cui 5
iudicio eum mors adeo opportuna, ut voluntariam magna
pars crederet, subtraxit.

B.C. 389. *After one* interregnum, *Camillus as* interrex *procures the
election of military tribunes, six in number. Surviving documents
are collected and certain days, marked by disaster, are included among* 10
dies nefasti. *The Volscians and Etruscans take advantage of the
condition of Rome to begin war. The Latins and Hernicans also
threaten to rebel. Camillus named dictator divides the army raised
into three divisions. He himself takes the field against the Volscians
and Aequians, and defeats both.* 15

8 Interregnum initum; P. Cornelius Scipio interrex, et
post eum M. Furius Camillus. is tribunos militum consulari potestate creat L. Valerium Publicolam iterum, L.
Verginium, P. Cornelium, A. Manlium, L. Aemilium, L.
Postumium. 20

9 Hi ex interregno cum extemplo magistratum inissent,
nulla de re prius quam de religionibus senatum consuluere.
10 in primis foedera ac leges (erant autem eae duodecim
tabulae et quaedam regiae leges) conquiri, quae compa-
rerent, iusserunt; alia ex eis edita etiam in vulgus; quae 25
autem ad sacra pertinebant, a pontificibus maxime, ut
religione obstrictos haberent multitudinis animos, sup-
11 pressa. tum de diebus religiosis agitari coeptum, diemque
a. d. xv Kal. Sextiles, duplici clade insignem, quo die ad
Cremeram Fabii caesi, quo deinde ad Aliam cum exitio 30
urbis foede pugnatum, a posteriore clade Aliensem appel-
larunt, insignemque rei nulli publice privatimque agendae

fecerunt. quidam, quod postridie idus Quintiles non 12
litasset Sulpicius tribunus militum, neque inventa pace
deum post diem tertium obiectus hosti exercitus Romanus
esset, etiam postridie idus rebus divinis supersederi iussum,
5 inde, ut postridie calendas quoque ac nonas eadem religio
esset, traditum putant.

Nec diu licuit quietis consilia erigendae ex tam gravi 2
casu rei publicae secum agitare. hinc Volsci, veteres 2
hostes, ad exstinguendum nomen Romanum arma cepe-
10 rant; hinc Etruriae principum ex omnibus populis coni-
urationem de bello ad fanum Voltumnae factam mercatores
afferebant. novus quoque terror accesserat defectionis 3
Latinorum Hernicorumque, qui post pugnam ad lacum
Regillum factam per annos prope centum nunquam ambigua
15 fide in amicitia populi Romani fuerant. itaque cum tanti 4
undique terrores circumstarent appareretque omnibus, non
odio solum apud hostes, sed contemptu etiam inter socios
nomen Romanum laborare, placuit, eiusdem auspiciis 5
defendi rem publicam, cuius recuperata esset, dictatoremque
20 dici M. Furium Camillum. is dictator C. Servilium Ahalam 6
magistrum equitum dixit; iustitioque indicto dilectum
iuniorum habuit, ita ut seniores quoque, quibus aliquid
roboris superesset, in verba sua iuratos centuriaret. exer- 7
citum conscriptum armatumque trifariam divisit. partem
25 unam in agro Veiente Etruriae opposuit, alteram ante
urbem castra locare iussit; tribuni militum his A. Manlius, 8
illis, qui adversus Etruscos mittebantur, L. Aemilius prae-
positus. tertiam partem ipse ad Volscos duxit, nec procul
a Lanuvio (ad Mecium is locus dicitur) castra oppugnare
30 est adortus. quibus ab contemptu, quod prope omnem 9
deletam a Gallis Romanam iuventutem crederent, ad
bellum profectis tantum Camillus auditus imperator terroris
intulerat, ut vallo se ipsi, vallum congestis arboribus

saepirent, ne qua intrare ad munimenta hostis posset.
10 quod ubi animadvertit Camillus, ignem in obiectam saepem
coniici iussit; et forte erat vis magna venti versa in hostem;
11 itaque non aperuit solum incendio viam, sed, flammis in
castra tendentibus, vapore etiam ac fumo crepituque viridis 5
materiae flagrantis ita consternavit hostes, ut minor moles
superantibus vallum militibus munitum in castra Volscorum
Romanis fuerit, quam transcendentibus saepem incendio
12 absumptam fuerat. fusis hostibus caesisque cum castra
impetu cepisset dictator, praedam militi dedit, quo minus 10
13 speratam minime largitore duce, eo militi gratiorem. per-
secutus deinde fugientes, cum omnem Volscum agrum
depopulatus esset, ad deditionem Volscos septuagesimo
14 demum anno subegit. victor ex Volscis in Aequos
transiit, et ipsos bellum molientes; exercitum eorum ad 15
Bolas oppressit, nec castra modo, sed urbem etiam aggressus impetu primo cepit.

3 *Sutrium is besieged by the Etruscans and forced to surrender. But on
the very day of its capture Camillus appears on the scene and recovers
it.*
20

Cum in ea parte, in qua caput rei Romanae Camil'us
erat, ea fortuna esset, aliam in partem terror ingens
2 ingruerat. Etruria prope omnis armata Sutrium, socios
populi Romani, obsidebat; quorum legati, opem rebus
affectis orantes, cum senatum adissent, decretum tulere, ut 25
dictator primo quoque tempore auxilium Sutrinis ferret.
3 cuius spei moram cum pati fortuna obsessorum non
potuisset, confectaque paucitas oppidanorum opere, vigiliis,
vulneribus, quae semper eosdem urgebant, per pactionem
urbe hostibus tradita, inermis cum singulis emissa vesti- 30
4 mentis miserabili agmine penates relinqueret, eo forte
tempore Camillus cum exercitu Romano intervenit. cui

cum se maesta turba ad pedes provolvisset, principumque
orationem necessitate ultima expressam fletus mulierum ac
puerorum, qui exsilii comites trahebantur, excepisset, parcere
lamentis Sutrinos iussit : Etruscis se luctum lacrimasque
5 ferre. sarcinas inde deponi Sutrinosque ibi considere 5
modico praesidio relicto, arma secum militem ferre iubet.
ita expedito exercitu profectus ad Sutrium, id quod rebatur,
soluta omnia rebus, ut fit, secundis invenit, nullam stationem
ante moenia, patentes portas, victorem vagum praedam ex
10 hostium tectis egerentem. iterum igitur eodem die Sutrium 6
capitur ; victores Etrusci passim trucidantur ab novo hoste,
neque se conglobandi coeundique in unum aut arma
capiundi datur spatium. cum pro se quisque tenderent ad 7
portas, si qua forte se in agros eiicere possent, clausas (id
15 enim primum dictator imperaverat) portas inveniunt. inde 8
alii arma capere, alii, quos forte armatos tumultus occu-
paverat, convocare suos, ut proelium inirent ; quod accensum ab desperatione hostium fuisset, ni praecones per
urbem dimissi poni arma et parci inermi iussissent nec
20 praeter armatos quemquam violari. tum etiam quibus 9
animi in spe ultima obstinati ad decertandum fuerant,
postquam data spes vitae est, iactare passim arma iner-
mesque, quod tutius fortuna fecerat, se hosti offerre.
magna multitudo in custodias divisa; oppidum ante noctem 10
25 redditum Sutrinis inviolatum integrumque ab omni clade
belli, quia non vi captum, sed traditum per condiciones
fuerat.

Camillus celebrates a triumph. The remainder of his spoils, after repay- 4
ing the matrons (cf. v. 50), *is dedicated in the form of three golden*
30 *paterae to Jupiter of the Capitol. Such Veientines, Capenatians, and*
Faliscans as had assisted Rome receive citizenship and land. The
emigrants are recalled from Veii.

Camillus in urbem triumphans rediit, trium simul bel-
2 lorum victor. longe plurimos captivos ex Etruscis ante
currum duxit, quibus sub hasta venundatis tantum aeris
redactum est, ut, pretio pro auro matronis persoluto, ex eo,
3 quod supererat, tres paterae aureae factae sint, quas cum 5
titulo nominis Camilli ante Capitolium incensum in Iovis
cella constat ante pedes Iunonis positas fuisse.
4   Eo anno in civitatem accepti, qui Veientium Cape-
natiumque ac Faliscorum per ea bella transfugerant ad
5 Romanos, agerque his novis civibus assignatus. revocati 10
quoque in urbem senatus consulto a Veiis, qui aedificandi
Romae pigritia, occupatis ibi vacuis tectis, Veios se contulerant. et primo fremitus fuit aspernantium imperium ;
dies deinde praestituta capitalisque poena, qui non remi-
grasset Romam, ex ferocibus universis singulos, metu suo 15
6 quemque, obedientes fecit ; et Roma cum frequentia
crescere, tum tota simul exsurgere aedificiis, et re publica
impensas adiuvante et aedilibus velut publicum exigentibus
opus et ipsis privatis (admonebat enim desiderium usus)
festinantibus ad effectum operis ; intraque annum nova urbs 20
stetit.

B.C. 388. *Military tribunes are elected, six in number. One army is
occupied in ravaging the lands of the Aequians. A second enters
Etruria, where the towns Cortuosa and Contenebra are taken. The
Capitol is strengthened with a massive stone substruction. The* 25
*tribunes agitate for the distribution of the Pomptine land, but without
success.*

7   Exitu anni comitia tribunorum militum consulari potestate habita. creati T. Quinctius Cincinnatus, Q. Servilius
Fidenas quintum, L. Iulius Iulus, L. Aquilius Corvus, L. 30
8 Lucretius Tricipitinus, Ser. Sulpicius Rufus exercitum alterum in Aequos, non ad bellum (victos namque se fateban-

tur), sed ab odio ad pervastandos fines, ne quid ad nova
consilia relinquerent virium, duxere, alterum in agrum
Tarquiniensem. ibi oppida Etruscorum Cortuosa et Con- 9
tenebra vi capta. ad Cortuosam nihil certaminis fuit:
5 improviso adorti primo clamore atque impetu cepere;
direptum oppidum atque incensum est. Contenebra paucos 10
dies oppugnationem sustinuit, laborque continuus, non die,
non nocte remissus, subegit eos. cum in sex partes divisus
exercitus Romanus senis horis in orbem succederet proelio,
10 oppidanos eosdem integro semper certamini paucitas fessos
obiiceret, cessere tandem, locusque invadendi urbem Romanis datus est. publicari praedam tribunis placebat; sed 11
imperium quam consilium segnius fuit; dum cunctantur,
iam militum praeda erat nec nisi per invidiam adimi po-
15 terat.

Eodem anno, ne privatis tantum operibus cresceret urbs, 12
Capitolium quoque saxo quadrato substructum est, opus vel
in hac magnificentia urbis conspiciendum. iam et tribuni 5
plebis, civitate aedificando occupata, contiones suas frequen-
20 tare legibus agrariis conabantur. ostentabatur in spem 2
Pomptinus ager, tum primum post accisas a Camillo
Volscorum res possessionis haud ambiguae. criminaban- 3
tur, multo eum infestiorem agrum ab nobilitate esse, quam
a Volscis fuerit; ab illis enim tantum, quoad vires et arma
25 habuerint, incursiones eo factas; nobiles homines in pos- 4
sessionem agri publici grassari, nec, nisi, antequam omnia
praecipiant, divisus sit, locum ibi plebi fore. haud magno 5
opere plebem moverunt, et infrequentem in foro propter
aedificandi curam et eodem exhaustam impensis, eoque agri
30 immemorem, ad quem instruendum vires non essent.

B.C. 387. *After more than one* interregnum *military tribunes are elected,
six in number. Four new tribes are formed. Renewed agitation
about the Pomptine land.*

6   In civitate plena religionum, tunc etiam ab recenti
clade superstitiosis principibus, ut renovarentur auspicia,
res ad interregnum rediit. interreges deinceps M. Manlius
Capitolinus, Ser. Sulpicius Camerinus, L. Valerius Potitus;
7 hic demum tribunorum militum consulari potestate comitia 5
habuit. L. Papirium, *C. Cornelium*, C. Sergium, L. Aemilium iterum, L. Menenium, L. Valerium Publicolam tertium
8 creat; ii ex interregno magistratum occepere. eo anno
aedes Martis Gallico bello vota dedicata est a T. Quinctio
duumviro sacris faciendis. tribus quattuor ex novis civibus 10
additae, Stellatina, Tromentina, Sabatina, Arniensis; eaeque
6 viginti quinque tribuum numerum explevere. de agro Pomptino ab L. Sicinio tribuno plebis actum ad frequentiorem
iam populum mobilioremque ad cupiditatem agri, quam
2 fuerat. et de Latino Hernicoque bello mentio facta in 15
senatu maioris belli cura, quod Etruria in armis erat, dilata
est.

B.C. 386. *Camillus military tribune, with five colleagues. News
arrives that Antium assisted by the Latins is in arms against
Rome. Camillus at the desire of his colleagues takes general 20
command of all the forces, which he divides into three divisions,
one to act against Antium, the second to watch the Etruscans, Latins,
and Hernicans, the third to guard Rome.*

3   Res ad Camillum tribunum militum consulari potestate
rediit; collegae additi quinque, Ser. Cornelius Maluginensis, 25
Q. Servilius Fidenas sextum, L. Quinctius Cincinnatus, L.
4 Horatius Pulvillus, P. Valerius. principio anni aversae
curae hominum sunt a bello Etrusco, quod fugientium ex
agro Pomptino agmen repente illatum in urbem attulit;
Antiates in armis esse Latinorumque populos iuventutem 30
5 suam misisse ad id bellum, eo abnuentes publicum fuisse
consilium, quod non prohibitos tantummodo voluntarios

dicerent militare, ubi vellent. desierant iam ulla contemni 6
bella. itaque senatus dis agere gratias, quod Camillus in
magistratu esset: dictatorem quippe dicendum eum fuisse,
si privatus esset; et collegae fateri, regimen omnium rerum,
5 ubi quid bellici terroris ingruat, in viro uno esse, sibique 7
destinatum in animo esse Camillo summittere imperium,
nec quicquam de maiestate sua detractum credere, quod
maiestati eius viri concessissent. collaudatis ab senatu
tribunis et ipse Camillus, confusus animo, gratias egit.
10 ingens inde ait onus a populo Romano sibi, qui se [dicta- 8
torem] iam quartum creasset, magnum a senatu talibus de
se iudiciis eius ordinis, maximum tam honorato collegarum
obsequio iniungi. itaque si quid laboris vigiliarumque 9
adiici possit, certantem secum ipsum annisurum, ut tanto
15 de se consensu civitatis opinionem, quae maxima sit, etiam
constantem efficiat. quod ad bellum atque Antiates atti- 10
neat, plus ibi minarum quam periculi esse; se tamen, ut
nihil timendi, sic nihil contemnendi auctorem esse. cir- 11
cumsederi urbem Romanam ab invidia et odio finitimorum;
20 itaque et ducibus pluribus et exercitibus administrandam
rem publicam esse. "te" inquit, "L. Valeri, socium 12
imperii consiliique legiones mecum adversus Antiatem
hostem ducere placet; te, Q. Servili, altero exercitu in- 13
structo paratoque ad urbem castra habere, intentum, sive
25 Etruria se interim, ut nuper, sive nova haec cura, Latini
atque Hernici moverint; pro certo habeo, ita rem gesturum,
ut patre, avo teque ipso ac sex tribunatibus dignum est.
tertius exercitus ex causariis senioribusque a L. Quinctio 14
scribatur, qui urbi moenibusque praesidio sit. L. Horatius
30 arma, tela, frumentum, quaeque alia belli tempora poscent,
provideat. te, Ser. Corneli, praesidem huius publici consilii, 15
custodem religionum, comitiorum, legum, rerum omnium
urbanarum, collegae facimus." cunctis in partem muneris 16

sui benigne pollicentibus operam, Valerius, socius imperii
lectus, adiecit, M. Furium sibi pro dictatore seque ei pro
17 magistro equitum futurum; proinde, quam opinionem de
unico imperatore, eam spem de bello haberent. se vero
bene sperare patres et de bello et de pace universaque re 5
18 publica erecti gaudio fremunt, nec dictatore unquam opus
fore rei publicae, si tales viros in magistratu habeat, tam
concordibus iunctos animis, parere atque imperare iuxta
paratos laudemque conferentes potius in medium quam ex
communi ad se trahentes.   10

7 *Camillus and Valerius set out for Satricum where a large force of*
Volscians, Latins, and Hernicans is collected. The soldiers being
disheartened by news of the overwhelming force of the enemy,
Camillus addresses them.

Iustitio indicto dilectuque habito, Furius ac Valerius ad 15
Satricum profecti, quo non Volscorum modo iuventutem
Antiates ex nova subole lectam, sed ingentem Latinorum
Hernicorumque *vim* conciverant ex integerrimis diutina
pace populis. itaque novus hostis veteri adiunctus com-
2 movit animos militis Romani. quod ubi aciem iam in- 20
struenti Camillo centuriones renuntiaverunt, turbatas militum mentes esse, segniter arma capta, cunctabundosque et
restitantes egressos castris esse, quin voces quoque auditas,
cum centenis hostibus singulos pugnaturos, et aegre iner-
mem tantam multitudinem, nedum armatam, sustineri posse, 25
3 in equum insilit et ante signa, obversus in aciem, ordines
interequitans: "quae tristitia, milites, haec, quae insolita
cunctatio est? hostem an me an vos ignoratis? hostis est
quid aliud quam perpetua materia virtutis gloriaeque ves-
4 trae? vos contra me duce, ut Falerios Veiosque captos et 30
in capta patria Gallorum legiones caesas taceam, modo
trigeminae victoriae triplicem triumphum ex his ipsis Volscis

et Aequis et ex Etruria egistis. an me, quod non dictator 5
vobis, sed tribunus signum dedi, non agnoscitis ducem?
neque ego maxima imperia in vos desidero, et vos in me
nihil praeter me ipsum intueri decet; neque enim dictatura
5 mihi unquam animos fecit, ut ne exsilium quidem ademit.
iidem igitur omnes sumus, et cum eadem omnia in hoc 6
bellum afferamus, quae in priora attulimus, eundem eventum belli exspectemus. simul concurreritis, quod quisque
didicit ac consuevit, faciet: vos vincetis, illi fugient."

10 *An engagement follows in which Camillus wins a decisive victory. The* 8
Latins and Hernicans return to their homes. The Volscians retire
into Satricum, but Camillus storms the city.

Dato deinde signo ex equo desilit et proximum signiferum
manu arreptum secum in hostem rapit, "infer, miles" cla-
15 mitans, "signum." quod ubi videre ipsum Camillum, iam 2
ad munera corporis senecta invalidum, vadentem in hostes,
procurrunt pariter omnes clamore sublato, "sequere imperatorem" pro se quisque clamantes. emissum etiam signum 3
Camilli iussu in hostium aciem ferunt, idque ut repeteretur,
20 concitatos antesignanos; ibi primum pulsum Antiatem, 4
terroremque non in primam tantum aciem, sed etiam ad
subsidiarios perlatum. nec vis tantum militum movebat, 5
excitata praesentia ducis, sed quod Volscorum animis nihil
terribilius erat quam ipsius Camilli forte oblata species; ita, 6
25 quocunque se intulisset, victoriam secum haud dubiam
trahebat. maxime id evidens fuit, cum in laevum cornu
prope iam pulsum arrepto repente equo cum scuto pedestri
advectus conspectu suo proelium restituit, ostentans vincen-
tem ceteram aciem. iam inclinata res erat, sed turba 7
30 hostium et fugam impediebat, et longa caede conficienda
multitudo tanta fesso militi erat, cum repente ingentibus
procellis fusus imber certam magis victoriam quam proelium

8 diremit. signo deinde receptui dato, nox insecuta quietis
Romanis perfecit bellum. Latini namque et Hernici relictis
Volscis domos profecti sunt, malis consiliis pares adepti
9 eventus; Volsci ubi se desertos ab eis videre, quorum
fiducia rebellaverant, relictis castris moenibus Satrici se 5
includunt. quos primo Camillus vallo circumdare et aggere
10 atque operibus oppugnare est adortus. quae postquam
nulla eruptione impediri videt, minus esse animi ratus in
hoste, quam ut in eo tam lentae spei victoriam exspectaret,
cohortatus milites, "ne tanquam Veios oppugnantes in opere 10
longinquo sese tererent: victoriam in manibus esse," ingenti
militum alacritate moenia undique aggressus scalis oppidum
cepit. Volsci abiectis armis sese dediderunt.

9 *Camillus returns to Rome to urge the Senate to provide means for the*
destruction of Antium. While he is speaking, ambassadors from 15
Nepĕte arrive imploring assistance. Camillus and Valerius proceed
to Sutrium, recapture the portion of it captured by the Etruscans,
and disperse the enemy. They then march to Nepĕte which is entirely
in the hands of the Etruscans.

Ceterum animus ducis rei maiori, Antio, imminebat: id 20
2 caput Volscorum, eam fuisse originem proximi belli. sed
quia nisi magno apparatu, tormentis machinisque, tam
valida urbs capi non poterat, relicto ad exercitum collega,
Romam est profectus, ut senatum ad excidendum Antium
3 hortaretur. inter sermonem eius (credo rem Antiatem 25
diuturniorem manere dis cordi fuisse) legati ab Nepete
ac Sutrio auxilium adversus Etruscos petentes veniunt,
brevem occasionem esse ferendi auxilii memorantes. eo
4 vim Camilli ab Antio fortuna avertit. namque cum ea
loca opposita Etruriae et velut claustra inde portaeque 30
essent, et illis occupandi ea, cum quid novi molirentur,
5 et Romanis recuperandi tuendique cura erat. igitur senatui

cum Camillo agi placuit, ut omisso Antio bellum Etruscum susciperet; legiones urbanae, quibus Quinctius praefuerat, ei decernuntur. quanquam expertum exercitum assue- 6 tumque imperio, qui in Volscis erat, mallet, nihil recusavit; 5 Valerium tantummodo imperii socium depoposcit. Quinctius Horatiusque successores Valerio in Volscos missi.

Profecti ab urbe Sutrium Furius et Valerius partem 7 oppidi iam captam ab Etruscis invenere, ex parte altera, intersaeptis itineribus, aegre oppidanos vim hostium ab se 10 arcentes. cum Romani auxilii adventus, tum Camilli nomen 8 celeberrimum apud hostes sociosque et in praesentia rem inclinatam sustinuit et spatium ad opem ferendam dedit. itaque diviso exercitu Camillus collegam, in eam partem 9 circumductis copiis, quam hostes tenebant, moenia aggredi 15 iubet, non tanta spe, scalis capi urbem posse, quam ut, aversis eo hostibus, et oppidanis iam pugnando fessis laxaretur labor et ipse spatium intrandi sine certamine moenia haberet. quod cum simul utrinque factum esset 10 ancepsque terror Etruscos circumstaret, et moenia summa 20 vi oppugnari et intra moenia esse hostem viderent, porta se, quae una forte non obsidebatur, trepidi uno agmine eiecere. magna caedes fugientium et in urbe et per agros est facta; 11 plures a Furianis intra moenia caesi; Valeriani expeditiores ad persequendos fuere nec ante noctem, quae conspectum 25 ademit, finem caedendi fecere. Sutrio recepto restitutoque 12 sociis, Nepete exercitus ductus, quod per deditionem acceptum iam totum Etrusci habebant.

In answer to a summons to surrender the city, the citizens declare their 10
inability to do so; thereupon the Romans first try to frighten them
30 *into surrender, and, failing in this, take the city by storm. The*
citizens who have been guilty of betraying the city to the Etruscans,
and all the Etruscans, are put to death. The Latins and Hernicans

in reply to a demand to account for their late conduct disclaim connexion with their citizens, who served with the Volscians, and explain that fear of the Volscians has been their only reason for not supplying their contingent of soldiers.

Videbatur plus in ea urbe recipienda laboris fore, non eo 5 solum, quod tota hostium erat, sed etiam quod parte Nepe-
2 sinorum prodente civitatem facta erat deditio; mitti tamen ad principes eorum placuit, ut secernerent se ab Etruscis fidemque, quam implorassent ab Romanis, ipsi praestarent.
3 unde cum responsum allatum esset, nihil suae potestatis 10 esse, Etruscos moenia custodiasque portarum tenere, primo
4 populationibus agri terror est oppidanis admotus; deinde, postquam deditionis quam societatis fides sanctior erat, fascibus sarmentorum ex agro collatis, ductus ad moenia exercitus, completisque fossis scalae admotae, et clamore 15
5 primo impetuque oppidum capitur. Nepesinis inde edictum, ut arma ponant, parcique iussum inermi; Etrusci pariter armati atque inermes caesi. Nepesinorum quoque auctores deditionis securi percussi; innoxiae multitudini redditae
6 res, oppidumque cum praesidio relictum. ita duabus 20 sociis urbibus ex hoste receptis, victorem exercitum tribuni cum magna gloria Romam reduxerunt.

Eodem anno ab Latinis Hernicisque res repetitae quaesitumque, cur per eos annos militem ex instituto non
7 dedissent. responsum frequenti utriusque gentis concilio 25 est, nec culpam in eo publicam nec consilium fuisse, quod
8 suae iuventutis aliqui apud Volscos militaverint; eos tamen ipsos pravi consilii poenam habere, nec quemquam ex iis reducem esse; militis autem non dati causam terrorem assiduum a Volscis fuisse, quam pestem adhaerentem lateri 30
9 suo tot super alia aliis bellis exhauriri nequisse. Quae relata patribus magis tempus quam causam non visa belli habere.

Insequenti anno, A. Manlio, P. Cornelio, T. et L.
5 Quinctiis Capitolinis, L. Papirio Cursore iterum, *C. Sergio
iterum* tribunis consulari potestate, grave bellum foris,
gravior domi seditio exorta, bellum a Volscis, adiuncta 2
Latinorum atque Hernicorum defectione, seditio, unde
minime timeri potuit, a patriciae gentis viro et inclitae
10 famae, M. Manlio Capitolino. qui nimius animi cum alios 3
principes sperneret, uni invideret eximio simul honoribus
atque virtutibus, M. Furio, aegre ferebat, solum eum in
magistratibus, solum apud exercitus esse: tantum iam
eminere, ut iisdem auspiciis creatos non pro collegis, sed 4
15 pro ministris habeat, cum interim, si quis vere aestimare
velit, a M. Furio recuperari patria ex obsidione hostium non
potuerit, nisi a se prius Capitolium atque arx servata esset,
et ille inter aurum accipiendum et in spem pacis solutis 5
animis Gallos aggressus sit, ipse armatos capientesque
20 arcem depulerit, illius gloriae pars virilis apud omnes
milites sit, qui simul vicerint, suae victoriae neminem
omnium mortalium socium esse. his opinionibus inflato 6
animo, ad hoc vitio quoque ingenii vehemens et impotens,
postquam inter patres non, quantum aequum censebat,
25 excellere suas opes animadvertit, primus omnium ex 7
patribus popularis factus cum plebeiis magistratibus consilia
communicare; criminando patres, alliciendo ad se plebem,
iam aura, non consilio ferri famaeque magnae malle quam
bonae esse. et non contentus agrariis legibus, quae materia 8
30 semper tribunis plebi seditionum fuisset, fidem moliri
coepit: acriores quippe aeris alieni stimulos esse, qui non
egestatem modo atque ignominiam minentur, sed nervo ac
vinclis corpus liberum territent. et erat aeris alieni magna 9

vis re damnosissima etiam divitibus, aedificando, contracta.
bellum itaque Volscum, grave per se, oneratum Latinorum
atque Hernicorum defectione, in speciem causae iactatum,
10 ut maior potestas quaereretur; sed nova consilia Manlii
magis compulere senatum ad dictatorem creandum. creatus 5
A. Cornelius Cossus magistrum equitum dixit T. Quinctium
Capitolinum.

12 *The dictator postponing the home contest marches into the Pomptine terri-*
tory to meet the Volscians. The question how the Volscians procured
the vast number of men required for their wars discussed. The 10
address of Cossus to his soldiers before the battle.

Dictator etsi maiorem dimicationem propositam domi
quam foris cernebat, tamen, seu quia celeritate ad bellum
opus erat, seu victoria triumphoque dictaturae ipsi vires se
additurum ratus, dilectu habito in agrum Pomptinum, quo 15
2 a Volscis exercitum inductum audierat, pergit. non dubito,
praeter satietatem, tot iam libris assidua bella cum Volscis
gesta legentibus illud quoque succursurum, quod mihi per-
censenti propiores temporibus harum rerum auctores mira-
culo fuit, unde toties victis Volscis et Aequis suffecerint 20
3 milites. quod cum ab antiquis tacitum praetermissum sit,
cuius tandem ego rei praeter opinionem, quae sua cuique
4 coniectanti esse potest, auctor sim? simile veri est, aut
intervallis bellorum, sicut nunc in dilectibus fit Romanis,
alia atque alia subole iuniorum ad bella instauranda toties 25
usos esse, aut non ex iisdem semper populis exercitus
scriptos, quanquam eadem semper gens bellum intulerit,
5 aut innumerabilem multitudinem liberorum capitum in eis
fuisse locis, quae nunc, vix seminario exiguo militum relicto,
6 servitia Romana ab solitudine vindicant. ingens certe, 30
quod inter omnes auctores conveniat, quanquam nuper
Camilli ductu atque auspicio accisae res erant, Volscorum

exercitus fuit; ad hoc Latini Hernicique accesserant et
Circeiensium quidam et coloni etiam a Velitris Romani.
Dictator, castris eo die positis, postero quum auspicato 7
prodisset hostiaque caesa pacem deum adorasset, laetus ad
5 milites iam arma ad propositum pugnae signum, sicut
edictum erat, luce prima capientes processit. "nostra 8
victoria est, milites" inquit, "si quid di vatesque eorum in
futurum vident. itaque, ut decet certae spei plenos et cum
imparibus manus conserturos, pilis ante pedes positis,
10 gladiis tantum dextras armemus. ne procurri quidem ab
acie velim, sed obnixos vos stabili gradu impetum hostium
excipere. ubi illi vana iniecerint missilia et effusi stantibus 9
vobis se intulerint, tum micent gladii, et veniat in mentem
unicuique, deos esse, qui Romanum adiuvent, deos, qui
15 secundis avibus in proelium miserint. tu, T. Quincti, 10
equitem intentus ad primum initium moti certaminis tene;
at ubi haerere iam aciem collato pede videris, tum terrorem
equestrem occupatis alio pavore infer, invectusque ordines
pugnantium dissipa." sic eques, sic pedes, ut praeceperat, 11
20 pugnant; nec dux legiones nec fortuna fefellit ducem.

The enemy trusting in their numbers are easily defeated. The pursuit 13
lasts till nightfall. A very large number of prisoners are taken and
vast spoil. From the number of Latin and Hernican prisoners
taken, and the social position of some of them, it is clearly proved
25 *that those two peoples have publicly assisted the enemy.*

Multitudo hostium, nulli rei praeterquam numero freta et
oculis utramque metiens aciem, temere proelium iniit,
temere omisit; clamore tantum missilibusque telis et primo 2
pugnae impetu ferox, gladios et collatum pedem et vultum
30 hostis ardore animi micantem ferre non potuit. impulsa 3
frons prima et trepidatio subsidiis illata; et suum terrorem
intulit eques; rupti inde multis locis ordines motaque

omnia, et fluctuanti similis acies erat. dein postquam
cadentibus primis iam ad se quisque perventuram caedem
4 cernebat, terga vertunt. instare Romanus; et donec armati
confertique abibant, peditum labor in persequendo fuit;
postquam iactari arma passim fugaque per agros spargi 5
aciem hostium animadversum est, tum equitum turmae
emissae, dato signo, ne in singulorum morando caede
5 spatium ad evadendum interim multitudini darent: satis
esse missilibus ac terrore impediri cursum obequitandoque
agmen teneri, dum assequi pedes et iusta caede conficere 10
6 hostem posset. fugae sequendique non ante noctem finis
fuit. capta quoque ac direpta eodem die castra Volscorum,
praedaque omnis praeter libera corpora militi concessa est.
7 pars maxima captivorum ex Latinis atque Hernicis fuit, nec
hominum de plebe, ut credi posset mercede militasse, sed 15
principes quidam iuventutis inventi, manifesta fides, publica
8 ope Volscos hostes adiutos. Circeiensium quoque quidam
cogniti et coloni a Velitris; Romamque omnes missi
percontantibus primoribus patrum eadem, quae dictatori,
defectionem sui quisque populi, haud perplexe indicavere. 20

14 *Continued agitations at Rome. Manlius releases a centurion, condemned
to servitude for debt. Violent emotion of the people roused by the centurion's account of his services and sufferings. Manlius sells his estate
for the benefit of the people. He attacks the patricians accusing them
of appropriating the gold recovered from the Gauls.* 25

Dictator exercitum in stativis tenebat, minime dubius,
bellum cum iis populis patres iussuros, cum maior domi
exorta moles coegit acciri Romam eum, gliscente in dies
seditione, quam solito magis metuendam auctor faciebat.
2 non enim iam orationes modo M. Manlii, sed facta popularia 30
in speciem, tumultuosa eadem, qua mente fierent, intuenti
3 erant. centurionem, nobilem militaribus factis, iudicatum

pecuniae cum duci vidisset, medio foro cum caterva sua
accurrit et manum iniecit, vociferatusque de superbia patrum
ac crudelitate feneratorum et miseriis plebis, virtutibus eius
viri fortunaque, "tum vero ego" inquit "nequicquam hac 4
5 dextra Capitolium arcemque servaverim, si civem com-
militonemque meum, tanquam Gallis victoribus captum, in
servitutem ac vincla duci videam." inde rem creditori 5
palam populo solvit, libraque et aere liberatum emittit, deos
atque homines obtestantem, ut M. Manlio, liberatori suo,
10 parenti plebis Romanae, gratiam referant. acceptus ex- 6
templo in tumultuosam turbam et ipse tumultum augebat,
cicatrices acceptas Veienti, Gallico aliisque deinceps bellis
ostentans : se militantem, se restituentem eversos penates, 7
multiplici iam sorte exsoluta, mergentibus semper sortem
15 usuris, obrutum fenore esse ; videre lucem, forum, civium
ora M. Manlii opera ; omnia parentium beneficia ab illo se 8
habere ; illi devovere corporis vitaeque ac sanguinis quod
supersit ; quodcunque sibi cum patria, penatibus publicis ac
privatis iuris fuerit, id cum uno homine esse. his vocibus 9
20 instincta plebes cum iam unius hominis esset, addita alia
commodioris ad omnia turbanda consilii res. fundum in 10
Veienti, caput patrimonii, subiecit praeconi, "ne quem
vestrum" inquit, "Quirites, donec quicquam in re mea
supererit, iudicatum addictumve duci patiar." id vero ita
25 accendit animos, ut per omne fas ac nefas secuturi vindicem
libertatis viderentur. ad hoc domi, contionantis in modum, 11
sermones pleni criminum in patres ; inter quos, [cum]
omisso discrimine, vera an vana iaceret, thesauros Gallici
auri occultari a patribus iecit, nec iam possidendis publicis
30 agris contentos esse, nisi pecuniam quoque publicam avertant ; ea res si palam fiat, exsolvi plebem aere alieno posse.
quae ubi obiecta spes est, enimvero indignum facinus videri, 12
cum conferendum ad redimendam civitatem a Gallis aurum

fuerit, tributo collationem factam, idem aurum ex hostibus
13 captum in paucorum praedam cessisse. itaque exsequebantur quaerendo, ubi tantae rei furtum occultaretur;
differentique et tempore suo se indicaturum dicenti, ceteris
omissis eo versae erant omnium curae, apparebatque, nec 5
veri indicii gratiam mediam nec falsi offensionem fore.

15 *The Dictator is recalled to Rome. He summons Manlius before him, and
orders him on pain of arrest to make good his accusations and his
promises. The reply of Manlius.*

Ita suspensis rebus, dictator accitus ab exercitu in urbem 10
venit. postero die senatu habito, cum satis periclitatus
voluntates hominum discedere senatum ab se vetuisset,
2 stipatus ea multitudine, sella in comitio posita, viatorem
ad M. Manlium misit; qui dictatoris iussu vocatus, cum
signum suis dedisset, adesse certamen, agmine ingenti ad 15
3 tribunal venit. hinc senatus, hinc plebs, suum quisque
4 intuentes ducem, velut in acie constiterant. tum dictator,
silentio facto, "utinam" inquit "mihi patribusque Romanis
ita de ceteris rebus cum plebe conveniat, quemadmodum,
quod aα te attinet eamque rem, quam de te sum quaesiturus, 20
5 conventurum satis confido. spem factam a te civitati video,
fide incolumi ex thesauris Gallicis, quos primores patrum
occultent, creditum solvi posse. cui ego rei tantum abest
ut impedimento sim, ut contra te, M. Manli, adhorter,
liberes fenore plebem Romanam et istos incubantes publicis 25
6 thesauris ex praeda clandestina evolvas. quod nisi facis,
sive ut et ipse in parte praedae sis, sive quia vanum
indicium est, in vincla te duci iubebo nec diutius patiar, a
7 te multitudinem fallaci spe concitari." ad ea Manlius nec
se fefellisse ait, non adversus Volscos, toties hostes, quoties 30
patribus expediat, nec adversus Latinos Hernicosque, quos
falsis criminibus in arma agant, sed adversus se ac plebem

Romanam dictatorem creatum esse; iam omisso bello, 8
quod simulatum sit, in se impetum fieri; iam dictatorem
profiteri patrocinium feneratorum adversus plebem; iam
sibi ex favore multitudinis crimen et perniciem quaeri.
5 "offendit" inquit "te, A. Corneli, vosque, patres conscripti, 9
circumfusa turba lateri meo? quin eam diducitis a me
singuli vestris beneficiis, intercedendo, eximendo de nervo
cives vestros, prohibendo iudicatos addictosque duci, ex eo,
quod afluit opibus vestris, sustinendo necessitates aliorum?
10 sed quid ego vos, de vestro impendatis, hortor? sortem 10
reliquam ferte; de capite deducite, quod usuris pernumeratum est; iam nihilo mea turba quam ullius conspectior erit.
at enim quid ita solus ego civium curam ago? nihilo 11
magis, quod respondeam, habeo, quam si quaeras, quid ita
15 solus Capitolium arcemque servaverim. et tum universis,
quam potui, opem tuli et nunc singulis feram. nam quod 12
ad thesauros Gallicos attinet, rem suapte natura facilem
difficilem interrogatio facit. cur enim quaeritis, quod scitis?
cur, quod in sinu vestro est, excuti iubetis potius, quam
20 ponatis, nisi aliqua fraus subest? quo magis argui prae- 13
stigias iubetis vestras, eo plus vereor, ne abstuleritis obser-
vantibus etiam oculos. itaque non ego vobis, ut indicem
praedas vestras, sed vos id cogendi estis, ut in medium
proferatis."

25 *Manlius is arrested and thrown into prison. The people though indignant* 16
  dare not resist the authority of the dictator. Many however put on
  mourning, and show other signs of grief. The general indignation is
  stimulated by the dictator's triumph. To quiet the people a colony is
  despatched to Satricum, but it makes matters rather worse than better.
30 *The dictator resigns.*

Cum mittere ambages dictator iuberet et aut peragere
verum indicium cogeret aut fateri facinus insimulati falso

crimine senatus oblataeque vani furti invidiae, negantem
arbitrio inimicorum se locuturum in vincla duci iussit.
2 arreptus a viatore "Iuppiter" inquit "optime maxime
Iunoque regina ac Minerva ceterique di deaeque, qui
Capitolium arcemque incolitis, sicine vestrum militem ac 5
praesidem sinitis vexari ab inimicis? haec dextra, qua
Gallos fudi a delubris vestris, iam in vinclis et catenis erit?"
3 nullius nec oculi nec aures indignitatem ferebant; sed
invicta sibi quaedam patientissima iusti imperii civitas
fecerat, nec adversus dictatoriam vim aut tribuni plebis aut 10
4 ipsa plebs attollere oculos aut hiscere audebant. coniecto
in carcerem Manlio, satis constat magnam partem plebis
vestem mutasse, multos mortales capillum ac barbam
promisisse, obversatamque vestibulo carceris maestam tur-
5 bam. dictator de Volscis triumphavit, invidiaeque magis 15
triumphus quam gloriae fuit; quippe domi, non militiae
partum eum actumque de cive, non de hoste fremebant;
unum defuisse tantum superbiae, quod non M. Manlius
6 ante currum sit ductus. iamque haud procul seditione res
erat; cuius leniendae causa, postulante nullo, largitor 20
voluntarius repente senatus factus Satricum coloniam duo
millia civium Romanorum deduci iussit. bina iugera et
7 semisses agri assignati; quod cum et parvum et paucis
datum et mercedem esse prodendi M. Manlii interpreta-
8 rentur, remedio irritatur seditio. et iam magis insignis 25
sordibus et facie reorum turba Manliana erat, amotusque
post triumphum abdicatione dictaturae terror et linguam
et animos liberaverat hominum.

17 *Reproaches hurled against the people* (*Livy does not say by whom*) *for
deserting their champions. Manlius is released by the Senate only* 30
*in time to prevent his liberation by force. Ambassadors from the
Hernicans, from Circeii and Velitrae demanding the surrender of*

their prisoners, in order that they may deal with their offence before
their own tribunals, receive a stern reply, warning them to leave the
city at once.

Audiebantur itaque propalam voces exprobrantium
5 multitudini, quod defensores suos semper in praecipitem
locum favore tollat, deinde in ipso discrimine periculi
destituat: sic Sp. Cassium in agros plebem vocantem, sic 2
Sp. Maelium ab ore civium famem suis impensis propul-
santem oppressos; sic M. Manlium, mersam et obrutam
10 fenore partem civitatis in libertatem ac lucem extrahentem,
proditum inimicis. saginare plebem [populares] suos, ut 3
iugulentur. hocine patiendum fuisse, si ad nutum dictatoris
non responderit vir consularis? fingerent, mentitum ante,
atque ideo non habuisse, quod tum responderet; cui servo
15 unquam mendacii poenam vincla fuisse? non obversatam 4
esse memoriam noctis illius, quae paene ultima atque
aeterna nomini Romano fuerit? non speciem agminis Gallorum per Tarpeiam rupem scandentis? non ipsius M.
Manlii, qualem eum armatum, plenum sudoris ac sanguinis,
20 ipso paene Iove erepto ex hostium manibus, vidissent?
selibrisne farris gratiam servatori patriae relatam? et quem 5
prope caelestem, cognomine certe Capitolino Iovi parem
fecerint, eum pati vinctum in carcere, in tenebris obnoxiam
carnificis arbitrio ducere animam? adeo in uno omnibus
25 satis auxilii fuisse, nullam opem in tam multis uni esse?
iam ne nocte quidem turba ex eo loco dilabebatur, re- 6
fracturosque carcerem minabantur, cum remisso, quod
erepturi erant, ex senatus consulto Manlius vinclis libe-
ratur; quo facto non seditio finita, sed dux seditioni datus
30 est.

Per eosdem dies Latinis et Hernicis, simul colonis 7
Circeiensibus et a Velitris, purgantibus se Volsci crimine
belli captivosque repetentibus, ut suis legibus in eos anim-

adverterent, tristia responsa reddita, tristiora colonis, quod cives Romani patriae oppugnandae nefanda consilia inissent.

8 non negatum itaque tantum de captivis, sed, in quo ab sociis tamen temperaverant, denuntiatum senatus verbis, facesserent propere ex urbe ab ore atque oculis populi 5 Romani, ne nihil eos legationis ius, externo, non civi comparatum, tegeret.

18 B.C. 384. *Military tribunes elected, six in number. With peace abroad the struggle at home gains strength. Manlius inviting the plebs to his house urges them to use their power as the army of the State 10 to free themselves from the tyranny of the patricians. For the first time now Manlius is accused of aiming at royalty.*

Recrudescente Manliana seditione, sub exitum anni comitia habita, creatique tribuni militum consulari potestate Ser. Cornelius Maluginensis iterum, P. Valerius Potitus 15 iterum, M. Furius Camillus quintum, Ser. Sulpicius Rufus iterum, C. Papirius Crassus, T. Quinctius Cincinnatus 2 iterum. cuius principio anni et patribus et plebi peropportune externa pax data, plebi, quod non avocata dilectu spem cepit, dum tam potentem haberet ducem, fenoris 20 expugnandi, patribus, ne quo externo terrore avocarentur 3 animi ab sanandis domesticis malis. igitur cum pars utraque acrior aliquanto coorta esset, iam propinquum certamen aderat. et Manlius, advocata domum plebe, cum principibus novandarum rerum interdiu noctuque consilia 25 agitat, plenior aliquanto animorum irarumque, quam antea 4 fuerat. iram accenderat ignominia recens in animo ad contumeliam inexperto; spiritus dabat, quod nec ausus esset idem in se dictator, quod in Sp. Maelio Cincinnatus Quinctius fecisset, et vinclorum suorum invidiam non 30 dictator modo abdicando dictaturam fugisset, sed ne senatus 5 quidem sustinere potuisset. his simul inflatus exacerbatus-

que iam per se accensos incitabat plebis animos. "quousque tandem ignorabitis vires vestras, quas natura ne beluas
quidem ignorare voluit? numerate saltem, quot ipsi sitis,
quot adversarios habeatis. si singuli singulos aggressuri 6
5 essetis, tamen acrius crederem vos pro libertate quam illos
pro dominatione certaturos; quot enim clientes circa singulos
fuistis patronos, tot nunc adversus unum hostem eritis.
ostendite modo bellum; pacem habebitis. videant vos 7
paratos ad vim; ius ipsi remittent. audendum est aliquid
10 universis, aut omnia singulis patienda. quousque me circum- 8
spectabitis? ego quidem nulli vestrum deero; ne fortuna
mea desit, videte. ipse vindex vester, ubi visum inimicis
est, nullus repente fui, et vidistis in vincla duci universi
eum, qui a singulis vobis vincla depuleram. quid sperem, 9
15 si plus in me audeant inimici? an exitum Cassii Maeliique
exspectem? bene facitis, quod abominamini. di prohibe-
bunt haec; sed nunquam propter me de caelo descendent;
vobis dent mentem oportet, ut prohibeatis, sicut mihi
dederunt armato togatoque, ut vos a barbaris hostibus, a
20 superbis defenderem civibus. tam parvus animus tanti 10
populi est, ut semper vobis auxilium adversus inimicos satis
sit, nec ullum, nisi quatenus imperari vobis sinatis, certamen adversus patres noritis? nec hoc natura insitum vobis
est, sed usu possidemini. cur enim adversus externos 11
25 tantum animorum geritis, ut imperare illis aequum cense-
atis? quia consuestis cum eis pro imperio certare, adversus
hos tentare magis quam tueri libertatem. tamen, qualescun- 12
que duces habuistis, qualescunque ipsi fuistis, omnia adhuc,
quantacunque petistis, obtinuistis seu vi seu fortuna vestra.
30 tempus est [et]iam maiora conari. experimini modo et 13
vestram felicitatem et me, ut spero, feliciter expertum;
minore negotio, qui imperet patribus imponetis quam, qui
resisterent imperantibus, imposuistis. solo aequandae sunt 14

dictaturae consulatusque, ut caput attollere Romana plebes
possit. proinde adeste; prohibete ius de pecuniis dici;
ego me patronum profiteor plebis, quod mihi cura mea et
15 fides nomen induit; vos si quo insigni magis imperii
honorisve nomine vestrum appellabitis ducem, eo utemini 5
16 potentiore ad obtinenda ea, quae vultis." inde de regno
agendi ortum initium dicitur; sed nec cum quibus nec
quem ad finem consilia pervenerint, satis planum traditur.

19 *The Senate pass a decree ordering the magistrates to protect the common-*
wealth from the fatal designs of M. Manlius. The military tribunes, 10
assisted by the tribunes of the plebs, who are convinced of Manlius'
criminal ambition, determine to impeach him.

At in parte altera senatus de secessione in domum
privatam plebis, forte etiam in arce positam, et imminenti
2 mole libertati agitat. magna pars vociferantur, Servilio 15
Ahala opus esse, qui non in vincla duci iubendo irritet
publicum hostem, sed unius iactura civis finiat intestinum
3 bellum. decurritur ad leniorem verbis sententiam, vim
tamen eandem habentem, ut videant magistratus, ne quid
ex perniciosis consiliis M. Manlii res publica detrimenti 20
4 capiat. tum tribuni consulari potestate tribunique plebi
(nam et *ei*, quia eundem et suae potestatis, quem libertatis
omnium, finem cernebant, patrum auctoritati se dediderant)
5 hi tum omnes, quid opus facto sit, consultant. cum
praeter vim et caedem nihil cuiquam occurreret, eam autem 25
ingentis dimicationis fore appareret, tum M. Menenius et
6 Q. Publilius tribuni plebis: "quid patrum et plebis
certamen facimus, quod civitatis esse adversus unum
pestiferum civem debet? quid cum plebe aggredimur eum,
quem per ipsam plebem tutius aggredi est, ut suis ipse 30
7 oneratus viribus ruat? diem dicere ei nobis in animo est.
nihil minus populare quam regnum est. simul multitudo

illa non secum certari viderint et ex advocatis iudices facti
erunt et accusatores de plebe, patricium reum intuebuntur
et regni crimen in medio, nulli magis quam libertati
favebunt suae."

5 *Manlius is put on his trial. He is deserted by all his friends and relations.* 20
    His moving appeal to the people, which could not counterbalance the
    prejudice against him. However, in the Campus Martius *in full*
    sight of the Capitol it is clear that the citizens cannot bring themselves
    to condemn him. The trial is therefore adjourned to another place
10   *and time. He is condemned and executed. A pestilence follows, as-*
    cribed by some to the anger of the gods at the execution of the preserver
    of the Capitoline temple.

Approbantibus cunctis diem Manlio dicunt. quod ubi
est factum, primo commota plebs est, utique postquam
15 sordidatum reum viderunt nec cum eo non modo patrum 2
quemquam, sed ne cognatos quidem aut affines, postremo
ne fratres quidem A. et T. Manlios, quod ad eum diem
nunquam usu venisset, ut in tanto discrimine non et
proximi vestem mutarent: App. Claudio in vincla ducto 3
20 C. Claudium inimicum Claudiamque omnem gentem sordi-
datam fuisse; consensu opprimi popularem virum, quod
primus a patribus ad plebem defecisset. cum dies venit, 4
quae praeter coetus multitudinis seditiosasque voces et
largitionem et fallax indicium pertinentia proprie ad regni
25 crimen ab accusatoribus obiecta sint reo, apud neminem
auctorem invenio; nec dubito, haud parva fuisse, cum 5
damnandi mora plebi non in causa, sed in loco fuerit.
illud notandum videtur, ut sciant homines, quae et quanta
decora foeda cupiditas regni non ingrata solum, sed invisa
30 etiam reddiderit: homines prope quadringentos produxisse 6
dicitur, quibus sine fenore expensas pecunias tulisset,
quorum bona venire, quos duci addictos prohibuisset; ad 7
haec decora quoque belli non commemorasse tantum, sed

protulisse etiam conspicienda, spolia hostium caesorum
ad triginta, dona imperatorum ad quadraginta, in quibus
8 insignes duas murales coronas, civicas octo; ad hoc servatos
ex hostibus cives [produxit], inter quos C. Servilium
magistrum equitum absentem nominatim; et cum ea 5
quoque, quae bello gesta essent, pro fastigio rerum oratione
etiam magnifica, facta dictis aequando, memorasset, nudasse
9 pectus insigne cicatricibus bello acceptis et identidem
Capitolium spectans Iovem deosque alios devocasse ad
auxilium fortunarum suarum precatusque esse, ut, quam 10
mentem sibi Capitolinam arcem protegenti ad salutem
populi Romani dedissent, eam populo Romano in suo
discrimine darent, et orasse singulos universosque, ut
Capitolium atque arcem intuentes, ut ad deos immortales
10 versi de se iudicarent. in campo Martio cum centuriatim 15
populus citaretur, et reus ad Capitolium manus tendens ab
hominibus ad deos preces avertisset, apparuit tribunis, nisi
oculos quoque hominum liberassent tanti memoria decoris,
nunquam fore in praeoccupatis beneficio animis vero
11 crimini locum. ita prodicta die, in Petelinum lucum 20
extra portam Flumentanam, unde conspectus in Capitolium
non esset, concilium populi indictum est. ibi crimen
valuit, et obstinatis animis triste iudicium invisumque etiam
12 iudicibus factum. sunt, qui per duumviros, qui de per-
duellione anquirerent, creatos auctores sint damnatum. 25
tribuni de saxo Tarpeio deiecerunt, locusque idem in uno
homine et eximiae gloriae monumentum et poenae ultimae
13 fuit. adiectae mortuo notae sunt, publica una, quod, cum
domus eius fuisset, ubi nunc aedes atque officina Monetae
est, latum ad populum est, ne quis patricius in arce aut 30
14 Capitolio habitaret, gentilicia altera, quod gentis Manliae
decreto cautum est, ne quis deinde M. Manlius vocaretur.
hunc exitum habuit vir, nisi in libera civitate natus esset,

memorabilis. populum brevi, postquam periculum ab eo 15
nullum erat, per se ipsas recordantem virtutes desiderium
eius tenuit. pestilentia etiam brevi consecuta, nullis occur-
rentibus tantae cladis causis, ex Manliano supplicio magnae
5 parti videri orta: violatum Capitolium esse sanguine ser- 16
vatoris, nec dis cordi fuisse, poenam eius oblatam prope
oculis suis, a quo sua templa erepta e manibus hostium
essent.

B.C. 383. *The burden of foreign war is aggravated by the defection of the* 21
10   *Lanuvini. The senate, in order to conciliate the* plebs *and induce*
them to consent to war with the Lanuvini, appoint commissioners to
distribute the Pomptine land, and to plant a colony at Nepĕte. Mili-
tary operations are delayed by the pestilence. Rumoured defection of
Praeneste.

15   Pestilentiam inopia frugum et vulgatam utriusque mali
famam anno insequente multiplex bellum excepit, L.
Valerio quartum, A. Manlio tertium, Ser. Sulpicio tertium,
L. Lucretio, L. Aemilio tertium, M. Trebonio tribunis
militum consulari potestate. hostes novi, praeter Volscos, 2
20 velut sorte quadam prope in aeternum exercendo Romano
militi datos, Circeiosque et Velitras colonias, iam diu
molientes defectionem, et suspectum Latium, Lanuvini
etiam, quae fidelissima urbs fuerat, subito exorti. id patres 3
rati contemptu accidere, quod Veliternis civibus suis tam
25 diu impunita defectio esset, decreverunt, ut primo quoque
tempore ad populum ferretur de bello eis indicendo. ad 4
quam militiam quo paratior plebes esset, quinqueviros
Pomptino agro dividendo et triumviros Nepete coloniae
deducendae creaverunt. tum, ut bellum iuberent, latum ad 5
30 populum est, et nequicquam dissuadentibus tribunis plebis
omnes tribus bellum iusserunt. apparatum eo anno bellum 6
est, exercitus propter pestilentiam non eductus; eaque

cunctatio colonis spatium dederat deprecandi senatum ; et
magna hominum pars eo, ut legatio supplex Romam
7 mitteretur, inclinabat, ni privato, ut fit, periculo publicum
implicitum esset auctoresque defectionis ab Romanis metu,
ne soli crimini subiecti piacula irae Romanorum dederentur, 5
8 avertissent colonias a consiliis pacis. neque in senatu
solum per eos legatio impedita est, sed magna pars plebis
incitata, ut praedatum in agrum Romanum exirent. haec
9 nova iniuria exturbavit omnem spem pacis. de Praenestinorum quoque defectione eo anno primum fama exorta ; 10
arguentibusque eos Tusculanis et Gabinis et Lavicanis,
quorum in fines incursatum erat, ita placide ab senatu
responsum est, ut minus credi de criminibus, quia nollent
ea vera esse, appareret.

22 B.C. 382. *Two of the six military tribunes of this year lead an army* 15
against Velitrae. The Veliterni assisted by a force of Praenestines
outnumbering their own are defeated. War is declared against the
Praenestines, who in the following year in conjunction with the
Volscians capture Satricum, and cruelly ill-treat the inhabitants.

Insequenti anno Sp. et L. Papirii novi tribuni militum 20
consulari potestate Velitras legiones duxere, quattuor collegis, Ser. Cornelio Maluginensi tertium, Q. Servilio, C.
Sulpicio, L. Aemilio quartum tribunis, ad praesidium urbis
et si qui ex Etruria novi motus nuntiarentur (omnia enim
2 inde suspecta erant), relictis. Ad Velitras adversus maiora 25
paene auxilia Praenestinorum quam ipsam colonorum
multitudinem secundo proelio pugnatum est ita, ut propin-
quitas urbis hosti et causa maturioris fugae et unum ex
3 fuga receptaculum esset. oppidi oppugnatione tribuni
abstinuere, quia et anceps erat nec in perniciem coloniae 30
pugnandum censebant. litterae Romam ad senatum cum
victoriae nuntiis acriores in Praenestinum quam in Veliter-

num hostem missae. itaque ex senatus consulto populique 4
iussu bellum Praenestinis indictum; qui coniuncti Volscis
anno insequente Satricum, coloniam populi Romani, per-
tinaciter a colonis defensam, vi expugnarunt foedeque in
5 captis exercuere victoriam.

B.C. 381. *Camillus, elected military tribune for the sixth time, is
appointed to the command of the Volscian war, and leads his army
against Satricum. The enemy are prepared for them, and anxious
to fight. L. Furius, colleague of Camillus, in spite of the latter's*
10 *advice, determines to give battle at once.*

Eam rem aegre passi Romani M. Furium Camillum 5
sextum tribunum militum creavere. additi collegae A. et
L. Postumii Regillenses ac L. Furius cum L. Lucretio et
M. Fabio Ambusto. Volscum bellum M. Furio extra 6
15 ordinem decretum; adiutor ex tribunis sorte L. Furius
datur, non tam e re publica, quam ut collegae materia ad
omnem laudem esset, et publice, quod rem temeritate eius
prolapsam restituit, et privatim, quod ex errore gratiam
potius eius sibi quam suam gloriam petiit. exactae iam 7
20 aetatis Camillus erat, comitiisque iurare parato in verba
excusandae valetudini solita consensus populi restiterat;
sed vegetum ingenium in vivido pectore vigebat, virebat-
que integris sensibus, et civiles iam res haud magnopere
obeuntem bella excitabant. quattuor legionibus quaternum 8
25 millium scriptis, exercitu indicto ad portam Esquilinam
in posteram diem, ad Satricum profectus. ibi eum expug- 9
natores coloniae haudquaquam perculsi, fidentes militum
numero, quo aliquantum praestabant, opperiebantur. postquam appropinquare Romanos senserunt, extemplo in
30 aciem procedunt, nihil dilaturi, quin periculum summae
rerum facerent : ita paucitati hostium nihil artes imperatoris
unici, quibus solis confiderent, profuturas esse. idem ardor **23**

et in Romano exercitu erat et in altero duce, nec praesentis
dimicationis fortunam ulla res praeterquam unius viri
consilium atque imperium morabatur, qui occasionem
2 iuvandarum ratione virium trahendo bello quaerebat. eo
magis hostis instare, nec iam pro castris tantum suis 5
explicare aciem, sed procedere in medium campi et vallo
prope hostium signa inferendo superbam fiduciam virium
3 ostentare.   id aegre patiebatur Romanus miles, multo
aegrius alter ex tribunis militum, L. Furius, ferox cum aetate
et ingenio, tum multitudinis ex incertissimo sumentis animos 10
4 spe inflatus. hic per se iam milites incitatos insuper
instigabat elevando, qua una poterat, aetate auctoritatem
collegae, iuvenibus bella data dictitans, et cum corporibus
5 vigere et deflorescere animos ; cunctatorem ex acerrimo
bellatore factum, et, qui adveniens castra urbesque primo 15
impetu rapere sit solitus, eum residem intra vallum tempus
terere, quid accessurum suis decessurumve hostium viribus
6 sperantem ? quam occasionem, quod tempus, quem insidiis
7 instruendis locum ? frigere ac torpere senis consilia. sed
Camillo cum vitae satis, tum gloriae esse ; quid attinere 20
cum mortali corpore uno civitatis, quam immortalem esse
8 deceat, pati consenescere vires ? his sermonibus tota in se
averterat castra ; et cum omnibus locis posceretur pugna,
"sustinere," inquit, " M. Furi, non possumus impetum
militum, et hostis, cuius animos cunctando auximus, iam 25
minime toleranda superbia insultat ; cede unus omnibus et
9 patere te vinci consilio, ut maturius bello vincas." ad ea
Camillus, quae bella suo unius auspicio gesta ad eam diem
essent, negare in eis neque se neque populum Romanum
aut consilii sui aut fortunae paenituisse ; nunc scire se, 30
collegam habere iure imperioque parem, vigore aetatis
10 praestantem ; itaque se, quod ad exercitum attineat, regere
consuesse, non regi ; collegae imperium se non posse

impedire. dis bene iuvantibus ageret, quod e re publica
duceret; aetati suae se veniam eam petere, ne in prima acie 11
esset; quae senis munia in bello sint, iis se non defuturum.
id a dis immortalibus precari, ne qui casus suum consilium
5 laudabile efficiat. nec ab hominibus salutaris sententia nec 12
a dis tam piae preces auditae sunt. primam aciem auctor
pugnae instruit, subsidia Camillus firmat validamque
stationem pro castris opponit; ipse edito loco spectator
intentus in eventum alieni consilii constitit.

10 *The Romans are outmanœuvred, and retreat in disorder. Camillus* **24**
rallies them, and gains a splendid victory.

Simul primo concursu concrepuere arma, hostis dolo,
non metu pedem rettulit. lenis ab tergo clivus erat inter 2
aciem et castra; et, quod multitudo suppeditabat, aliquot
15 validas cohortes in castris armatas instructasque reliquerant,
quae inter commissum iam certamen, ubi vallo appropinquasset hostis, erumperent. Romanus cedentem hostem 3
effuse sequendo in locum iniquum pertractus opportunus
huic eruptioni fuit; versus itaque in victorem terror et
20 novo hoste et supina valle Romanam inclinavit aciem.
instant Volsci recentes, qui e castris impetum fecerant; 4
integrant et illi pugnam, qui simulata cesserant fuga. iam
non recipiebat se Romanus miles, sed immemor recentis
ferociae veterisque decoris terga passim dabat atque effuso
25 cursu castra repetebat, cum Camillus, subiectus ab circum- 5
stantibus in equum et raptim subsidiis oppositis, "haec
est" inquit, "milites, pugna, quam poposcistis? quis homo,
quis deus est, quem accusare possitis? vestra illa temeritas,
vestra ignavia haec est. secuti alium ducem sequimini 6
30 nunc Camillum et, quod ductu meo soletis, vincite. quid
vallum et castra spectatis? neminem vestrum illa nisi
victorem receptura sunt." pudor primo tenuit effusos; 7

3—2

inde, ut circumagi signa obvertique aciem viderunt in
hostem, et dux, praeterquam quod tot insignis triumphis,
etiam aetate venerabilis inter prima signa, ubi plurimus
labor periculumque erat, se offerebat, increpare singuli se
quisque et alios, et adhortatio in vicem totam alacri clamore 5
8 pervasit aciem. neque alter tribunus rei defuit, sed missus
a collega restituente peditum aciem ad equites, non castigando, ad quam rem leviorem auctorem eum culpae
societas fecerat, sed ab imperio totus ad preces versus orare
singulos universosque, ut se reum fortunae eius diei crimine 10
9 eximerent: "Abnuente ac prohibente collega, temeritati
me omnium potius socium quam unius prudentiae dedi.
Camillus in utraque vestra fortuna suam gloriam videt; ego,
ni restituitur pugna, quod miserrimum est, fortunam cum
10 omnibus, infamiam solus sentiam." optimum visum est in 15
fluctuante acie † tradi equos et pedestri pugna invadere
hostem. Eunt insignes armis animisque, qua premi parte
maxime peditum copias vident. nihil neque apud duces
neque apud milites remittitur a summo certamine animi.
11 sensit ergo eventus virtutis enixae opem, et Volsci, qua 20
modo simulato metu cesserant, ea in veram fugam effusi,
magna pars et in ipso certamine et post in fuga caesi,
ceteri in castris, quae capta eodem impetu sunt; plures
tamen capti quam occisi.

25 *Some Tusculans being discovered among the captives, war is declared* 25
against Tusculum. Camillus and L. Furius proceed thither, but
find no signs of warlike intentions on the part of the Tusculans, who
persistently refuse to offer resistance.

Ubi in recensendis captivis cum Tusculani aliquot
noscitarentur, secreti ab aliis ad tribunos adducuntur, 30
2 percontantibusque fassi, publico consilio se militasse. cuius
tam vicini belli metu Camillus motus extemplo se Romam

captivos ducturum ait, ne patres ignari sint, Tusculanos ab
societate descisse: castris exercituique interim, si videatur,
praesit collega. documento unus dies fuerat, ne sua 3
consilia melioribus praeferret; nec tamen aut ipsi aut in
5 exercitu cuiquam satis placato animo Camillus laturus
culpam eius videbatur, qua data in tam praecipitem casum
res publica esset; et cum in exercitu, tum Romae constans 4
omnium fama erat, cum varia fortuna in Volscis gesta res
esset, adversae pugnae fugaeque in L. Furio culpam,
10 secundae decus omne penes M. Furium esse. introductis 5
in senatum captivis, cum bello persequendos Tusculanos
patres censuissent Camilloque id bellum mandassent, adiu-
torem sibi ad eam rem unum petit, permissoque, ut ex
collegis optaret, quem vellet, contra spem omnium L.
15 Furium optavit, qua moderatione animi cum collegae 6
levavit infamiam, tum sibi gloriam ingentem peperit. nec
fuit cum Tusculanis bellum; pace constanti vim Romanam
arcuerunt, quam armis non poterant. intrantibus fines 7
Romanis non demigratum ex propinquis itineri locis, non
20 cultus agrorum intermissus; patentibus portis urbis togati
obviam frequentes imperatoribus processere; commeatus
exercitui comiter in castra ex urbe et ex agris devehitur.
Camillus, castris ante portas positis, eademne forma pacis, 8
quae in agris ostentaretur, etiam intra moenia esset, scire
25 cupiens, ingressus urbem, ubi patentes ianuas et tabernis 9
apertis proposita omnia in medio vidit, intentosque opifices
suo quemque operi, et ludos litterarum strepere discentium
vocibus, ac repletas semitas inter vulgus aliud puerorum et
mulierum huc atque illuc euntium, qua quemque suorum
30 usuum causae ferrent, nihil usquam non pavidis modo, sed 10
ne mirantibus quidem simile, circumspiciebat omnia, in-
quirens oculis, ubinam bellum fuisset; adeo nec amotae rei 11
usquam nec oblatae ad tempus vestigium ullum erat, sed ita

omnia constanti tranquilla pace, ut eo vix fama belli perlata
videri posset.

26 *Camillus sends the Tusculan senate to Rome, where they declare their*
resolution to abstain from war, whatever the Romans do. They
obtain peace, and shortly afterwards receive the Roman franchise. 5

Victus igitur patientia hostium senatum eorum vocari iussit. "soli adhuc" inquit, "Tusculani, vera arma
verasque vires, quibus ab ira Romanorum vestra tu-
2 taremini, invenistis. ite Romam ad senatum; aestima-
bunt patres, utrum plus ante poenae an nunc veniae meriti 10
sitis. non praecipiam gratiam publici beneficii; deprecandi
potestatem a me habueritis; precibus eventum vestris
3 senatus, quem videbitur, dabit." postquam Romam Tusculani venerunt senatusque paulo ante fidelium sociorum
maestus in vestibulo curiae est conspectus, moti extemplo 15
patres vocari eos iam tum hospitaliter magis quam hostiliter
4 iussere. dictator Tusculanus ita verba fecit: "quibus
bellum indixistis intulistisque, patres conscripti, sicut nunc
videtis nos stantes in vestibulo curiae vestrae, ita armati
paratique obviam imperatoribus legionibusque vestris pro- 20
5 cessimus. hic noster, hic plebis nostrae habitus fuit,
eritque semper, nisi si quando a vobis proque vobis arma
acceperimus. gratias agimus et ducibus vestris et exercitibus, quod oculis magis quam auribus crediderunt et, ubi
6 nihil hostile erat, ne ipsi quidem fecerunt. pacem, quam 25
nos praestitimus, eam a vobis petimus; bellum eo, sicubi
est, avertatis precamur; in nos quid arma polleant vestra, si
patiendo experiundum est, inermes experiemur. haec mens
7 nostra est, di immortales faciant, tam felix, quam pia. quod
ad crimina attinet, quibus moti bellum indixistis, etsi 30
revicta rebus verbis confutare nihil attinet, tamen, etiamsi
vera sint, vel fateri nobis ea, cum tam evidenter paenituerit,

tutum censemus. peccetur in vos, dum digni sitis, quibus
ita satisfiat." tantum fere verborum ab Tusculanis factum. 8
pacem in praesentia, nec ita multo post civitatem etiam
impetraverunt. ab Tusculo legiones reductae.

5 B.C. 380. *Censors are created on account of a 'vague rumour about* 27
debts'. But no census is taken, one of the censors first elected dying,
and the election of two fresh ones having been vitiated. Tribunician
agitations. On news of war from Praeneste the tribunes forbid the
arrest of debtors, and the citizens refuse to serve.

10 Camillus, consilio et virtute in Volsco bello, felicitate in
Tusculana expeditione, utrobique singulari adversus collegam
patientia et moderatione insignis, magistratu abiit, creatis 2
tribunis militaribus in insequentem annum L. et P. Valeriis,
Lucio quintum, Publio tertium, et C. Sergio tertium,
15 L. Menenio iterum, P. Papirio, Ser. Cornelio Maluginense.
censoribus quoque eguit annus, maxime propter incertam 3
famam aeris alieni, aggravantibus summam etiam invidiosius
tribunis plebis, cum ab iis elevaretur, quibus fide magis
quam fortuna debentium laborare creditum videri expedie-
20 bat. creati censores C. Sulpicius Camerinus, Sp. Postumius 4
Regillensis, coeptaque iam res morte Postumii, quia collegam suffici censori religio erat, interpellata est. igitur 5
cum Sulpicius abdicasset se magistratu, censores alii vitio
creati non gesserunt magistratum; tertios creari, velut dis
25 non accipientibus in eum annum censuram, religiosum fuit.
eam vero ludificationem plebis tribuni ferendam negabant: 6
fugere senatum testes tabulas publicas census cuiusque, quia
nolint conspici summam aeris alieni, quae indicatura sit,
demersam partem a parte civitatis, cum interim obaeratam
30 plebem obiectari aliis atque aliis hostibus. passim iam sine 7
ullo discrimine bella quaeri: ab Antio Satricum, ab Satrico
Velitras, inde Tusculum legiones ductas; Latinis, Hernicis,

Praenestinis iam intentari arma, civium magis quam hostium
odio, ut in armis terant plebem nec respirare in urbe aut
per otium libertatis meminisse sinant aut consistere in
contione, ubi aliquando audiant vocem tribuniciam de
8 levando fenore et fine aliarum iniuriarum agentem. quod 5
si sit animus plebi memor patrum libertatis, se nec addici
quemquam civem Romanum ob creditam pecuniam passuros neque dilectum haberi, donec, inspecto aere alieno
initaque ratione minuendi eius, sciat unusquisque, quid sui,
quid alieni sit, supersit sibi liberum corpus an id quoque 10
9 nervo debeatur. merces seditionis proposita confestim
seditionem excitavit. nam et addicebantur multi, et ad
Praenestini famam belli novas legiones scribendas patres
censuerant; quae utraque simul auxilio tribunicio et con-
10 sensu plebis impediri coepta; nam neque duci addictos 15
tribuni sinebant, neque iuniores nomina dabant. cum
patribus minor *in* praesens cura creditae pecuniae iuris
exsequendi quam dilectus esset (quippe iam a Praeneste
profectos hostes in agro Gabino consedisse nuntiabatur),
11 interim tribunos plebis fama ea ipsa irritaverat magis ad 20
susceptum certamen quam deterruerat, neque aliud ad
seditionem exstinguendam in urbe quam prope illatum
moenibus ipsis bellum valuit.

28 *The Praenestines hearing what was going on, advance as far as the*
Colline gate. Trepidation in the city. T. Quinctius Cincinnatus 25
is named dictator; and the citizens give in their names for military
service readily. The Praenestines fall back upon the Alia.

Nam cum esset Praenestinis nuntiatum, nullum exercitum conscriptum Romae, nullum ducem certum esse,
2 patres ac plebem in semet ipsos versos, occasionem rati 30
duces eorum, raptim agmine acto, pervastatis protinus agris,
3 ad portam Collinam signa intulere. ingens in urbe trepi-

datio fuit. conclamatum "ad arma," concursumque in
muros atque portas est; tandemque ab seditione ad bellum
versi dictatorem T. Quinctium Cincinnatum creavere. is 4
magistrum equitum A. Sempronium Atratinum dixit. quod
5 ubi auditum est, (tantus eius magistratus terror erat) simul
hostes a moenibus recessere et iuniores Romani ad edictum
sine retractatione convenere. dum conscribitur Romae 5
exercitus, castra interim hostium haud procul Alia flumine
posita; inde agrum late populantes, fatalem se urbi
10 Romanae locum cepisse, inter se iactabant; similem 6
pavorem inde ac fugam fore, ac bello Gallico fuerit;
etenim si diem contactum religione insignemque nomine
eius loci timeant Romani, quanto magis Aliensi die Aliam
ipsam, monumentum tantae cladis, reformidaturos? species
15 profecto iis ibi truces Gallorum sonumque vocis in oculis
atque auribus fore. has inanium rerum inanes ipsas vol- 7
ventes cogitationes, fortunae loci delegaverant spes suas.
Romani contra, ubicunque esset Latinus hostis, satis scire,
eum esse, quem ad Regillum lacum devictum centum
20 annorum pace obnoxia tenuerint: locum insignem memoria 8
cladis irritaturum se potius ad delendam memoriam dede-
coris, quam ut timorem faciat, ne qua terra sit nefasta
victoriae suae; quin ipsi sibi Galli si offerantur illo loco, se 9
ita pugnaturos, ut Romae pugnaverint in repetenda patria,
25 ut postero die ad Gabios, tunc cum effecerint, ne quis
hostis, qui moenia Romana intrasset, nuntium secundae
adversaeque fortunae domum perferret.

A battle is fought on the Alia, in which Cincinnatus defeats the Praenes- **29**
tines. Eight cities subject to Praeneste are captured. Then Velitrae
30 *is stormed. Lastly Praeneste surrenders. Triumph of Cincinnatus.*

His utrinque animis ad Aliam ventum est. dictator
Romanus, postquam in conspectu hostes erant instructi

intentique, "videsne tu" inquit, "A. Semproni, loci fortuna illos fretos ad Aliam constitisse? nec illis di immortales
certioris quicquam fiduciae, maiorisve quod sit auxilii,
2 dederint. at tu, fretus armis animisque, concitatis equis
invade mediam aciem; ego cum legionibus in turbatos 5
trepidantesque inferam signa. adeste, di testes foederis, et
expetite poenas debitas simul vobis violatis nobisque per
3 vestrum numen deceptis." non equitem, non peditem
sustinuere Praenestini. primo impetu ac clamore dissipati
ordines sunt; dein postquam nullo loco constabat acies, 10
terga vertunt, consternatique et praeter castra etiam sua
pavore praelati non prius se ab effuso cursu sistunt, quam
4 in conspectu Praeneste fuit. ibi ex fuga dissipati locum,
quem tumultuario opere communirent, capiunt, ne, si intra
moenia se recepissent, extemplo ureretur ager depopulatis- 15
5 que omnibus obsidio urbi inferretur. sed postquam, di-
reptis ad Aliam castris, victor Romanus aderat, id quoque
munimentum relictum, et vix moenia tuta rati oppido se
6 Praeneste includunt. octo praeterea oppida erant sub
dicione Praenestinorum; ad ea circumlatum bellum, dein- 20
cepsque haud magno certamine captis, Velitras exercitus
7 ductus. eae quoque expugnatae. tum ad caput belli
Praeneste ventum. id non vi, sed per deditionem receptum
8 est. T. Quinctius, semel acie victor, binis castris hostium,
novem oppidis vi captis, Praeneste in deditionem accepto, 25
Romam revertit, triumphansque signum Praeneste devectum
9 Iovis imperatoris in Capitolium tulit. dedicatum est inter
cellam Iovis ac Minervae, tabulaque sub eo fixa, monumentum rerum gestarum, his ferme incisa litteris fuit:
10 "Iuppiter atque divi omnes hoc dederunt, ut T. Quinctius 30
dictator oppida novem caperet." die vicesimo, quam
creatus erat, dictatura se abdicavit.

B.C. 379. *Six military tribunes elected, three of them plebeians. The* 30
*two Manlii, acting against the Volscians, are inveigled into an
ambuscade. A dictator is appointed. The Volscians however take
no advantage of their victory. The Praenestines rouse the Latins to*
5 *assist them in renewing war. Fresh colonists sent to Setia.*

Comitia inde habita tribunorum militum consulari
potestate, quibus aequatus patriciorum plebeiorumque nu-
merus. ex patribus creati P. et C. Manlii cum L. Iulio; 2
plebes C. Sextilium, M. Albinium, L. Antistium dedit.
10 Manliis, quod genere plebeios, gratia Iulium anteibant, 3
Volsci provincia sine sorte, sine comparatione extra ordinem
data; cuius et ipsos postmodo et patres, qui dederant,
paenituit. inexplorato pabulatum cohortes misere; quibus 4
velut circumventis, cum id falso nuntiatum esset, dum,
15 praesidio ut essent, citati feruntur, ne auctore quidem
asservato, qui eos hostis Latinus pro milite Romano
frustratus erat, ipsi in insidias praecipitavere. ibi dum 5
iniquo loco, sola virtute militum restantes, caedunt caedunturque, castra interim Romana, iacentia in campo, ab
20 altera parte hostes invasere. ab ducibus utrobique proditae 6
temeritate atque inscitia res; quicquid superfuit fortunae
populi Romani, id militum etiam sine rectore stabilis virtus
tutata est. quae ubi Romam sunt relata, primum dicta- 7
torem dici placebat; deinde, postquam quietae res ex
25 Volscis afferebantur et apparuit, nescire eos victoria et
tempore uti, revocati etiam inde exercitus ac duces, otium- 8
que inde, quantum a Volscis, fuit; id modo extremo anno
tumultuatum, quod Praenestini, concitatis Latinorum populis, rebellarunt. eodem anno Setiam, ipsis querentibus 9
30 penuriam hominum, novi coloni adscripti; rebusque haud
prosperis bello domestica quies, quam tribunorum militum
ex plebe gratia maiestasque inter suos obtinuit, solatium
fuit.

31 B.C. 378. *Renewed disturbances at home owing to the prevalence of debt.
Invasion by the Volscians. The senate are obliged to suspend the*
tributum, *and forbid proceedings to be taken against debtors during
the continuance of the war, before an army can be raised. The
Roman army, unable to bring the Volscians to an engagement,* 5
*thoroughly devastates their land. Proceedings against debtors begin
again, and the* tributum *is again levied.*

Insequentis anni principia statim seditione ingenti
arsere, tribunis militum consulari potestate Sp. Furio,
Q. Servilio iterum, L. Menenio tertium, P. Cloelio, M. 10
2 Horatio, L. Geganio. erat autem et materia et causa
seditionis aes alienum; cuius noscendi gratia Sp. Servilius
Priscus, Q. Cloelius Siculus censores facti, ne rem agerent,
3 bello impediti sunt; namque trepidi nuntii primo, fuga
deinde ex agris legiones Volscorum ingressas fines populari- 15
4 que passim Romanum agrum attulere. in qua trepidatione
tantum afuit, ut civilia certamina terror externus cohiberet,
ut contra eo violentior potestas tribunicia impediendo
dilectu esset, donec condiciones impositae patribus, ne
quis, quoad debellatum esset, tributum daret aut ius de 20
5 pecunia credita diceret. eo laxamento plebi sumpto, mora
dilectui non est facta. legionibus novis scriptis, placuit
duos exercitus in agrum Volscum legionibus divisis duci.
Sp. Furius, M. Horatius dextrorsus *in* maritimam oram
atque Antium, Q. Servilius et L. Geganius laeva ad montes 25
6 Ecetram pergunt. neutra parte hostis obvius fuit. popu-
latio itaque non illi vagae similis, quam Volscus latrocinii
more, discordiae hostium fretus et virtutem metuens, per
trepidationem raptim fecerat, sed ab iusto exercitu iusta ira
7 facta, spatio quoque temporis gravior. quippe a Volscis, 30
timentibus, ne interim exercitus ab Roma exiret, incursiones
in extrema finium factae erant; Romano contra etiam in

hostico morandi causa erat, ut hostem ad certamen eliceret.
itaque omnibus passim tectis agrorum vicisque etiam 8
quibusdam exustis, non arbore frugifera, non satis in spem
frugum relictis, omni, quae extra moenia fuit, hominum
5 pecudumque praeda abacta, Romam utrinque exercitus
reducti.

Parvo intervallo ad respirandum debitoribus dato, post- 32
quam quietae res ab hostibus erant, celebrari de integro
iurisdictio, et tantum abesse spes veteris levandi fenoris, ut
10 tributo novum fenus contraheretur in murum a censoribus
locatum saxo quadrato faciundum; cui succumbere oneri 2
coacta plebes, quia, quem dilectum impedirent, non habebant tribuni plebis.

B.C. 377—371. *The next military tribunes elected, six in number, are*
15 *all patricians. Three armies are raised without opposition for war*
against the Volscians and Latins. A battle is fought before
Satricum, where the Latins and Volscians are encamped, in which
after a severe struggle the Romans are successful. The enemy retreat
first to Satricum, and thence to Antium.

20 Tribunos etiam militares patricios omnes coacta prin- 3
cipum opibus fecit, L. Aemilium, P. Valerium quartum,
C. Veturium, Ser. Sulpicium, L. et C. Quinctios Cincin-
natos. iisdem opibus obtinuere, ut adversus Latinos 4
Volscosque, qui coniunctis legionibus ad Satricum castra
25 habebant, nullo impediente omnibus iunioribus sacramento
adactis, tres exercitus scriberent, unum ad praesidium urbis, 5
alterum, qui, si qui alibi motus exstitisset, ad subita belli
mitti posset; tertium longe validissimum P. Valerius et
L. Aemilius ad Satricum duxere. ubi cum aciem instructam 6
30 hostium loco aequo invenissent, extemplo pugnatum; et ut
nondum satis certam victoriam, sic prosperae spei pugnam
imber ingentibus procellis fusus diremit. postero die iterata 7

pugna, et aliquamdiu aequa virtute fortunaque Latinae
maxime legiones, longa societate militiam Romanam e-
8 doctae, restabant. eques immissus ordines turbavit; turbatis
signa peditum illata, quantumque Romana se invexit acies,
tantum hostes gradu demoti; et ut semel inclinavit pugna, 5
9 iam intolerabilis Romana vis erat. fusi hostes cum Satricum,
quod duo millia inde aberat, non castra peterent, ab equite
10 maxime caesi; castra capta direptaque. ab Satrico nocte,
quae proelio proxima fuit, fugae simili agmine petunt
Antium; et cum Romanus exercitus prope vestigiis seque- 10
11 retur, plus tamen timor quam ira celeritatis habuit. prius
itaque moenia intravere hostes, quam Romanus extrema
agminis carpere aut morari posset. inde aliquot dies
vastando agro absumpti, nec Romanis satis instructis
apparatu bellico ad moenia aggredienda nec illis ad 15
subeundum pugnae casum.

33 *The Latins and Antiates quarrel, and the latter surrender to Rome.
The Latins in a rage burn Satricum, and surprise and capture
Tusculum. The inhabitants however hold the citadel, and the
Romans coming to their assistance recover the city and massacre the* 20
Latins.

Seditio tum inter Antiates Latinosque coorta, cum
Antiates victi malis subactique bello, in quo et nati erant et
2 consenuerant, deditionem spectarent, Latinos ex diutina
pace nova defectio recentibus adhuc animis ferociores ad 25
perseverandum in bello faceret. finis certaminis fuit, postquam utrisque apparuit, nihil per alteros stare, quo minus
3 incepta persequerentur. Latini profecti a societate pacis,
ut rebantur, inhonestae sese vindicaverunt; Antiates, in-
commodis arbitris salutarium consiliorum remotis, urbem 30
4 agrosque Romanis dedunt. ira et rabies Latinorum, quia
nec Romanos bello laedere nec Volscos in armis retinere

potuerant, eo erupit, ut Satricum urbem, quae receptaculum
primum eis adversae pugnae fuerat, igni concremarent.
nec aliud tectum eius superfuit urbis, cum faces pariter
sacris profanisque iniicerent, quam matris Matutae tem-
5 plum; inde eos nec sua religio nec verecundia deum 5
arcuisse dicitur, sed vox horrenda edita templo cum
tristibus minis, ni nefandos ignes procul delubris amovis-
sent. incensos ea rabie impetus Tusculum tulit ob iram, 6
quod deserto communi concilio Latinorum non in socie-
10 tatem modo Romanam, sed etiam in civitatem se dedissent.
patentibus portis cum improviso incidissent, primo clamore 7
oppidum praeter arcem captum est. in arcem oppidani
refugere cum coniugibus ac liberis, nuntiosque Romam, qui
certiorem de suo casu senatum facerent, misere. haud 8
15 segnius, quam fide populi Romani dignum fuit, exercitus
Tusculum ductus; L. Quinctius et Ser. Sulpicius tribuni
militum duxere. clausas portas Tusculi, Latinosque simul 9
obsidentium atque obsessorum animo hinc moenia Tusculi
tueri vident, illinc arcem oppugnare, terrere una ac pavere.
20 adventus Romanorum mutaverat utriusque partis animos: 10
Tusculanos ex ingenti metu in summam alacritatem, Latinos
ex prope certa fiducia mox capiendae arcis, quoniam oppido
potirentur, in exiguam de se ipsis spem verterat. tollitur 11
ex arce clamor ab Tusculanis; excipit aliquanto maior ab
25 exercitu Romano. utrinque urgentur Latini; nec impetus
Tusculanorum decurrentium ex superiore loco sustinent nec
Romanos subeuntes moenia molientesque obices portarum
arcere possunt. scalis prius moenia capta, inde effracta 12
claustra portarum; et cum anceps hostis et a fronte et a
30 tergo urgeret, nec ad pugnam ulla vis nec ad fugam loci
quicquam superesset, in medio caesi ad unum omnes.
recuperato ab hostibus Tusculo, exercitus Romam est
reductus.

34 *Increasing misery of debtors at Rome. The story of the younger Fabia and her sister. The plans of her father M. Fabius and her husband C. Licinius Stolo.*

Quanto magis prosperis eo anno bellis tranquilla omnia foris erant, tantum in urbe vis patrum in dies miseriaeque 5 plebis crescebant, cum eo ipso, quod necesse erat solvi, 2 facultas solvendi impediretur. itaque cum iam ex re nihil dari posset, fama et corpore, iudicati atque addicti, creditoribus satisfaciebant, poenaque in vicem fidei cesserat. 3 adeo ergo obnoxios summiserant animos non infimi solum, 10 sed principes etiam plebis, ut non modo ad tribunatum 4 militum inter patricios petendum, quod tanta vi ut liceret tetenderant, sed ne ad plebeios quidem magistratus capessendos petendosque ulli viro acri experientique animus esset, possessionemque honoris usurpati modo a plebe per 15 paucos annos recuperasse in perpetuum patres viderentur. 5 ne id nimis laetum parti alteri esset, parva, ut plerumque solet, rem ingentem moliundi causa intervenit. M. Fabii Ambusti, potentis viri cum inter sui corporis homines, tum etiam ad plebem, quod haudquaquam inter id genus con- 20 temptor eius habebatur, filiae duae nuptae, Ser. Sulpicio maior, minor C. Licinio Stoloni erat, illustri quidem viro, tamen plebeio ; eaque ipsa affinitas haud spreta gratiam 6 Fabio ad vulgum quaesierat. forte ita incidit, ut in Ser. Sulpicii tribuni militum domo sorores Fabiae cum inter se, 25 ut fit, sermonibus tempus tererent, lictor Sulpicii, cum is de foro se domum reciperet, forem, ut mos est, virga percuteret. cum ad id, moris eius insueta, expavisset minor 7 Fabia, risui sorori fuit, miranti ignorare id sororem ; ceterum is risus stimulos parvis mobili rebus animo muliebri 30 subdidit. frequentia quoque prosequentium rogantiumque, num quid vellet, credo fortunatum matrimonium ei sororis

visum, suique ipsam malo arbitrio, quo a proximis quisque
minime anteiri vult, paenituisse. confusam eam ex recenti 8
morsu animi cum pater forte vidisset, percontatus "satin'
salve?" avertentem causam doloris, quippe nec satis piam
5 adversus sororem nec admodum in virum honorificam,
elicuit comiter sciscitando, ut fateretur, eam esse causam 9
doloris, quod iuncta impari esset, nupta in domo, quam nec
honos nec gratia intrare posset. consolans inde filiam 10
Ambustus bonum animum habere iussit: eosdem prope-
10 diem domi visuram honores, quos apud sororem videat.
inde consilia inire cum genero coepit, adhibito L. Sextio, 11
strenuo adolescente et cuius spei nihil praeter genus patricium deesset.

C. Licinius and L. Sextius elected tribunes of the plebs. They promulgate 35
15 *three bills (1) to relieve debtors (2) to limit occupation of domain land
(3) to abolish military tribunes and provide that one consul at
least should be a plebeian. Other tribunes are engaged by the
patricians to veto the proposals. Licinius and Sextius veto all,
except plebeian, elections.*

20 Occasio videbatur rerum novandarum propter ingentem
vim aeris alieni, cuius levamen mali plebes, nisi suis in
summo imperio locatis, nullum speraret: accingendum ad 2
eam cogitationem esse; conando agendoque iam eo gradum
fecisse plebeios, unde si porro annitantur, pervenire ad
25 summa et patribus aequari tam honore quam virtute possent. in praesentia tribunos plebis fieri placuit, quo in 3
magistratu sibimet ipsi viam ad ceteros honores aperirent.
creatique tribuni C. Licinius et L. Sextius promulgavere 4
leges omnes adversus opes patriciorum et pro commodis
30 plebis, unam de aere alieno, ut, deducto eo de capite, quod
usuris pernumeratum esset, id, quod superesset, triennio
aequis pensionibus persolveretur; alteram de modo agro- 5

rum, ne quis plus quingenta iugera agri possideret, tertiam,
ne tribunorum militum comitia fierent, consulumque utique
alter ex plebe crearetur; cuncta ingentia et quae sine
6 certamine maximo obtineri non possent. omnium igitur
simul rerum, quarum immodica cupido inter mortales est, 5
agri, pecuniae, honorum, discrimine proposito, conterriti
patres cum trepidassent publicis privatisque consiliis, nullo
remedio alio praeter expertam multis iam ante certaminibus
intercessionem invento, collegas adversus tribunicias roga-
7 tiones comparaverunt. qui ubi tribus ad suffragium ineun- 10
dum citari a Licinio Sextioque viderunt, stipati patrum
praesidiis nec recitari rogationes nec sollemne quicquam
8 aliud ad sciscendum plebi fieri passi sunt. iamque frustra
saepe concilio advocato, cum pro antiquatis rogationes
essent, "bene habet" inquit Sextius; "quando quidem 15
tantum intercessionem pollere placet, isto ipso telo tutabi-
9 mur plebem. agite dum, comitia indicite, patres, tribunis
militum creandis; faxo, ne iuvet vox ista 'veto,' qua nunc
10 concinentes collegas nostros tam laeti auditis." haud
irritae cecidere minae; comitia, praeter aedilium tribuno- 20
rumque plebi, nulla sunt habita.

Licinius and Sextius are re-elected for five years in succession. An attack
of the Veliternians on Tusculum forces the tribunes to give way, and
military tribunes are elected for B.C. *370.*

Licinius Sextiusque tribuni plebis refecti nullos curules 25
magistratus creari passi sunt, eaque solitudo magistratuum,
et plebe reficiente duos tribunos et iis comitia tribunorum
militum tollentibus, per quinquennium urbem tenuit.

36   Alia bella opportune quievere; Veliterni coloni gestientes
otio, quod nullus exercitus Romanus esset, et agrum Roma- 30
num aliquoties incursavere et Tusculum oppugnare adorti
2 sunt; eaque res, Tusculanis veteribus sociis, novis civibus

opem orantibus, verecundia maxime non patres modo, sed
etiam plebem movit.

B.C. 370. *Great difficulty is experienced in levying an army. Tusculum
is relieved and Velitrae besieged but not taken.*

5 Remittentibus tribunis plebis comitia per interregem 3
sunt habita; creatique tribuni militum L. Furius, A. Manlius, Ser. Sulpicius, Ser. Cornelius, P. et C. Valerii haudquaquam tam obedientem in dilectu quam in comitiis
plebem habuere; ingentique contentione exercitu scripto, 4
10 profecti non ab Tusculo modo summovere hostem, sed
intra suamet ipsum moenia compulere, obsidebanturque 5
haud paulo vi maiore Velitrae, quam Tusculum obsessum
fuerat. nec tamen ab eis, a quibus obsideri coeptae erant,
expugnari potuere; ante novi creati sunt tribuni militum, 6
15 Q. Servilius, C. Veturius, A. et M. Cornelii, Q. Quinctius,
M. Fabius.

B.C. 369. *The new military tribunes succeed no better at Velitrae. The
tribunes re-elected for the eighth time renew their agitation under
more favorable circumstances, M. Fabius Ambustus being one of the
20 six military tribunes this year. They add to their previous proposals
a bill to appoint ten instead of two commissioners* sacris faciundis, *five
of them to be plebeians.*

Nihil ne ab iis quidem tribunis ad Velitras memorabile
factum. in maiore discrimine domi res vertebantur. nam 7
25 praeter Sextium Liciniumque latores legum, iam octavum
tribunos plebis refectos, Fabius quoque tribunus militum,
Stolonis socer, quarum legum auctor fuerat, earum suasorem
se haud dubium ferebat, et cum octo ex collegio tribunorum 8
plebi primo intercessores legum fuissent, quinque soli erant,
30 et, ut ferme solent, qui a suis desciscunt, capti et stupentes
animi vocibus alienis, id modo, quod domi praeceptum erat,

4—2

9 intercessioni suae praetendebant: Velitris in exercitu plebis
magnam partem abesse; in adventum militum comitia
differri debere, ut universa plebes de suis commodis
10 suffragium ferret. Sextius Liciniusque cum parte collegarum et uno ex tribunis militum Fabio, artifices iam tot 5
annorum usu tractandi animos plebis, primores patrum
productos interrogando de singulis, quae ferebantur ad
11 populum, fatigabant: auderentne postulare, ut, cum bina
iugera agri plebi dividerentur, ipsis plus quingenta iugera
habere liceret, ut singuli prope trecentorum civium posside- 10
rent agros, plebeio homini vix ad tectum necessarium aut
12 locum sepulturae suus pateret ager? an placeret, fenore
circumventam plebem, potius quam sorte creditum solvat,
corpus in nervum ac supplicia dare, et gregatim quotidie de
foro addictos duci, et repleri vinctis nobiles domus et, 15
ubicunque patricius habitet, ibi carcerem privatum esse?
37 haec indigna miserandaque auditu cum apud timentes
sibimet ipsos, maiore audientium indignatione quam sua,
2 increpuissent, atqui nec agros occupandi modum nec fenore
trucidandi plebem alium patribus unquam fore affirmabant, 20
nisi alterum ex plebe consulem, custodem suae libertatis,
3 plebes fecisset. contemni iam tribunos plebis, quippe
quae potestas iam suam ipsa vim frangat intercedendo.
4 non posse aequo iure agi, ubi imperium penes illos, penes
se auxilium tantum sit; nisi imperio communicato, nun- 25
quam plebem in parte pari rei publicae fore. nec esse,
quod quisquam satis putet, si plebeiorum ratio comitiis
consularibus habeatur; nisi alterum consulem utique ex
5 plebe fieri necesse sit, neminem fore. an iam memoria
exisse, cum tribunos militum idcirco potius quam consules 30
creari placuisset, ut et plebeiis pateret summus honos,
quattuor et quadraginta annis neminem ex plebe tribunum
6 militum creatum esse? quid crederent? duobusne in locis

sua voluntate impertituros plebi honorem, qui octona loca
tribunis militum creandis occupare soliti sint, et ad consulatum viam fieri passuros, qui tribunatum saeptum tam diu
habuerint? lege obtinendum esse, quod comitiis per gra- 7
5 tiam nequeat, et seponendum extra certamen alterum
consulatum, ad quem plebi sit aditus, quoniam in certamine
relictus praemium semper potentioris futurus sit. nec iam 8
posse dici id, quod antea iactare soliti sint, non esse in
plebeiis idoneos viros ad curules magistratus. numquid
10 enim socordius aut segnius rem publicam administrari post
P. Licinii Calvi tribunatum, qui primus ex plebe creatus sit,
quam per eos annos gesta sit, quibus praeter patricios nemo
tribunus militum fuerit? quin contra patricios aliquot dam- 9
natos post tribunatum, neminem plebeium. quaestores
15 quoque, sicut tribunos militum, paucis ante annis ex plebe
coeptos creari, nec ullius eorum populum Romanum paenituisse. consulatum superesse plebeiis; eam esse arcem 10
libertatis, id columen. si eo perventum sit, tum populum
Romanum vere exactos ex urbe reges et stabilem libertatem
20 suam existimaturum; quippe ex illa die in plebem ventura 11
omnia, quibus patricii excellant, imperium atque honorem,
gloriam belli, genus, nobilitatem, magna ipsis fruenda,
maiora liberis relinquenda. huius generis orationes ubi 12
accipi videre, novam rogationem promulgant, ut pro duum-
25 viris sacris faciundis decemviri creentur, ita ut pars ex plebe,
pars ex patribus fiat; omniumque earum rogationum comitia
in adventum eius exercitus differunt, qui Velitras obsidebat.

B.C. 368. *The struggle over the Licinian laws continues: Camillus is* **38**
appointed dictator. Licinius and Sextius refuse to recognise their
30 *colleagues' veto. Camillus threatens to administer the military oath*
to all the iuniores, *and lead them out of the city, but presently*
resigns, his reason for doing so being uncertain.

Prius circumactus est annus, quam a Velitris reduce-

rentur legiones; ita suspensa de legibus res ad novos
tribunos militum dilata; nam plebis tribunos eosdem, duos
2 utique, qui legum latores erant, plebes reficiebat. tribuni
militum creati T. Quinctius, Ser. Cornelius, Ser. Sulpicius,
3 Sp. Servilius, L. Papirius, L. Veturius. principio statim 5
anni ad ultimam dimicationem de legibus ventum; et cum
tribus vocarentur nec intercessio collegarum latoribus ob-
staret, trepidi patres ad duo ultima auxilia, summum
4 imperium summumque [ad] civem decurrunt. dictatorem
dici placet; dicitur M. Furius Camillus, qui magistrum 10
equitum L. Aemilium cooptat. legum quoque latores
adversus tantum apparatum adversariorum et ipsi causam
plebis ingentibus animis armant, concilioque plebis indicto,
5 tribus ad suffragium vocant. cum dictator, stipatus agmine
patriciorum, plenus irae minarumque consedisset, atque 15
ageretur res solito primum certamine inter se tribunorum
plebi ferentium legem intercedentiumque, et, quanto iure
potentior intercessio erat, tantum vinceretur favore legum
ipsarum latorumque, et "uti rogas" primae tribus dicerent,
6 tum Camillus "quando quidem" inquit, "Quirites, iam vos 20
tribunicia libido, non potestas regit, et intercessionem,
secessione quondam plebis partam, vobis eadem vi facitis
irritam, qua peperistis, non rei publicae magis universae
quam vestra causa dictator intercessioni adero eversumque
7 vestrum auxilium imperio tutabor. itaque si C. Licinius et 25
L. Sextius intercessioni collegarum cedunt, nihil patricium
magistratum inseram concilio plebis; si adversus intercessionem tanquam captae civitati leges imponere tendent,
8 vim tribuniciam a se ipsa dissolvi non patiar." adversus ea
cum contemptim tribuni plebis rem nihilo segnius perage- 30
rent, tum percitus ira Camillus lictores, qui de medio
plebem emoverent, misit et addidit minas, si pergerent,
sacramento omnes iuniores adacturum exercitumque extem-

plo ex urbe educturum. terrorem ingentem incusserat 9
plebi; ducibus plebis accendit magis certamine animos
quam minuit. sed re neutro inclinata magistratu se abdicavit, seu quia vitio creatus erat, ut scripsere quidam, seu
5 quia tribuni plebis tulerunt ad plebem idque plebs scivit,
ut, si M. Furius pro dictatore quid egisset, quingentum
milium ei multa esset; sed auspiciis magis quam novi 10
exempli rogatione deterritum ut potius credam, cum ipsius
viri facit ingenium, tum quod ei suffectus est extemplo
10 P. Manlius dictator, quem quid creari attinebat ad id 11
certamen, quo M. Furius victus esset? et quod eundem
M. Furium dictatorem insequens annus habuit, haud sine
pudore certe fractum priore anno in se imperium repeti-
turum; simul quod eo tempore, quo promulgatum de multa 12
15 eius traditur, aut et huic rogationi, qua se in ordinem cogi
videbat, obsistere potuit aut ne illas quidem, propter quas 13
et haec lata erat, impedire, et quod usque ad memoriam
nostram tribuniciis consularibusque certatum viribus est,
dictaturae semper altius fastigium fuit.

20 *Manlius is named dictator. In the interval between the two dictatorships,* **39**
the tribunes bring their proposals before the concilium plebis. *The
plebeians vote for the debt and agrarian proposals, but reject the one
touching the consulship. Licinius and Sextius declare that they will
not stand for the tribuneship again, unless the plebs accept and*
25 *support all the proposals. Appius Claudius Crassus delivers a
violent speech against the tribunician proposals. Licinius and
Sextius are re-elected for the tenth time, and carry their bill touching
the commissioners* sacris faciundis.

Inter priorem dictaturam abdicatam novamque a Manlio
30 initam ab tribunis velut per interregnum concilio plebis
habito, apparuit, quae ex promulgatis plebi, quae latoribus
gratiora essent. nam de fenore atque agro rogationes 2
iubebant, de plebeio consule antiquabant; et perfecta utra-

que res esset, ni tribuni se in omnia simul consulere plebem
3 dixissent. P. Manlius deinde dictator rem in causam plebis
inclinavit, C. Licinio, qui tribunus militum fuerat, magistro
4 equitum de plebe dicto. id aegre patres passos accipio;
dictatorem propinqua cognatione Licinii se apud patres 5
excusare solitum, simul negantem, magistri equitum maius
5 quam tribuni consularis imperium esse. Licinius Sextiusque,
cum tribunorum plebi creandorum indicta comitia essent,
ita se gerere, ut negando, iam sibi velle continuari honorem,
acerrime accenderent ad· id, quod dissimulando petebant, 10
6 plebem. nonum se annum iam velut in acie adversus
optimates maximo privatim periculo, nullo publice emolumento stare. consenuisse iam secum et rogationes promul-
7 gatas et vim omnem tribuniciae potestatis. primo interces-
sione collegarum in leges suas pugnatum esse, deinde 15
ablegatione iuventutis ad Veliternum bellum; postremo
8 dictatorium fulmen in se intentatum. iam nec collegas
nec bellum nec dictatorem obstare, quippe qui etiam omen
plebeio consuli magistro equitum ex plebe dicendo dederit;
9 se ipsam plebem et commoda morari sua. liberam urbem 20
ac forum a creditoribus, liberos agros ab iniustis possessori-
10 bus extemplo, si velit, habere posse. quae munera quando
tandem satis grato animo aestimaturos, si inter accipiendas
de suis commodis rogationes spem honoris latoribus earum
incidant? non esse modestiae populi Romani id postulare, 25
ut ipse fenore levetur et in agrum iniuria possessum a
potentibus inducatur, per quos ea consecutus sit, senes
tribunicios non sine honore tantum, sed etiam sine spe
11 honoris relinquat. proinde ipsi primum statuerent apud
animos, quid vellent, deinde comitiis tribuniciis declararent 30
voluntatem. si coniuncte ferri ab se promulgatas rogationes vellent, esse, quod eosdem reficerent tribunos plebis;
12 perlaturos enim, quae promulgaverint; sin, quod cuique

privatim opus sit, id modo accipi velint, opus esse nihil
invidiosa continuatione honoris; nec se tribunatum nec illos
ea, quae promulgata sint, habituros.

Adversus tam obstinatam orationem tribunorum cum **40**
5 prae indignitate rerum stupor silentiumque inde ceteros
patrum defixisset, App. Claudius Crassus, nepos decemviri, 2
dicitur odio magis iraque quam spe ad dissuadendum pro-
cessisse et locutus in hanc fere sententiam esse. "neque 3
novum neque inopinatum mihi sit, Quirites, si, quod unum
10 familiae nostrae semper obiectum est ab seditiosis tribunis,
id nunc ego quoque audiam, Claudiae genti iam inde ab
initio nihil antiquius in re publica patrum maiestate fuisse,
semper plebis commodis adversatos esse. quorum alterum 4
neque nego neque infitias eo, nos, ex quo adsciti sumus
15 simul in civitatem et patres, enixe operam dedisse, ut per
nos aucta potius quam imminuta maiestas earum gentium,
inter quas nos esse voluistis, dici vere posset; illud alterum 5
pro me maioribusque meis contendere ausim, Quirites, nisi,
quae pro universa re publica fiant, ea plebi tanquam aliam
20 incolenti urbem adversa quis putet, nihil nos neque privatos
neque in magistratibus, quod incommodum plebi esset,
scientes fecisse, nec ullum factum dictumve nostrum contra
utilitatem vestram, etsi quaedam contra voluntatem fuerint,
vere referri posse. an hoc, si Claudiae familiae non sim 6
25 nec ex patricio sanguine ortus, sed unus Quiritium quilibet,
qui modo me duobus ingenuis ortum et vivere in libera
civitate sciam, reticere possim, L. illum Sextium et C. 7
Licinium, perpetuos, si dis placet, tribunos, tantum licentiae
novem annis, quibus regnant, sumpsisse, ut vobis negent
30 potestatem liberam suffragii, non in comitiis, non in legibus
iubendis, se permissuros esse? 'sub condicione' inquit 8
'nos reficietis decimum tribunos.' quid est aliud dicere:
'quod petunt alii, nos adeo fastidimus, ut sine mercede

9 magna non accipiamus'? sed quae tandem ista merces
est, qua vos semper tribunos plebis habeamus? 'ut rogationes' inquit 'nostras, seu placent seu displicent, seu utiles
10 seu inutiles sunt, omnes coniunctim accipiatis.' obsecro vos,
Tarquinii tribuni plebis, putate me ex media contione unum 5
civem succlamare: 'bona venia vestra liceat ex his rogationibus legere, quas salubres nobis censemus esse, antiquare
11 alias.' 'non' inquit 'licebit, ut de fenore atque agris,
quod ad vos omnes pertinet, iubeas, et hoc portenti non
fiat in urbe Romana, uti L. Sextium atque hunc C. Licinium 10
consules, quod indignaris, quod abominaris, videas; aut
12 omnia accipe, aut nihil fero.' ut si quis ei, quem urgeat
fames, venenum ponat cum cibo et aut abstinere eo, quod
vitale sit, iubeat aut mortiferum vitali admisceat. ergo si
esset libera haec civitas, non tibi frequentes succlamassent: 15
'abi hinc cum tribunatibus ac rogationibus tuis'? quid?
si tu non tuleris, quod commodum est populo accipere,
13 nemo erit, qui ferat? illud si quis patricius, si quis, quod
illi volunt invidiosius esse, Claudius diceret: 'aut omnia
accipite, aut nihil fero,' quis vestrum, Quirites, ferret? 20
14 nunquamne vos res potius quam auctores spectabitis, sed
omnia semper, quae magistratus ille dicet, secundis auribus,
15 quae ab nostrum quo dicentur, adversis accipietis? at
hercule sermo est minime civilis; quid? rogatio qualis est,
quam a vobis antiquatam indignantur? sermoni, Quirites, 25
simillima. 'consules' inquit, 'rogo, ne vobis, quos velitis,
16 facere liceat.' an aliter rogat, qui utique alterum ex plebe
fieri consulem iubet nec duos patricios creandi potestatem
17 vobis permittit? si hodie bella sint, quale Etruscum fuit,
cum Porsinna Ianiculum insedit, quale Gallicum modo, 30
cum praeter Capitolium atque arcem omnia haec hostium
erant, et consulatum cum hoc M. Furio et quolibet alio ex
patribus L. ille Sextius peteret, possetisne ferre, Sextium

haud pro dubio consule esse, Camillum de repulsa dimicare?
hocine est in commune honores vocare, ut duos plebeios 18
fieri consules liceat, duos patricios non liceat? et alterum ex
plebe creari necesse sit, utrumque ex patribus praeterire
5 liceat? quaenam ista societas, quaenam consortio est? parum
est, si, cuius pars tua nulla adhuc fuit, in partem eius venis,
nisi partem petendo totum traxeris? 'timeo' inquit, 'ne, 19
si duos licebit creari patricios, neminem creetis plebeium.'
quid est dicere aliud: 'quia indignos vestra voluntate crea-
10 turi non estis, necessitatem vobis creandi, quos non vultis,
imponam'? quid sequitur, nisi ut ne beneficium quidem 20
debeat populo, si cum duobus patriciis unus petierit plebeius,
et lege se, non suffragio creatum dicat? quomodo extor- 41
queant, non quomodo petant honores, quaerunt; et ita
15 maxima sunt adepturi, ut nihil ne pro minimis quidem
debeant; et occasionibus potius quam virtute petere honores
malunt. est aliquis, qui se inspici, aestimari fastidiat, qui 2
certos sibi uni honores inter dimicantes competitores aequum
censeat esse, qui se arbitrio vestro eximat, qui vestra neces-
20 saria suffragia pro voluntariis et serva pro liberis faciat.
omitto Licinium Sextiumque, quorum annos in perpetua 3
potestate tanquam regum in Capitolio numeratis; quis est
hodie in civitate tam humilis, cui non via ad consulatum
facilior per istius legis occasionem quam nobis ac liberis
25 nostris fiat? si quidem nos ne cum volueritis quidem creare
interdum poteritis, istos, etiamsi nolueritis, necesse erit. de 4
indignitate satis dictum est; etenim dignitas ad homines
pertinet. quid de religionibus atque auspiciis, quae propria
deorum immortalium contemptio atque iniuria est, loquar?
30 auspiciis hanc urbem conditam esse, auspiciis bello ac pace,
domi militiaeque omnia geri, quis est, qui ignoret? penes 5
quos igitur sunt auspicia more maiorum? nempe penes
patres; nam plebeius quidem magistratus nullus auspicato

6 creatur; nobis adeo propria sunt auspicia, ut non solum,
quos populus creat patricios magistratus, non aliter quam
auspicato creet, sed nos quoque ipsi sine suffragio populi
auspicato interregem prodamus, et privati auspicia habea-
7 mus, quae isti ne in magistratibus quidem habent. quid 5
igitur aliud quam tollit ex civitate auspicia, qui plebeios
consules creando a patribus, qui soli ea habere possunt,
8 aufert? eludant nunc licet religiones: quid enim esse, si
pulli non pascantur, si ex cavea tardius exierint, si occecinerit avis? parva sunt haec; sed parva ista non contem- 10
9 nendo maiores nostri maximam hanc rem fecerunt; nunc
nos, tanquam iam nihil pace deorum opus sit, omnes
caerimonias polluimus. vulgo ergo pontifices, augures,
sacrificuli reges creentur; cuilibet apicem Dialem, dum-
modo homo sit, imponamus; tradamus ancilia, penetralia, 15
10 deos deorumque curam, quibus nefas est; non leges auspicato ferantur, non magistratus creentur; nec centuriatis nec
curiatis comitiis patres auctores fiant; Sextius et Licinius
tanquam Romulus ac Tatius in urbe Romana regnent, quia
11 pecunias alienas, quia agros dono dant. tanta dulcedo est 20
ex alienis fortunis praedandi, nec in mentem venit, altera
lege solitudines vastas in agris fieri pellendo finibus dominos,
altera fidem abrogari, cum qua omnis humana societas
12 tollitur? omnium rerum causa vobis antiquandas censeo
istas rogationes. quod faxitis, deos velim fortunare." 25

42   Oratio Appii ad id modo valuit, ut tempus rogationum
2 iubendarum proferretur. refecti decimum iidem tribuni,
Sextius et Licinius, de decemviris sacrorum ex parte de
plebe creandis legem pertulere. creati quinque patrum,
quinque plebis, graduque eo iam via facta ad consulatum 30
3 videbatur. hac victoria contenta plebes cessit patribus, ut
in praesentia consulum mentione omissa tribuni militum
crearentur.

B.C. 367. *On news of a Gallic war Camillus is appointed dictator.*
After the Gauls are defeated, the struggle over the Licinian rogations
is renewed, and ends in their becoming law. L. Sextius is elected
first plebeian consul. The praetorship, confined to patricians, is
5 *instituted.*

Creati A. et M. Cornelii iterum, M. Geganius, P. Manlius, L. Veturius, P. Valerius sextum.

Cum praeter Velitrarum obsidionem, tardi magis rem 4
exitus quam dubii, quietae externae res Romanis essent,
10 fama repens belli Gallici allata perpulit civitatem, ut M.
Furius dictator quintum diceretur. is T. Quinctium Poe-
num magistrum equitum dixit. bellatum cum Gallis eo 5
anno circa Anienem flumen, auctor est Claudius, inclitam-
que in ponte pugnam, qua T. Manlius Gallum, cum quo
15 provocatus manus conseruit, in conspectu duorum exer-
cituum caesum torque spoliavit, tum pugnatam. pluribus 6
auctoribus magis adducor ut credam, decem haud minus
post annos ea acta, hoc autem anno in Albano agro cum
Gallis dictatore M. Furio signa collata. nec dubia nec 7
20 difficilis Romanis, quanquam ingentem Galli terrorem memoria pristinae cladis attulerant, victoria fuit. multa millia
barbarorum in acie, multa captis castris caesa; palati alii, 8
Apuliam maxime petentes, cum fuga se longinqua, tum
quod passim eos simul pavor terrorque distulerant, ab
25 hoste [sese] tutati sunt. dictatori consensu patrum plebis-
que triumphus decretus.

Vixdum perfunctum eum bello atrocior domi seditio ex- 9
cepit, et per ingentia certamina dictator senatusque victus,
ut rogationes tribuniciae acciperentur; et comitia consu-
30 lum adversa nobilitate habita, quibus L. Sextius de plebe
primus consul factus. et ne is quidem finis certaminum 10
fuit. quia patricii se auctores futuros negabant, prope

secessionem plebis res terribilesque alias minas civilium
11 certaminum venit, cum tandem per dictatorem condicioni-
bus sedatae discordiae sunt, concessumque ab nobilitate
plebi de consule plebeio, a plebe nobilitati de praetore uno,
12 qui ius in urbe diceret, ex patribus creando. ita ab diutina 5
ira tandem in concordiam redactis ordinibus, cum dignam
eam rem senatus censeret esse, meritoque id, si quando
unquam alias, deum immortalium fore, ut ludi maximi
13 fierent et dies unus ad triduum adiiceretur, recusantibus id
munus aedilibus plebis, conclamatum a patriciis est iuveni- 10
bus, se id honoris deum immortalium causa libenter facturos
14 ut aediles fierent. quibus cum ab universis gratiae actae
essent, factum senatus consultum, ut duo viros aediles ex
patribus dictator populum rogaret, patres auctores omnibus
eius anni comitiis fierent. 15

PERIOCHA LIBRI VI.

Res adversus Volscos et Aequos et Praenestinos prospere gestas
continet. quattuor tribus adiectae: Stellatina, Tromentina, Sabatina,
Arniensis. M. Manlius, qui Capitolium a Gallis defenderat, cum
obstrictos aere alieno liberaret, nexos exsolveret, crimine affectati regni
damnatus de saxo deiectus est; in cuius notam senatus consultum factum
est, ne cui de Manlia gente Marco nomen esset. C. Licinius et
L. Sextius tribuni plebis legem promulgaverunt, ut consules ex plebe
fierent, qui ex patribus creabantur; eamque cum magna contentione
repugnantibus patribus, cum iidem tribuni plebis per quinquennium soli
magistratus fuissent, pertulerunt; et primus ex plebe consul L. Sextius
creatus est. lata est et altera lex, ne cui plus quingentis iugeribus agri
liceret possidere.

NOTES.

CHAPTER I.

p. **1.** 1 §§ **1, 2.** The opening sentence is long and should be read through carefully before translation. The main outline is: 'I have set forth ..the history of Rome, a history at once (*cum*) obscure by reason of its exceeding antiquity,...and obscure also (*tum*) because the literary records...were scanty, and because whatever there was...perished.'

4 § **1. ab condita urbe**] This seems to support the common assumption that the title, under which Livy's history was published, was *Ab urbe condita libri*; cf. the title of the Annals of Tacitus, *Ab excessu divi Augusti libri*. Translate: 'from the foundation of the city.' The part. pass. in agreement with a subst. is frequently used instead of a subst. with another in the gen. depending on it.

ad captam eandem urbem] The capture of Rome by the Gauls had been narrated by Livy in Book V. Probably a new section of the work begins with Book VI, as is indicated by the short preface contained in this chapter. Cf. Introd. § 1.

5 **consulibus...ac dictatoribus, decemviris...tribunis consularibus**] The two magistracies which were in the nature of experiments are placed in contrast with the consulship and dictatorship. The decemvirate lasted from 451–449 B.C.; its principal work was the drawing up of the code of laws known as the XII Tables. The consular tribunate was established in 444 B.C., partly with the object of opening up to the plebeians the powers of the consulship without its more external dignities, and partly with a view to creating a larger number of military commanders.

8 § **2. velut quae**]=*velut ea sunt quae*, 'as is the case with things which.'

9   **parvae**] 'scanty,' referring to meagre annalistic notices. For Livy's use of the earliest sources of Roman history, see Introd. § 2.

10   **una custodia fidelis memoriae rerum gestarum**] Very characteristic of Livy, who was by no means a lover of archaeological research. But 'the Record of the Human Past is not all contained in printed books,' and monuments are often more faithful recorders of the past than are written documents.

11   **in commentariis pontificum**] These books contained primarily the decrees of the *pontifices* touching religious matters. But Livy evidently regards them as also concerned with historical records, though perhaps only incidentally. Cf. 4. 3. 9, where Canuleius, in proposing his laws, says: *si non ad fastos, non ad commentarios pontificum admittimur, ne ea quidem scimus, quae omnes peregrini etiam sciunt, consules in locum regum successisse?* At the same time we cannot help suspecting that Livy is confusing the *commentarii* with the *annales maximi*, the latter being a record of the chief events of each year, drawn up by the Pontifex Maximus.

12   **publicis**] Such as laws (e.g. the XII Tables) and treaties.

    privatis] Family records, *laudationes* or funeral orations, which were a frequent cause of the falsification of history, and the inscriptions (*tituli*) placed beneath the *imagines* or masks of distinguished members of a family. These last were also in many cases mere fabrications; cf. 8. 40. 4: *falsis imaginum titulis.*

    § 3. The sentence is a little complicated. Rome, after the burning, is likened to a tree which has been cut down, whose roots, however, are still sound. Translate: 'clearer thenceforward and more certain will be the record of the history of the city both at home and abroad, from the time of its second foundation, when it sprang afresh as it were from the roots with greater promise of vigour and fruitfulness.' *clariora* is held by some to mean 'more brilliant.' It would be possible to take *ab secunda origine velut ab stirpibus* closely together, but this seems to involve considerable awkwardness.

16   **§ 4. adminiculo**] As Weissenborn remarks, this carries on the image of the plant or tree. Trans. 'prop,' or 'support.'

    M. Furio principe] M. Furius Camillus, with whose speech against the proposed migration to Veii the Fifth Book had closed. *Princeps* is an unofficial title, and means 'foremost citizen.' Augustus made a dexterous use of the word in founding his system of government.

17   **anno**] i.e. Camillus, after celebrating his triumph, remained dictator till the end of June, when he quitted office with the consular tribunes.

The 'year' meant is that of the magistrates. No dictator could lawfully remain in office beyond a period of six months; he usually resigned immediately after his special task had been carried out; cf. c. 29. 10 (of T. Quinctius Cincinnatus): *die vicesimo, quam creatus erat, dictatura se abdicavit.* Plutarch (*Cam.* 31) is wrong in saying that Camillus remained dictator for a whole year: ἡ βουλὴ τὸν Κάμιλλον οὐκ εἴασε βουλόμενον ἀποθέσθαι τὴν ἀρχὴν ἐντὸς ἐνιαυτοῦ, καίπερ ἓξ μῆνας οὐδενὸς ὑπερβαλόντος ἑτέρου δικτάτορος.

19   **§ 5. tribunos]** Owing to the disaster which had happened during their term of office the consular tribunes were held *vitio creati*, i.e. it was supposed that there must have been some flaw in the taking of the auspices at the time of their election. They were therefore called upon to resign, as being incapable of presiding at the election of their successors and of taking the auspices; cf. 8. 3. 4. The dictator, as nominated by one of these consular tribunes, would be considered equally incapable of holding the elections.

p. 2.   1. **res ad interregnum rediit]** Upon the resignation of the consuls or consular tribunes the government passed temporarily into the hands of the patrician portion of the Senate (*patres*). In the regal period this had been the case upon the death of the King. This state of affairs was known as an *interregnum.* The patrician portion of the Senate then nominated from their number an *interrex* (*interregem prodere*), who held office for five days; it should be noted that the first *interrex* never held the elections, probably because he had not received office directly from the hands of a magistrate. He nominated a second *interrex*, who, if the omens were favourable, could hold the elections. But there was nothing to prevent the succession of any number of *interreges*, should circumstances so require.

2   **§ 6. opere ac labore]** Cf. § 3: *laetius feraciusque.* A certain amount of tautology is characteristic of Livy's style. Cf. Introd. § 3.

3   **Q. Fabio]** Cf. 5. 36. 7. Fabius, though ambassador, had assisted the people of Clusium in battle against the Gauls.

   simul primum] So frequently in Livy for *simulac primum.*

4   **dicta dies est]** In the case of trials before the Comitia (*iudicia populi*), the prosecutor, who was necessarily a magistrate, gave formal notice in a *contio* or mass-meeting of his intention to summon the accused for enquiry on a certain day. Hence *diem dicere=*'to give formal notice of a prosecution.' The preliminary enquiry (*anquisitio*) led up to the trial proper before the Comitia Centuriata or Tributa, which took the form of a *rogatio* or bill of pains and penalties

introduced by the magistrate for acceptance or rejection by the
assembly.

legatus] This word may well be retained in addition to *orator*;
stress is laid upon the fact that Fabius had fought while in the capacity
of envoy. Livy's style is full, and he does not hesitate to use two words,
though only one is absolutely necessary. See Appendix.

5   **orator**] For the meaning 'envoy,' cf. Verg. *Aen.* 7. 153: *centum
oratores augusta ad moenia regis | ire iubet.*

ius gentium] 'The law of nations,' *not* 'international law' in the
modern sense. The *ius gentium* was a body of rules generally observed among the various peoples with whom the Romans were brought
in contact, and was contrasted with the *ius civile* or laws specially
affecting Roman citizens. See Maine, *Ancient Law*, ch. iii, and
cf. c. 17. 8 n.

17   **§ 8. Camillus**] See Appendix.

18   **creat**] Livy never troubles to use very accurate terms in relation to
constitutional points. The *interrex* presided at the elections, took the
auspices, and duly returned (*renuntiare*) the elected candidates. Hence
creat simply = 'obtains the election of.'

21   **§ 9. magistratum inissent**] The ordinary date upon which consuls
or consular tribunes entered office was at this period July 1st; but,
owing to the *interregnum*, the date on the present occasion must have
been July 6th or later. It may be noted in this connection that the
tribunes of the *plebs* always entered upon office on December 10th.

23   **§ 10. foedera**] Treaties were reckoned under the head of *religiones*,
as being concluded with elaborate religious ceremonies. See especially
1. 24. 4, where the ceremony at the conclusion of a treaty between the
Romans and Albans is fully described.

duodecim tabulae] The famous code of laws drawn up by the
decemviri legibus scribundis in 451, 450 B.C. The original tables were
set up in the Forum; cf. 3. 57. 10: *leges...in aes incisas in publico
proposuerunt.*

24   **regiae leges**] Very little is known of these 'royal laws,' but it
seems probable that they were certain rules, partly of a secular, partly
of a religious character, which were published by the *pontifices* under
the Kings' directions for the guidance of the public. The pontifical
rules were usually kept a close secret, and the present opportunity was
seized upon to suppress those relating to religion, which had previously
been published; these most likely concerned the calendar and festivals.
Cf. 9. 46. 5, where the scribe-aedile Flavius (304 B.C.) *civile ius, repo-*

situm in penetralibus pontificum, evulgavit, fastosque circa forum in albo proposuit, ut quando lege agi posset, sciretur.

It seems possible that we have an actual specimen of a *lex regia* preserved in a fragmentary Latin inscription, a cast of which is in the British Museum. It was discovered in 1899 on the site of the Comitium and is written in archaic Greek letters. It perhaps gives directions as to the place and time at which certain sacrifices are to be made and indicates the penalty in case of contravention. The date of the inscription is probably to be placed early in the 6th century B.C., and it is likely that its mutilation took place at the time of the Gallic invasion. The interpretation, however, is very uncertain.

quae comparerent] 'So far as they were to be found.' Or. recta: *conquirantur, (si) quae compareant.*

28 **§ 11. diebus religiosis]** Cf. Gellius 4. 9. 5. He defines *dies religiosi* as *tristi omine et infames impeditique, in quibus et res divinas facere et rem quampiam novam exordiri temperandum est.* Upon these days it was considered extremely unlucky to embark upon any important business. The *dies nefasti*, on the other hand, were the days upon which the law-courts were closed. *Dies religiosi* were also known as *dies atri.*

29 **a. d. xv Kal. Sextiles]** July 18th. So Tacitus *Hist.* 2. 91 speaks of *infausto die Cremerensi Alliensique cladibus*; cf. also Lucan 7. 409: *et damnata diu Romanis Allia fastis.*

ad Cremeram] The disaster to the Fabii is assigned to the year 477 B.C. (II. 50). The Cremera was a tributary of the Tiber, and flowed past Veii. See map.

32 **insignemque rei nulli...agendae]** Trans.: 'and marked it out for doing no business, public or private.' The dat. after *insignis* is one of purpose, as in 10. 39. 14: *ut...spolia ea referrent, quae insignia publicis etiam locis decorandis essent*: 'which were marked out for the decoration...' For various emendations which have been suggested see Appendix.

p. 3. 1 **§ 12. postridie idus Quintiles]** July 16th. Quintilis was the 5th month of the old Roman year, which began with March. Later on Quintilis was changed into Julius in honour of Julius Caesar. Similarly Sextilis, originally the 6th month, had its name changed in honour of Augustus.

The acc. after *postridie* and *pridie* is on the analogy of that after *post* and *ante.* The gen. is found rarely, e.g. in Caes. *B. G.* 1. 47. 2: *pridie eius diei.*

2　　**litasset]** *litare* means 'to offer a favourable sacrifice.' Cf. 5. 38. 1 *nec auspicato nec litato instruunt aciem.* When the omens were un-favourable, it was the duty of the general to endeavour by every means in his power to avoid an engagement, until by renewal (*instauratio*) of sacrifice favourable omens were obtained ; cf. 7. 8. 5 : *diu non perlitatum tenuerat dictatorem, ne ante meridiem signum dare posset.* Cf. also Gellius 5. 17. 2.

　　neque] = *et non.*

　　pace deum] ' the support,' or ' favour of heaven.'

3　　**post diem tertium]** ' two days afterwards,' as we should say. The Romans included the day reckoned from in their calculation.

4　　**rebus divinis supersederi]** ' that public sacrifice should be refrained from.' As a result no *comitia* could be held and no battle (at all events in offence) could be fought, since a public sacrifice was a necessary prelude to these. The days following the Kalends, Nones, and Ides, are called by post-classical writers *dies postridiani.*

CHAPTER II.

7　　**§ 1. quietis]** sc. *eis,* ' the Romans.'

　　erigendae...rei publicae] gen. defining *consilia.* ' Plans,' viz. ' of raising the state.'

8　　**§ 2. Volsci, veteres hostes]** The Volscians occupied the territory to the S. of Latium, beyond the Rutuli. Their land extended along the coast nearly to the river Liris. See map. In 396 B.C. they had con-cluded peace with Rome (5. 23. 12).

9　　**ceperant...afferebant]** Note the difference of tense. ' Had (actually) taken...kept bringing news.'

10　　**Etruriae principum ex omnibus populis]** The *populi* were the 12 autonomous cities, which were united in a federation. The *principes* would be drawn from the Lucumones, the ruling aristocratic class.

11　　**ad fanum Voltumnae]** Voltumna was the patron goddess of the Etruscan federation, and had her shrine at Volsinii. Here representatives from the different cities met every year to do honour to the goddess ; here also common councils were held, whenever need arose ; cf. 4. 23. 5 : *cum duae civitates legatis circa duodecim populos missis impetrassent, ut ad Voltumnae fanum indiceretur omni Etruriae concilium.*

　　mercatores] Cf. 4. 24. 2. A great fair was held simultaneously with the yearly meeting of the Etruscan League at Volsinii, and this fair was attended by Roman merchants ; cf. the fair held by the Sabines *ad Feroniae fanum* (1. 30. 5).

12   § **3. defectionis**]   See Appendix.

13   **Latinorum Hernicorumque**]   The Latins had joined the exiled
Tarquins, but, as tradition asserted, had been defeated at Lake Regillus.
The original league between Rome and the Latins, which had thus been
temporarily dissolved, is said to have been renewed by Spurius Cassius
in 493 B.C.   The same man effected an alliance between Rome and the
Hernicans in 486 B.C. : this was of great importance owing to the
geographical position of the latter people, whose territory parted
Rome's two great enemies, the Volscians and the Aequians.   See
map.

14   **ambigua fide**]   Ablative expressing a characteristic or quality,
frequently used with *esse*; cf. Cic. *ad Fam.* 6. 14. 3: *quam ob rem fac
animo magno fortique sis.*

18   § **5. eiusdem auspiciis**]   The real meaning of the phrase should be
carefully noted.   The *auspicia* were the means whereby the will of the
gods was ascertained, and the dictator, as supreme magistrate, consulted
the gods by taking them on behalf of the community.

19   **dictatoremque dici**]   The dictator was nominated by one of the
consular tribunes, or in ordinary periods by one of the consuls, after a
decree of the Senate (implied here in *placuit*).

21   § **6. iustitioque indicto**]   A suspension of all legal business, which
seems usually to have accompanied the appointment of a dictator :
cf. 4. 31. 9: *iustitium in foro tabernaeque clausae, fiuntque omnia castris
quam urbi similiora.*   Any of the higher magistrates could announce a
iustitium upon an emergency, usually after a decree of the Senate ;
cf. 3. 5. 4: *et quod necesse erat in tanto tumultu, iustitium per aliquot
dies servatum.*   The end of the *iustitium* was announced by decree of
the magistrate (*iustitium remittere*).

22   **iuniorum**]   The *iuniores* were men between the ages of 17 and 46,
the *seniores* between 47 and 60.   It was not customary to call out the
latter for service in the field, hence the qualification *ita, ut.*   ' He held
a levy of *iuniores*, and actually enrolled...' Lit. ' in such a way, that.'
Cf. 1. 43. 2: *seniores* (sc. *confecit*) *ad urbis custodiam ut praesto essent,
iuvenes ut foris bella gererent.*

23   **in verba sua iuratos**]   They were required to take the *sacramentum*,
or military oath.   One man appears to have repeated the formula
(*verba concepta*) of the oath, and then the rest merely added the words
' *idem in me.*' For the phrase *iurare in verba*=' to swear according to a
formula,' cf. c. 22. 7 : *comitiisque iurare parato in verba excusandae
valetudini.*

centuriaret] 'formed into centuries'; cf. Cic. *ad Att.* 16. 9: *rem gerit palam, centuriat Capuae, dinumerat.*

24 § **7. trifariam**] Not found before Livy ; cf. Gk τριφάσιος.

29 § **8. ad Mecium**] Diodorus (14. 117. 1) says : ἐν τῷ καλουμένῳ Μαρκίῳ κατεστρατοπέδευσαν, ἀπέχοντες ἀπὸ 'Ρώμης σταδίους διακοσίους : cf. Plut. *Cam.* 34 : περὶ τὸ Μάρκιον ὄρος. No doubt the *tribus Maecia* founded in 332 B.C. derived its name from the same source as the present place, perhaps from some conspicuous hill, as Plutarch's language suggests. The MSS. vary with regard to the name ; see Appendix.

30 § **9. ab**] Here practically = *propter*, giving the motive of the action. Cf. c. 4. 8 : *ab odio.*

31 **crederent**] By a curious usage the word introducing the or. obliqua is itself put into the subjunctive. We might have expected. *quod ...credebant* ; there is no logical justification for using the subjunctive *crederent*. The constr., however, is found elsewhere in Latin ; cf. 21. 1. 3 and Cic. *de off.* 1. 13. 40 : *rediit paulo post, quod se oblitum nescio quid diceret* ; c. 6. 5 is not parallel, since *dicerent* there occurs in true or. obliqua.

32 **auditus...**] 'The news that Camillus was in command'; cf. c. 1. 1 n.

33 **vallum**] This was properly the palisade. (*valli* = Gk χάρακες), which crowned the outer edge of the earthwork (*agger*) ; but *vallum* is frequently used for the earthwork itself, as here.

p. **4. 4** § **11. aperuit...viam**] The enemy had erected a barricade of logs outside the earth-mound. Camillus set fire to this barricade, the smoke from which blew into the faces of the defenders and threw them into confusion ; but the Romans themselves found considerable difficulty in crossing the glowing embers.

5 **vapore**] Very likely means 'heat' here, as always in Lucretius : cf. 5. 48. 2 : *loco...ab incendiis torrido et vaporis pleno.* It may of course bear the more usual meaning of ' steam,' ' vapour.'

6 **moles**] 'trouble.' *Moles* means originally ' mass,' and then 'trouble,' ' effort,' cf. Verg. *Aen.* 1. 33 : *Tantae molis erat Romanam condere gentem.* With this may be compared the English ' moil ' in the phrase ' toil and moil,' etc. Cf. Bacon, Essay ' of Plantations': ' but moile not too much under ground,' although the connection between *moles* and moil is disputed by philologists.

7 **militibus munitum**] See Appendix.

10 § **12. militi**] Collective singular = ' soldiers.' Livy makes a very extensive use of these collective singulars. Besides words like *eques,*

pedes, etc., we find *Romanus* = ' Romans' (c. 31. 7) and many similar usages.

11   **largitore**] Practically equivalent to an adjective, ' open-handed'; cf. c. 10. 6: *victorem exercitum*, 'the victorious army.' The allusion is to Camillus' disposal of the booty taken at Veii.

12   **§ 13. fugientes**] 'the fugitives.' The free use of present participles as substantives is a characteristic of Livy's style; cf. c. 25. 9 *discentium*, c. 37. 1 *audientium*.

13   **septuagesimo...anno**] It seems impossible to make out why Livy set the duration of the Volscian war at 70 years. There had been perpetual forays between the Romans and the Volscians since the regal period; cf. 1. 53. 2: *Is* (*Tarquinius Superbus*) *primus Volscis bellum in ducentos amplius post suam aetatem annos movit*. Apparently Livy has been betrayed into self-contradiction by combining the accounts of different annalists.

ad deditionem...subegit] But we very soon find the Volscians in arms again (c. 6. 4 etc.). It is, however, certain that the Volscians really received crushing blows from Rome about this period. Thus Diodorus Siculus, whose references to Roman history are probably based on the older and more trustworthy annals, says : τὸν ἔμπροσθεν χρόνον ἰσχυροὶ δοκοῦντες εἶναι, διὰ τὴν συμφορὰν ταύτην ἀσθενέστατοι τῶν περιοικούντων ἐθνῶν ἐγενήθησαν (14. 117. 3): cf. Introd. § 4.

15   **§ 14. molientes**] *Moliri* is used in so many different ways, that it is worth while to distinguish some of them. The primary notion involved is that of effort. In Livy we find amongst others the following uses of the word. (1) Absolute, ' to put oneself in motion,' 'to depart,' cf. 37. 11. 12 (of ships): *dum moliuntur a terra*. (2) ' To work on' a thing : so 28. 17. 15: *ancoras moliri* 'to hoist anchor'; 9. 3. 3: *montes moliri sede sua*, ' to remove mountains from their seat'; c. 34. 5 : *rem ingentem moliundi causa*. (3) A more general sense ' to undertake,' as in the present case, 'designing war.' In c. 11. 8 meaning (2) is extended in a bold manner in *moliri fidem* = ' to attack or tamper with credit.'

CHAPTER III.

23   **§ 1. ingruerat**] Not used by Cicero or Caesar. The word perhaps = *inruere*. Hence its meaning ' to threaten,' ' to assail.'

§ 2. Sutrium, socios] Livy writes *socios* in apposition to the word ' citizens' implied in the name of the town. A bold use of these sense-constructions marks the beginning of the decline from classical Latin. Cf. c. 30. 9: *Setiam, ipsis querentibus.*

Sutrium was a place of great importance, commanding as it did the route between N. and S. Etruria. Livy does not say when it entered into alliance with Rome, but it probably did so shortly after the fall of Veii (396 B.C.). Later on, in 383 B.C. (Vell. Pat. 1. 14. 2), Sutrium became a Latin colony, and, together with Nepete, marked for some time the boundary of Roman territory to the N.; cf. Introd. § 4, and see map.

26   **primo quoque tempore**] 'at the first possible opportunity.' Distinguish between this meaning and that of 'one after another,' which sometimes attaches to *primus quisque*, e.g. in 42. 32. 7: *cum tribuni militum, qui centuriones essent, primum quemque citarent.* *Primo quoque tempore* is explained by Kühner (*Ausführ. Gramm.* 2, p. 474) thus:—If possible, the thing shall be done on the first day; failing that, on the second, and so on. Hence 'at each first opportunity' is equivalent to 'as soon as possible.'

27   § **3. spei moram**] 'the postponement of the looked for relief.'

30   **singulis**] might mean either 'with one change of raiment' or 'with only one garment on them.' Plutarch evidently took it to mean the latter (*Cam.* 35): αὐτοὶ δὲ πάντων ἐνδεεῖς ἐν ἱματίοις μόνον ἀφειμένοι (ἔτυχον), and Livy's general usage favours this interpretation.

32   § **4. cui...ad pedes**] 'at whose feet.' In 34. 11. 5 we have the gen. *flentes ad genua consulis provolvuntur.*

p. 5. 3 **excepisset**] 'followed.' *Excipere* is used to express succession of events; cf. 2. 4. 5: *sermonem excepit* (of the ear following and catching up a sound); also 5. 13. 4: *tristem hiemem pestilens aestas excepit* (of summer following upon winter).

4   **luctum lacrimasque**] 'woe and weeping.' Livy is fond of alliteration; cf. c. 14. 8: *cum patria, penatibus publicis ac privatis,* and c. 17. 2: *libertatem ac lucem.*

7   § **5. ad Sutrium**] may mean 'to the neighbourhood of Sutrium,' but Livy constantly uses prepositions with the names of towns, where the normal constr. would be the simple acc. or abl.; cf. c. 26. 8: *ab Tusculo legiones reductae*; c. 27. 7 *ab Antio Satricum, ab Satrico Velitras...legiones ductas.* The prepositions are probably inserted with a view to clearness; cf. Suet. *Aug.* 86, where Augustus is said to have made an increased use of prepositions in order to express his meaning with greater exactness.

8   **soluta omnia**] 'all discipline relaxed.'

ut fit] 'as is generally the case.' This is the usual form of expression in Livy; cf. c. 21. 7 and c. 34. 6. The fuller phrase *ut fere fit* is not so common.

9   **ante moenia, patentes portas**] See Appendix.

14   **§ 7. si qua...possent**] 'in the hope...that they might be able.' *Si qua*='if by any means'; the subj. *possent* is due to the notion of wish involved. Cf. the Greek εἰ with the opt., e.g. in *Il.* 3. 449, 450: Ἀτρείδης δ' ἀν' ὅμιλον ἐφοίτα θηρὶ ἐοικώς, | εἴ που ἐσαθρήσειεν Ἀλέξανδρον θεοειδέα. Notice the past tenses side by side with the historic present *inveniunt*.

15   **portas**] See Appendix.

17   **§ 8. accensum...fuisset**] Strictly speaking *fuisset* (instead of *esset*) should indicate a state, 'would have been kindled and remained so.' But Livy is by no means careful to maintain the distinction between *fueram* and *eram*, and between *fuissem* and *essem*. Below (§ 10) *traditum fuerat*=*traditum erat* (a simple act). In the case of *fui* and *fuisse* the idea of a state is more often present; cf. 1. 19. 3: *bis deinde post Numae regnum clausus fuit*, lit. 'was in a closed condition.' The rule, however, is not a hard and fast one in Latin, for a sentence such as *Omnis Gallia divisa est* has clearly more reference to the ensuing state than to a specific act of division. In some cases *fui* indicates that a state has existed, but has now ceased to exist, as in c. 29. 9, *tabula...his ferme incisa litteris fuit*, and in 38. 56. 3, *Literni monumentum monumentoque statua superimposita fuit, quam tempestate disiectam nuper vidimus ipsi.*

18   **ab desperatione**] *Desperatio* is practically personified, hence the *ab*; 'would have been kindled by the desperate foe'; cf. c. 6. 11: *circumsederi...ab invidia et odio*. Others translate 'in consequence of the desperation,' as in c. 2. 9: *ab contemptu*.

20   **§ 9. quibus**]=*ei quibus*.

21   **in spe ultima**] 'so long as hope was very remote.' *In* expresses the circumstances in which a person is placed; cf. *in re trepida*.

CHAPTER IV.

p. 6. 1   **§ 1. trium simul bellorum**] i.e. wars against the Volscians, Aequians, and Etruscans. *Simul* is practically an attribute 'simultaneous.' Livy is very fond of using adverbs in this way, placing them often between an adj. and a subst.; cf. c. 39. 6: *maximo privatim periculo, nullo publice emolumento*. Perhaps this is an imitation of the Gk constr.; cf. ὁ πάνυ Περικλῆς, οἱ νῦν ἄνθρωποι, etc.

3   **§ 2. sub hasta venundatis**] When property captured in war was
sold, a spear was set up. No doubt owing to this custom a spear was
erected at auctions and in the Centumviral Court, which dealt chiefly
with cases relating to inheritance of property; cf. Cic. *de off.* 2. 8. 29 and
especially Gaius 4. 16: *Festuca autem utebantur quasi hastae loco, signo
quodam iusti dominii, (quod maxime) sua esse credebant quae ex hostibus
cepissent; unde in centumviralibus iudiciis hasta proponitur*; cf. also
24. 18. 11: *convenere frequentes, qui hastae huius generis adsueverant.*

4   **auro**] See 5. 50. 7, and cf. 5. 25. 8–10. It is said that the Roman
matrons provided from their ornaments the gold requisite for an offering
to Apollo, and also for the ransom paid to the Gauls. In return, they
received the right of riding in carriages in the city and of the *laudatio* at
their funerals.

6   **§ 3. ante Capitolium incensum**] The original temple (said to have
been dedicated in 509 B.C.) was burnt down in 83 B.C., during, though
not immediately in consequence of, the Sullan wars; cf. Tac. *Hist.* 3. 72:
arserat et ante Capitolium civili bello, sed fraude privata. This is the
conflagration to which Livy here refers. The site of the temple of
Jupiter Capitolinus has now been definitely located on the southern or
lower eminence of the Mons Capitolinus; on the northern eminence was
the *Arx*, and between the two was the depression known as *inter duos
lucos*. See map.

in Iovis cella...ante pedes Iunonis] Cf. c. 29. 9. The temple was
divided into three shrines (*cellae*) by parallel walls. The central *cella*
belonged to Jupiter, whose seated statue was placed there; the W. *cella*
contained a standing statue of Minerva, the E. one of Juno; cf. the coins
figured in Ramsay, *Roman Antiquities*[15], p. 41, and the description in
Dionysius of the temple as restored by Catulus (69 B.C.): ἐν αὐτῷ τρεῖς
σηκοὶ παράλληλοι, κοινὰς ἔχοντες πλευράς, μέσος μὲν ὁ τοῦ Διός, παρ'
ἐκάτερον δὲ τὸ μέρος ὅ τε τῆς "Ηρας καὶ ὁ τῆς 'Αθηνᾶς ὑφ' ἑνὸς ἀετοῦ
(pediment) καὶ μιᾶς στέγης καλυπτόμενοι. The question arises, How
could these *paterae* have been placed in the *cella* of Jupiter and yet before
the feet of Juno's statue? The explanation that there was a statue of Juno
in the *cella* of Jupiter seems an improbable one in the face of the above
evidence. Most probably Livy here uses *in Iovis cella* loosely for *in
Iovis templo*, and the *paterae* were placed in the chamber of Juno. That
Livy was not very careful to maintain the distinction between *templum*
and *cella* is shown by a passage in 7. 3. 5: *fixa fuit (lex) dextro lateri
aedis Iovis optimi maximi, ex qua parte Minervae templum est.* Here
templum = cella. Cf. Rolfe in *Class. Review*, 1893, p. 273.

9   **§ 4. ea bella]** The wars of 396, 395 B.C. described in Book V, as
well as those mentioned in cc. 2, 3. This notice is no doubt to be
brought into connection with the creation of the four new tribes (c. 5. 8).
It is therefore impossible to believe that the citizenship was given only
to a few deserters to the Roman cause; it must have been bestowed upon
practically all the members of the three communities mentioned.

14   **§ 5. capitalisque poena]** *Caput* was used technically to denote the
sum of the rights possessed by a Roman citizen. A *capitalis poena*
might affect one or all of these rights. Here the punishment threatened
was probably the loss of all active citizen rights, but not the loss of
personal freedom.

    qui]=*ei qui.* The subj. *remigrasset* is due to or. obliqua. The
form of the direct would be: *is, qui non remigraverit Romam, capitalem
poenam dabit*; cf. Hor. *Od.* 1. 10: *te, boves olim nisi* **reddidisses** | *per
dolum amotas, puerum minaci* | *voce dum terret.*

15   **ex ferocibus...obedientes]** 'He reduced them from united defiance
to individual obedience.' With this use of *ex*, denoting the passing from
one condition to another, cf. Gk ἐκ in phrases like τυφλὸς ἐκ δεδορκότος,
and καὶ λευκὸν ἦμαρ νυκτὸς ἐκ μελαγχίμου. Livy is very fond of contrast-
ing *singuli* and *universi*; cf. c. 18. 6, 7.

16   **§ 6. cum...tum]** 'both...and also.'

17   **re publica impensas adiuvante]** Cf. 5. 55. 3, where we are told
that the state provided tiles free of cost and gave special facilities for
quarrying stone.

18   **aedilibus velut publicum exigentibus opus]** 'the aediles inspecting
the work as though it were public'; cf. the phrase *sarta tecta exigere*,
which is used of censors, and means 'to inspect (and pass) work let out
to contract.' *Exigere* might here mean 'to make compulsory.' The
duty of letting out public works to contract lay with the censors, but
the aediles exercised a general supervision over the streets and public
buildings; in this case private buildings, as affecting public interests, fell
under their charge.

19   **usus]** Gen. 'of using them,' i.e. the buildings; *admonebat* is
absolute.

30   **§ 7. Fidenas]** *Cognomina* arose as a rule from some personal
peculiarity or some accidental circumstance; cf. Rufus, Cursor (9. 16. 13),
etc. The *cognomen* came into general use much later than the *praenomen* and *nomen*; it will be noticed that many of the consular tribunes
mentioned in this book are without it. As time went on, however, the
use of the *cognomen* became almost a necessity, in order to distinguish

the various branches of a *gens*. The present *cognomen* Fidenas is, exceptionally for this early period, derived from a place originally outside Roman territory. Very probably it was gained as the result of some military exploit, or it might possibly indicate a foreign origin for the Servilii.

32　§ **8. namque**] Strict classical prose writers always place *namque* first in a sentence. Livy departs from this rule. He also places *itaque* (c. 8. 8) and *igitur* (c. 9. 5) in positions unusual in prose writing, possibly as a result of the influence of the poets.

p. **7.**　1　**ab odio**] 'out of hatred'; cf. c. 2. 9 n.

2　**relinquerent**] See Appendix.

3　**Tarquiniensem**] Tarquinii lay in Etruria, W. of the Ciminian forest, not far from the sea-coast; Cortuosa and Contenebra would be townships dependent on it. Similarly Praeneste had eight smaller townships, which depended on it (c. 29. 6). It is noteworthy that this expedition took the Romans beyond the formidable barrier of the Mons Ciminius. Cf. 9. 36. 1, and see map.

5　§ **9. primo clamore**] Cf. Gk αὐτοβοεί.

7　§ **10. laborque**] The *-que* may have an adversative force, 'the town stood a siege for a few days, *yet* the unremitted efforts, etc.' (Weiss. compares c. 16. 5 : *dictator de Volscis triumphavit invidiaeque magis triumphus quam gloriae fuit*), or else it may express simple sequence of events.

8　**eos**]=*cives*; cf. c. 3. 2 n. The idea of the citizens is contained in the name of the town.

9　**senis horis in orbem**] 'for periods of six hours in rotation,' i.e. each division fought for six hours, and then rested for thirty. Cf. 5. 19. 11: *in partes sex munitorum numerum divisit: senae horae in orbem operi attributae sunt*. Luterbacher takes the meaning to be that each division fought for one hour only, and then had five hours' rest. But in that case we should expect rather *singulis horis*, and there is the further objection that such frequent changes in attack would lead to endless confusion. It must be admitted, however, that thirty hours is a long time for rest, and Mr Giles suggests that there may be some corruption in the numbers; possibly the army was divided into four not six parts.

12　§ **11. tribunis**] i.e. the military tribunes with consular powers.

sed imperium...fuit] 'but their orders lagged behind their purpose.'

17　§ **12. Capitolium...substructum**] The object would be partly to prevent the scaling of the citadel by a foe (the Gallic attempt had been a warning), and partly to lessen the danger of rocks falling from the rugged heights; cf. 35. 21. 6: *saxum ingens...in vicum Iugarium ex Capitolio procidit, et multos oppressit.*

18　**in hac magnificentia**] We can probably see here an allusion to the activity of Augustus in erecting magnificent buildings in Rome; at the time Livy was writing (between 27 and 20 B.C.; cf. Introd. § 1) that policy of rebuilding Rome would be taking shape, which caused Augustus to boast (*urbem*) *marmoream se relinquere, quam latericiam accepisset* (Suet. *Aug.* 28). Pliny (*N. H.* 36. 104) remarks the wonder excited by the supporting wall of the Capitolium: *senes...insanas Capitoli substructiones mirabantur.*

Chapter V.

19　**§ 1. contiones suas frequentare**] 'to fill their meetings.' The *contio* was an informal mass-meeting held by any magistrate; here it is opposed to the formal *concilium plebis* at which resolutions were passed after voting.

20　**legibus agrariis**] These laws dealt with the disposal of the *ager publicus*, or domain land, which had been acquired by conquest. Of the cultivated land thus gained large portions were from time to time given in full ownership to Roman citizens; the allotment to each was generally two *iugera* (about 1¼ acre), such allotment being frequently accompanied by the foundation of a colony. On the other hand, the state retained the ownership of the uncultivated lands, but allowed citizens to pasture cattle upon them at a proportionate rent (*scriptura*). The infrequent allotment of the *ager publicus*, and the abuse by the rich of the right of *occupatio*, gave rise to grave discontent. Cf. Introd. § 4 c.

21　**§ 2. Pomptinus ager**] seems to have been a fertile region bordering on the Pomptine marshes on the N., though Pliny's statement (*N. H.* 3. 9. 5), that there were once 24 flourishing towns in the *Palus Pomptina*, might lead us to think that it was the actual marsh district. The definite acquisition of this territory, so long disputed between the Romans and the Volscians, is a clear indication of the growing power of the former. See map.

23　**§ 3. infestiorem...ab nobilitate**] 'more threatened by the nobles.' *Infestus* here bears the passive sense natural to its form, though the active sense of 'hostile' became more common. For another instance of the passive meaning, cf. 10. 46. 9: *quia regio ea infesta ab Samnitibus erat.*

Livy is scarcely correct in saying that the occupation of the *ager publicus* was only the work of the nobles, i.e. of the patricians. It was rather the rich, whether patrician or plebeian, who contrived to exclude the poorer citizens.

24 **fuerit**] For Livy's habit of retaining the primary tenses in or. obliqua introduced by a verb in a secondary tense, see c. 39. 11 n.

25 **habuerint**] See Appendix.

§ **4. in possessionem...grassari**] 'took violent possession of': *grassari* is more commonly used with a person as object, cf. 2. 12. 15: *ut in te hac via grassaremur*; Suet. *Ner. 36 in externos grassari.* The subst. *grassator* means a 'footpad,' as in Juv. 3. 305: *grassator agit rem.*

28 § **5. moverunt**] See Appendix.

29 **eodem**] If this reading of the MSS. is retained, *eodem* must be referred to *aedificandi*, and the phrase = *exhaustam expensis in eandem rem.* But this explanation seems extremely unlikely. See Appendix.

30 **instruendum**] 'stocking.' *Instruere* here means to supply with *instrumenta.*

vires] = *copiae*, 'resources'; cf. 38. 21. 6: *obsides inde imperatos pro viribus inopis populi vicenos...dederunt.*

p. 8. 1 § **6. religionum**] 'religious fears' or 'scruples'; cf. 7. 28. 7: *librisque* (i.e. the Sibylline Books) *inspectis, cum plena religione civitas esset, placuit dictatorem feriarum constituendarum causa dici.*

2 **ut renovarentur auspicia**] Presumably the measures taken previously (c. 1) to appease the gods had not produced the desired result. As was pointed out in c. 2. 5 n., the *auspicia* were the means by which the will of heaven was consulted. These *auspicia* were taken by the chief magistrates of the community; if therefore it was considered that the conduct or mode of election of these magistrates had been in any way calculated to displease the gods, they were called upon to resign, as not being fit persons to hold intercourse with heaven. An *interregnum* followed (see c. 1. 5 n.), and the consultation of the gods was carried out afresh by the new magistrates; cf. 5. 17. 3: *unam expiationem esse, ut tribuni militum abdicarent se magistratu, auspicia de integro repeterentur, et interregnum iniretur.*

3 **M. Manlius Capitolinus**] The saviour of the Capitol. There can be no doubt that his *cognomen* was derived, not from the fact that he saved the Capitol, but that he dwelt upon the Capitoline hill; cf. Introd. § 4 c. Livy (5. 31. 2) gives M. Manlius, *cui Capitolino postea fuit cognomen*, as consul for 392 B.C., but Prof. Mommsen (*Röm. Forsch.* 2, p. 179) has shown that the statement is a doubtful one, and that this Manlius was very likely the A. Manlius given by Diod. 14. 103.

Such alterations and interpolations were by no means uncommon in the Roman annals.

8   § **7. occepere**]=*inierunt.* An archaism very likely borrowed from the annalists used by Livy. The word is fairly common in Plautus and Terence.

9   § **8. aedes Martis**] This temple cannot be identified with certainty. But most probably it was the one outside the Porta Capena (S. of Rome, beginning of the Via Appia) between the 1st and 2nd milestones. Cf. 7. 23. 3: *extra portam Capenam ad Martis aedem.* See map.

The notices at the end of this chapter illustrate well the short, dry character of the annals which furnished the basis of Roman History.

10   **duumviro sacris faciendis**] One of the keepers of the Sibylline Books, which were stored in the temple of Jupiter Capitolinus. The Sibylline Books were consulted on the occasion of any grave national crisis, and they were usually found to prescribe the introduction of some foreign rite. Hence it has been conjectured that the temple of Mars mentioned here was really a temple to the Greek Ares, whose worship was introduced at this time of national unrest. The number of the keepers of the Sibylline Books was raised from two to ten in 367 B.C., and the college was thrown open to plebeians (see c. 37. 12 n.). In 51 B.C. we find fifteen members of the college, probably in consequence of reforms introduced by Sulla.

The usual practice in dedicating temples was either to appoint a magistrate as dedicator, or to elect *duumviri aedi dedicandae,* extraordinary commissioners appointed from time to time as occasion required; cf. the III *viri coloniae deducendae* (c. 21. 4). Some have thought that Livy made a mistake here, and that he really meant to write *duumviro aedi dedicandae.*

ex novis civibus] Cf. n. on c. 4. 4. Rome was able to extend her territory in consequence of the conquests in S. Etruria.

11   **Stellatina**] Festus, an epitomator of the great Augustan scholar and antiquary M. Verrius Flaccus, has a mutilated note, probably to the following effect :—*Stellati*[*na tribus dicta non a campo eo*] *qui in Campania est, sed eo qui* [*prope abest ab urbe Ca*]*pena, ex quo Tusci profecti St*[*ellatinum illum*] *campum appellaverunt.* The *tribus Stellatina,* therefore, was in the neighbourhood of Capena, and the district is to be distinguished from the *ager Stellatinus* in Campania. The position of the *tribus Tromentina* is not exactly known, but it probably lay around Veii. The *tribus Sabatina* took its name from the *lacus Sabatinus* to the N. of Veii. The *tribus Arniensis* has, of course,

nothing to do with the river Arno, but may perhaps be connected with the river Aro in S. Etruria ; though in that case we should expect the spelling *Arnensis*, which is in fact the commoner form. But we have no right to depart from the reading of the MSS., since *Arniensis* is found in inscriptions. (*C. I. L.* VI. 2500, etc.) See map.

12 **viginti quinque tribuum numerum**] The local tribes of Rome began with the four city tribes created by Servius Tullius ; the next seventeen *tribus rusticae* were probably added gradually between that time and the present date (387 B.C.). Livy's statement in 2. 21. 7 : *tribus una et viginti factae*, must be received with caution. It is noteworthy that, whereas the present four tribes are all named after localities, the previous *tribus rusticae* (with the exception of the *tribus Crustumina*) were all named after patrician *gentes*. By 241 B.C. the number of the tribes had risen to 35, and no additional tribe was created after that date.

CHAPTER VI.

15 **§ 2. mentio...dilata est**] Rather careless writing. It was the discussion of the matter, or else action upon it, which was postponed.

30 **§ 4. Antiates**] Antium was the chief town of the Volscians, and occupied a commanding position upon a promontory; cf. c. 9. 2. According to Livy (2. 65. 7 and 3. 1. 5) the Romans had previously captured the town, and had made an attempt to colonize it. But it was not until 338 B.C. that it was effectually colonized. See map.

32 **§ 5. voluntarios**] Madvig would bracket this word as gloss on *ubi vellent*; but it may well be retained. Livy's style is essentially full, and he is not afraid of repetition ; cf. c. 1. 6: *legatus*.

p. 9. 1 dicerent] Subjunctive in or. obliqua after *attulit*; *quod dicerent* is a loose expression, which has its parallel in English. So we might say ' because they said they fought as volunteers,' meaning ' because, as they said, they fought.'

§ 6. desierant...contemni] This is an apparent violation of the rule that *desino* and *coepi* are attracted into the voice of the infinitive with which they are connected. We should have expected *desita erant ...contemni*, or *desierant...contemnere*; the explanation of this seeming irregularity is that the constr. is made with regard to the logical subject *Romani* or *patres*, rather than to the actual subject *bella*; cf. 5. 3. 2 : *id ego hoc anno desisse dubitari certum habeo.*

ulla] This is no exception to the rule that *ullus* is always used with a negative, since *desierant* is virtually negative. So we find *ullus* without a neg. after *vetare*; cf. Cic. *Rep.* i. 17. 27: *communis lex naturae, quae vetat ullam rem esse cuiusquam....*

3   quippe] 'for of course.'

6   § 7. in animo] As a rule Livy uses *animis* without *in* with *destinare*; but since we cannot be sure that he would *never* use *in animo*, it seems best to keep the reading of the MSS., especially as it is supported by 21. 44. 9: *destinatum in animo.* See Appendix.

9   confusus animo] 'overcome with emotion'; cf. c. 34. 8.

10   § 8. [dictatorem] Madvig was no doubt right in bracketing this word. Camillus' fourth dictatorship came later (368 B.C.; c. 38. 4); he was now consular tribune for the fourth time. The statement is, moreover, wrong from a constitutional point of view, since the dictator was not elected by the people, but nominated by a consul. Perhaps *dictatorem* has ousted *tribunum*. See Appendix.

12   honorato] 'complimentary.' The word is used in an active sense and = *honorificus*; cf. 27. 10. 6: *honoratissimo decreto.* See Appendix.

19   § 11. ab invidia et odio] Cf. c. 3. 8: *accensum ab desperatione hostium. Invidia* and *odium* are practically personified.

21   § 12. L. Valeri] This person must be identical with the P. Valerius mentioned above, so Livy seems to have made a slip in the name.

24   § 13. ad urbem] See Appendix.

        intentum, sive...] ' on the alert, in case of a rising...'

26   ita rem gesturum] sc. *te.* Mr Giles suggests that *te* has dropped out of the MSS. after *ita*, and this seems very likely.

28   § 14. ex causariis senioribusque] The *causarii* were men excused military service on account of ill-health or bodily infirmity. Weiss. quotes *Dig.* 3. 2. 2: *causaria (missio), quae propter valetudinem laboribus militiae solvit.* For *seniores,* cf. c. 2. 6 n.

29   praesidio] Predicative or final dat., expressing the purpose of the enrolment of the army. See Roby, Syntax pp. xxv ff.

30   frumentum] Observe that the singular as a rule denotes gathered grain, the plur. *frumenta* unharvested corn, cf. 23. 32. 14: *ut frumenta* (the crops) *ex agris...conveherent.* The plur. also denotes various kinds of corn.

        alia] See Appendix.

31   § 15. praesidem huius publici consilii] Not any extraordinary position, such as that of *praefectus urbi*, is meant. As Ser. Cornelius was the only consular tribune left in Rome, to him would naturally fall the task of summoning the Senate and of presiding in it, of superintending

certain religious ceremonies, of holding elections, and of **supervising**
justice.

33   **collegae facimus**] ' we, your colleagues, make you.'

    § 16. in partem] See Appendix.

p. 10. 9 **§ 18.** **conferentes...in medium**] 'giving for the common
weal.'

    in medium...ex communi] The use of the neut. adj. in substantival
sense is very extended in Livy. It is often so employed with prepositions
denoting place, as here; cf. c. 23. 3 : *ex incertissimo*, and c. 38. 8 *de
medio*.

CHAPTER VII.

15   **§ 1. iustitio**] See c. 2. 6 n.

16   **Satricum**] In the Ager Pomptinus, E. of Antium; it was a Latin
colony, but was constantly exposed to attacks from the Volscians, and
was at this time in their hands. See map.

17   **ex nova subole lectam**] 'enrolled from a new generation'; cf. c. 12. 4,
where Livy, in speculating upon the reasons why the Volscians were
enabled to keep up the struggle with Rome year after year, says:
*simile veri est...alia atque alia subole iuniorum ad bella instauranda
toties usos esse*.

    sed] sc. *etiam*. This omission of *etiam* is common in Livy.

20   **§ 2. quod ubi**] 'so when.' *Quod* is probably a connecting particle,
as in c. 8. 2. See c. 27. 8 n.

23   **restitantes**] 'loitering.' See Appendix.

    quin] introduces a climax: 'nay more.'

25   **nedum**] 'still less.' The word is used in neg. or virtually neg.
sentences, as here after *aegre*. In Cicero and other writers before Livy
we find *nedum* nearly always followed by a vb in the subj., e.g. Cic.
pro Clu. 35. 95: *optimis hercule temporibus ... clarissimi viri vim
tribuniciam sustinere non potuerunt : nedum his temporibus...salvi esse
possimus*. In the present case *nedum* is used as an adverb. The full
expression would have been: *nedum armata sustineri posset*; cf. the Gk
μὴ τί γε δή.

26   **§ 3. ante signa**] The legion was divided into three lines, the
hastati in front, the *principes* next, and the *triarii* third. The general
view is that the standards (*signa*) were carried in front of the army,
when it was on the march, but behind the first line (the *hastati*) in
battle. Thus the *antesignani*, the men in front of the standards, are the
same as the *hastati*. If, therefore, the army was here regularly drawn

up in line of battle, Camillus must have passed among the ranks of the *hastati*, facing the rest of the army. But, as the battle had not begun, it is possible that Livy considered the standards as still in front of the whole army.

The *signum* was a lance, furnished on the top with a crossbar, on which appeared the name of the legion and maniple: below the cross-bar was a series of metal disks (*phalerae*), probably awarded to the company (*manipulus*) for conspicuous valour. The division of the legions into maniples may with probability be assigned to the time of Camillus. For an illustration of the *signum*, see Ramsay, *Roman Antiqs.*[15], p. 426.

obversus] A poetical word, not found in prose before Livy. The simple *versus* occurs in c. 20. 9.

27   **quae tristitia...haec**] A departure from the usual order *quae haec tristitia* for the purpose of gaining effect. With a similar object *hostis est quid aliud* is put for the commoner *quid aliud est hostis?*

p. 11. 1 § **4. et Aequis**] See Appendix.

§ **5. an**] Notice that *an* introducing a question generally expects the answer 'no,' just as *num* does. The reason is that a previous question with *utrum* is omitted, while the question with *an* is the less probable alternative. Thus the full sentence here would have been: *utrum me agnoscitis an non* (*agnoscitis*) *ducem?* 'Do you recognize me as your general or can it be that you do not?' Cf. c. 36. 12.

2   **signum**] The signal that a fight would take place on that day. This was given by exposing a red flag over the general's tent; cf. Caesar *B. G.* 2. 20: *Caesari omnia uno tempore erant agenda: vexillum proponendum* (*quod erat insigne, cum ad arma concurri oporteret*); on the other hand, the signal to begin the fight was given with the trumpet (*signum tuba dare*). This is the signal referred to below, c. 8. 1.

5   **animos**] 'courage.'

8   § **6. simul**] = *simul ac*; cf. c. 1. 6 n.

CHAPTER VIII.

14   § **1. infer...signum**] Each standard formed the rallying point for a separate division of the Roman legion. The important part played by the standard may be gathered from the number of military phrases in which it occurs, e.g. *inferre signum* = to advance, *convertere signa* = to wheel (cf. c. 24. 7 *circumagi signa*), *signa servare* = to keep in rank, etc.; cf. c. 7. 3 n.

15 **§ 2. quod ubi]** *Quod* here, as in c. 7. 2, is simply a conjunction, 'when therefore they saw.'

16 **senecta]** In Cicero always *senectus*.

18 **§ 3. emissum...signum]** The loss of a standard was considered such a disgrace, that troops would use every exertion to recover one which had fallen into the enemy's hands; cf. 3. 70. 10, 11: *arrepta signa ab signiferis ipse inferre, quaedam iacere etiam in confertos hostes coepit; cuius ignominiae metu concitati milites invasere hostem*: cf. also the peculiar satisfaction of Augustus at the recovery (in 20 B.C.) of the standards captured by the Parthians at Carrhae; there are coins with the legend *signis Parthicis receptis*, and the event is particularly recorded on the *Monumentum Ancyranum*.

19 **ferunt]** 'it is said.'

20 **antesignanos]** The front line or *hastati*; cf. c. 7. 3 n., and 8. 11. 7· *caesos hastatos principesque, stragem et ante signa et post signa factam.*

22 **§ 4. subsidiarios]** These corresponded to the *triarii* of the Roman legion; cf. 8. 11. 7 where it is said that, after the defeat of the *hastati* and *principes, triarios postremo rem restituisse.*

§ 5. movebat] Used absolutely, 'made an impression.' Cf. 5. 55. 1. *movisse* (other MSS. read *movisse eos*) *Camillus cum alia oratione, tum ea, quae ad religiones pertinebat, maxime dicitur*; cf. also 3. 47. 4 and 26. 24. 8.

25 **§ 6. intulisset]** Subj. expressing frequency of action. Caesar and Cicero would have said *intulerat* or *intulit*. Livy and later prose writers prefer the subj.; cf. 1. 32. 13 *id ubi dixisset* (as often as he said it), *hastam in fines eorum emittebat*: cf. also c. 9. 4: *cum...molirentur.*

27 **scuto pedestri]** The heavy-armed Roman foot-soldier carried a large oblong shield, which covered the greater part of his body; on the other hand, the light-armed *velites* and the cavalry had a small round shield called *parma*; cf. 2. 46. 5, where the dismounted consul has only the *parma* to defend himself with in an infantry fight.

29 **§ 7. inclinata res erat]** 'the fortune of the day had turned,' i.e. in favour of the Romans. Livy also uses the active form absolutely of the turn of fortune's scale; cf. 3. 61. 4: *si fortuna belli inclinet*, and c. 32. 8: *ut semel inclinavit pugna.*

sed turba hostium, etc.] The connection of thought is as follows:— The Romans had clearly the best of matters, but they were unable to effect so complete a dispersion of their foes as had seemed probable. Trans.: 'but the numbers of the enemy served to delay even (*et*) their flight, and the multitude which remained to be despatched by the

wearied soldiers with a prolonged slaughter was exceedingly great,
when....' The point of the *et* is : the great numbers checked *even* that
easy thing, a flight. See Appendix.

31   **ingentibus procellis**] Probably there is a point in the plural : 'in
violent squalls.' Yet Livy often uses the plural in expressions relating
to weather, etc., where we should use the singular ; e.g. *nives* = snow,
pruinae = frost, etc. Cf. c. 32. 6.

p. 12.   1   § 8.   **quietis Romanis**] 'without an effort on the part of the
Romans.' Probably abl. abs., though it might be dat.

2   **namque**] For position, see c. 4. 8 n.

6   § 9.   **vallo...et aggere**] 'palisade and mound.' See c. 2. 9 n.

9   § 10.   **in eo**] 'in dealing with them (the enemy).' Lit. 'in their case.'
      tam lentae spei victoriam] 'a victory that promised to be so slow in
coming.' A free use of the gen. of quality.

CHAPTER IX.

20   § 1.   **imminebat**] 'was set upon.'

22   § 2.   **tormentis machinisque**] *Tormenta* (*torqueo*) = artillery, in-
cluding *catapultae* for discharging arrows, and *ballistae* for hurling
stones. Under *machinae*, a more general term, would come the
battering ram (*aries*), the shed for protecting besiegers (*vinea*), etc.

23   **ad exercitum**] 'with the army.' We might have expected *apud*.

25   § 3.   **credo...**] Livy is no Epicurean believing that the gods take
no interest in the affairs of this world ; he is far more in sympathy with
Stoicism, as is seen not merely in his views as to the divine influence,
but also as regards the power of fate and fortune; cf. below : *vim
Camilli ab Antio* **fortuna** *avertit*, and Cleanthes' expression of the Stoic
doctrine :

ἄγου δέ μ' ὦ Ζεῦ, καὶ σύγ' ἡ Πεπρωμένη,
ὅποι ποθ' ὑμῖν εἰμὶ διατεταγμένος.

26   **cordi fuisse**] 'to have been dear.' *Cordi* in this sense was probably
in origin a locative (cf. the Eng. 'to have at heart'), but was later
regarded as a dat., parallel to the other 'predicative' datives.

      ab Nepete] See c. 3. 5 n.

28   **brevem occasionem esse**] 'that the opportunity was but short.'

30   § 4.   **opposita Etruriae**] i.e. the Northern and non-Roman part of
Etruria. Sutrium and Nepete commanded the roads leading through
the forest-clad Ciminian mountains. See map.

      claustra inde portaeque] 'the keys oι the gates leading from it
(Etruria).' A hendiadys.

31   **illis]** The Etruscans.

molirentur] Subj. of frequent action: see c. 8. 6 n.   For the meaning of *moliri*, 'plotted,' cf. c. 2. 14 n. (3).

32   **§ 5. igitur]** More usually second or third in a sentence.   But, as with *itaque* and *namque*, Livy is inclined to diverge from the classical prose order ; cf. c. 4. 8 n.   In early Latin, Plautus for instance, *igitur* often begins a sentence.   Sallust also, who in many peculiarities of constr. closely resembles Livy, always places *igitur* first.

p. 13.   1   **cum Camillo agi]**   *Agere cum populo* is used technically of a magistrate laying proposals before an assembly of the people.   Hence we may translate 'that a proposal should be made to Camillus.'

2   **legiones urbanae]**   There can be little doubt that Livy has made a slip here.   Quinctius had (c. 6. 14) been placed in command of the infirm soldiers (*causarii*) and the *seniores*; it was not likely that Camillus would be represented as taking these troops on what promised to be a difficult campaign.   We must therefore suppose that the troops of Q. Servilius are really meant.

3   **§ 6. quanquam...mallet]**   *Mallet* can be explained as being the apodosis to *si liceret* or its equivalent understood.   Nevertheless Livy does use the subj. after *quanquam* in passages where such an explanation is impossible (e.g. in 45. 17. 7).   In this, as in other usages, he is leading the way to Silver Latinity.

6   **in Volscos]** See Appendix.

15   **§ 9. tanta]** See Appendix.

19   **§ 10. anceps]** 'from both sides.'   The word means literally 'double-headed,' hence its derived meaning ' doubtful.'   The Etruscans were exposed to attack both from within and from without the town.

22   **§ 11. fugientium]** 'the fugitives.'   See c. 2. 13 n.

in urbe et per agros]   Here there is some point in the change of preposition ; *per* gives the idea of the scattering over the face of the open country.   But Livy is constantly varying his prepositions for purely stylistic reasons.

CHAPTER X.

p. 14.   6   **§ 1. tota hostium erat]** 'was wholly in the enemy's hands.' The gen. is possessive.   Cf. *lucri totus esse*, ' to be entirely devoted to gain,' and c. 14. 9: *cum iam unius hominis esset.*

9   **§ 2. implorassent]**   Subj. due to indirect speech; the ambassadors sent to the people of Nepete would say '*fidem praestate quam implorastis.*'

10   **§ 3. unde**]=*a quibus.*

suae potestatis esse] Possessive gen., very similar to *hostium* above.

13   **§ 4. postquam...erat**] The normal constr. after *postquam* is the perf. indic. Livy frequently uses the imperf., sometimes (though not in this case) to denote the commencement of a state or action : cf. c. **13. 3,** *postquam...quisque...cernebat,* 'when each began to perceive.' Here *postquam* simply = *quia.*

23   **§ 6. res repetitae**] 'satisfaction was demanded.' *Repetere* is used of demanding back things unlawfully appropriated; cf. *lex repetundarum* sc. *pecuniarum,* which was a law providing for the recovery of wealth illegally extorted by a provincial governor.

24   **ex instituto**] i.e. in accordance with the terms of the treaties made by Cassius.

28   **§ 8. iis**] See Appendix.

29   **terrorem...a Volscis**] *a* here indicates the source of the apprehension ; cf. below, c. 11. **2**: *bellum ab Volscis,* which shows clearly how this use of *a* has arisen. In the latter case *ortum* is to be supplied from the preceding *exorta.* So here after *terrorem* some such word as *ortum* must be supplied mentally.

30   **adhaerentem lateri**] The dat. is poetical. Cicero uses *in* with abl. For the phrase, cf. Verg. *Aen.* 4. 73 : *haeret lateri letalis harundo.*

31   **§ 9. quae relata...habere**] 'this answer, when brought to the Senate, seemed to fail to afford an opportunity, rather than a ground, for war,' i.e. the answer of the Latins was so unsatisfactory that it might have been made a *casus belli,* but the Romans were not prepared for immediate hostilities. The order tends to make the sentence somewhat obscure ; *non* must be taken closely with *habere.*

CHAPTER XI.

p. 15. 5   **§ 1. C. Sergio iterum**] These words are omitted in the MSS., but are almost certainly to be supplied here, since the name of another consular tribune is required, and in c. **27. 2** C. Sergius is consular tribune for the third time, though his second year of office is nowhere else mentioned. The omission was no doubt brought about by the fact that the scribe had just written *iterum* after *Cursore*; as a result he passed over the second *iterum* with the name preceding it.

10   **§ 2. M. Manlio Capitolino**] Cf. c. 5. 6 n. For a general review of the story of M. Manlius, see Introd. § 4 c.

§ 3. nimius animi] Lit. 'intemperate in spirit,' so 'haughty.'

Animi is really a locative, as in the phrases *pendere animi, suspensus animi.* By false analogy the constr. was extended to real genitives, e.g. Tac. *Hist.* 3. 75: *sermonis nimius.*

alios]=*ceteros,* as frequently in Livy.

13 **esse**] There seems to be no occasion to omit *esse* as Madvig does; Camillus' moral influence was so great that in rhetorical language he was said to hold sole sway in the army, to be virtual, if not actual, dictator: cf. c. 6. 16: *M. Furium sibi pro dictatore...futurum.* The or. obliqua is continued after *aegre ferebat.* See Appendix.

14 **iisdem auspiciis creatos**] i.e. had been elected under the presidency of, and returned by, the same magistrate, who had consulted the will of the gods by taking the auspices. The whole system of Roman magistracies was a collegiate one and specially designed to prevent the undue prominence of any individual.

15 **§ 4. cum interim**] 'while all the time,' practically concessive. Dependent upon these words are *potuerit, aggressus sit, depulerit, sit,* and (irregularly) *esse* at the end of the sentence. For the sudden change from subj. to inf., cf. c. 27. 6, where we find *cum interim...obiectari,* though the natural constr. would have been the subj.; Ltb. in the present case adopts the conjectural reading *esse constet. Si...velit* is parenthetic: 'if only men would weigh things truly.'

17 **potuerit**] *Potuit* (in this case the subj. *potuerit*) is regularly used in unfulfilled conditions for *potuisset.* Parallel is the use of the perf. ind. of verbs expressing duty, and of gerundives and comparatives with *fuit*: cf. Cic. *pro Mil.* 22. 58: *quos nisi manumisisset, tormentis etiam dedendi fuerunt*; cf. also Juv. 10. 123 *Antoni potuit gladios contemnere, si sic| omnia dixisset.*

18 **§ 5. inter...solutis animis**] Note the variety of constr.; trans. 'while they were receiving the gold, and after their attention had been relaxed through expectation of peace.' For the gerundival constr. after *inter,* cf. c. 39. 10 *inter accipiendas...rogationes.* Such constructions are not found in strict classical prose writers.

in spem] *In* with the acc. denotes the direction towards which their minds turned.

20 **pars virilis**] 'a due share'; cf. the common *pro parte virili,* 'as far as a man can.'

apud] More regularly, *penes.* Cf. 2. 24. 2: *ut penes eosdem pericula belli, penes quos praemia essent.*

23 **§ 6. ad hoc**] 'in addition to this.'

impotens]=*non potens sui,* 'lacking in self-control.'

24   **patres**] Here=patricians. Livy's use of the word is by no means
constant, and it is important to note three distinct meanings : (1) as here
and in the next section *patres*=the patrician order as opposed to the
plebs. (2)=the Senate. (3) In *patrum auctoritas* and in a few other
phrases the word probably denotes the patrician portion of the Senate.
See c. 41. 10 n.

25   **§ 7. primus omnium**] The reading of the MSS., *primum omnium*,
cannot be retained. It is not strictly accurate for Livy to say that
Manlius was the first patrician who turned *popularis*. In 2. 8. 1 he
applies the term to Valerius Publicola, while Sp. Cassius was also a
patrician. Manlius, however, answers more thoroughly to the idea of
the *populares* of the last centuries of the Republic, professional agitators
who strove to raise themselves to power by working upon the ignorance
and passions of the lower orders. No doubt Livy had the character of
these later agitators in mind, while writing the story of Manlius. See
Appendix.

28   **aura**] sc. *populari*; cf. Verg. *Aen.* 6. 816 *nimium gaudens popula-*
ribus auris. In 22. 26. 4 occurs the fuller phrase, *aura favoris*
popularis.

      famaeque magnae] Gen. of quality or description. Cf. c. 22. 7 :
exactae iam aetatis Camillus erat.

29   **§ 8. agrariis legibus**] Not that Manlius had actually introduced
any agrarian proposals. These were dangerous enough in the hands of
the tribunes of the plebs (another anticipation of the later times of the
Republic, particularly those of the Gracchi), but Manlius had gone
further and had attempted to overthrow credit, one of the bases upon
which society rested. Cf. c. 5. 1 n.

30   **fuisset**] The subj. is to be explained as due to virtual or. obliqua ;
it expresses the thought in Manlius' mind : 'agrarian laws have been
always the weapon of mere tribunes of the plebs ; I, a patrician, must go
further.'

      fidem moliri] 'to tamper with credit': see c. 2. 14 n.

31   **aeris alieni stimulos**] The early Roman law of debt was of a
peculiarly harsh character, and pressed very hardly upon the poorer
plebeians, who were continually being compelled to borrow. By the
law of the XII Tables (Gell. 20. 1. 45) debtors were allowed 30 days'
grace after the time for payment became due ; they were then arrested
and formally adjudged (*addicti*) by the praetor to the creditors, who
might keep them in bonds (*vincito aut nervo aut compedibus quindecim*
pondo, ne maiore, aut si volet minore vincito). This imprisonment lasted

60 days, towards the end of which period the debtors were again brought before the praetor on three consecutive market days (*nundinae*). Then, if the debt still remained unpaid and no surety came forward, the debtors might be sold as slaves (or, as some maintain, actually be cut in pieces, and in this way distributed among their creditors); cf. the language of the XII Tables. *Tertiis nundinis partis secanto. Si plus minusve secuerunt, se* (=*sine*) *fraude esto.* It is therefore not surprising to find constant disturbance arising from the harsh operation of these laws : cf. Tac. *Ann.* 6. 16. 2 ff., and Introd. § 4 c.

32 **nervo**] Festus defines *nervus* as *ferreum vinculum quo pedes impediuntur,* but he goes on to say: *quamquam Plautus eo etiam cervices vinciri ait.* Thus the *nervus* seems to have corresponded pretty well to our stocks and pillory combined. Cf. the ξύλον πεντεσύριγγον of Aristoph. *Eq.* 1049.

33 **§ 9. et**] Notice the emphatic character of this *et* at the beginning of a sentence : 'and indeed,' cf. 2. 28. 8 : *et apparebat atrox cum plebe certamen.* In spite of assistance from the state the poorer plebeians must have borrowed largely in order to rebuild and restock their farms after the devastation wrought by the Gauls.

p. 16. 4 **§ 10. nova consilia**] 'revolutionary designs'; cf. the Gk νεωτερίζειν.

CHAPTER XII.

13 **§ 1. celeritate...opus erat**] The abl. is instrumental, as is the abl. after *fruor, fungor,* etc.; cf. the abl. after *usus est.* The alternative constr., in which *opus* is used as a secondary predicate and the thing needed is the subject, is also quite regular: cf. Cic. *ad Fam.* 2. 6. 4 : *dux nobis et auctor opus est.* But the gen., which occurs occasionally in Livy after *opus est,* is a constr. peculiar to him. Cf. **22. 51. 3**: *ad consilium pensandum temporis opus esse.*

16 **§ 2. non dubito**] The Ciceronian constr. after *non dubito* (meaning 'I do not doubt') is regularly *quin* with the subj. Livy constantly has the acc. and inf.; Cornelius Nepos (about 100–30 B.C.) also has this constr., but its use marks a decline from the standard of strict Latinity.

17 **bella cum Volscis**] Cf. Introd. § 4 b.

19 **propiores temporibus harum rerum auctores**] Livy probably refers particularly to Q. Fabius Pictor (about 200 B.C.), who wrote in Greek. Fabius was the earliest Roman historian, but even he wrote over a century and a half after the Volscian wars here recorded. The present statement might lead us to suppose that Livy had studied the

works of the earlier annalists for himself; the general opinion is, however, that he relied almost exclusively on the later annalists of the first
century B.C., upon Q. Claudius Quadrigarius, Valerius Antias, and
Licinius Macer, and that his acquaintance with Fabius is only at
second hand. See Introd. § 2.

21   § 3. tacitum] 'unmentioned,' 'in silence' (a passive sense); cf.
3. 45. 6: *ut tacitum feras quod celari vis.*

22   cuius tandem ...] Lit. 'of what thing, I ask, can I be the author?'
i.e. what can I bring forward, except an opinion? *Tandem* is used in
the common rhetorical sense of 'I pray'; *sim* is a deliberative subj.

None of Livy's conjectures is very convincing. The real reason,
in all probability, was that the so-called wars were generally mere
border forays, which resulted in comparatively little bloodshed. Besides
this, in the course of compilation from several annalists, the same war
might be repeated two or three times.

25   § 4. alia atque alia subole] 'successive generations'; cf. c. 7. 1.

26   populis...gens] As in the case of the Etruscans (see c. 2. 2 n.),
gens refers to the whole people, *populus* to the minor divisions within
the *gens*.

27   intulerit] subj. in or. obliqua after *simile veri est*; below, *vindicant*
is Livy's statement of fact.

29   § 5. seminario] 'a nursery' for soldiers. Lit. 'seed plot'; cf. 42.
61. 5: *equites seminarium senatus.*

30   servitia Romana] 'the Roman slave-gangs.' In tones of unmistak-
able sadness Livy utters the main cause of the ruin of Italy and the
Republic—the decay of the yeoman and the multiplying of the slave.
The contributing causes were many; not only had the civil wars cut off
great numbers of men, but there was a constant emigration to the
provinces, while a class of capitalists had arisen, who found that the
greatest profits were to be made by means of slave-labour; cf. Cic. *pro
Plancio* 9. 23: *Nisi forte te Labicana aut Gabina aut Bovillana vicinitas
adiuvabat, quibus e municipiis vix iam qui carnem Latinis petant re-
periuntur.* The once flourishing cities of Latium could scarcely find
representatives to send to the *Feriae Latinae.* Cf. also Plin. *N. H.*
18. 35: *verum confitentibus latifundia perdidere Italiam*; and Appian
B.C. I. 7. 11: τοὺς Ἰταλιώτας ὀλιγότης καὶ δυσανδρία κατελάμβανε, τρυχο-
μένους πενίᾳ τε καὶ εἰσφοραῖς καὶ στρατείαις. εἰ δὲ καὶ σχολάσειαν ἀπὸ
τούτων, ἐπὶ ἀργίας διετίθεντο, τῆς γῆς ὑπὸ τῶν πλουσίων ἐχομένης, καὶ
γεωργοῖς χρωμένων θεράπουσιν ἀντὶ ἐλευθέρων. See also 7. 25. 9.

§ 6. certe] 'at all events' (whatever the reason may be).

31   **conveniat**] **Potential** subj. 'A fact upon which all authorities would be agreed,' sc. if they were consulted ; cf. Tac. *Hist.* 3. 75 : *quod inter omnes* **constiterit**, *decus domus penes Sabinum erat.*

p. **17.** 2. **Circeiensium**] Circeii was a town on the sea-coast, S.W. of the Pomptine marshes. See map. Cf. 2. 39. 2, where the place, which had originally received Roman colonists, falls back into the hands of the Volscians. Diod. (14. 102) says (under the year 390 B.C.): ἀπέστη δὲ καὶ Σάτρικον ἀπὸ Ῥωμαίων, καὶ εἰς Κερκίους ἀποικίαν ἀπέστειλαν, so it appears to have been again a Latin colony at this time.

    a Velitris] Cf. 2. 31. 4: *Velitras coloni ab urbe missi.* The colony was Latin, not Roman (cf. c. 17. 7 n.), and lay a little to the S. of the Mons Albanus. See map. The variety of constr. should be noticed.

3   **§ 7. auspicato**] The gods were consulted before the commencement of a battle by means of the auspices; it was an accepted principle with the Romans that no important business should be entered upon without such consultation. The auspices before battle were generally drawn from the manner in which the sacred chickens (*pulli*) fed; cf. c. 41. 8 n. *Auspicato* is abl. abs., as *litato, augurato*; the usage, however, tends to become purely adverbial; cf. *falso, merito,* etc.

4   **hostiaque caesa**] It was of the utmost importance that the sacrifice of the victim should be attended by favourable signs. The loss of the battle on the Allia was partly attributed to fighting in the face of unfavourable omens ; cf. c. 1. 12 : *quod...non litasset Sulpicius.*

    pacem deum] Cf. c. 1. 12.

5   **signum**] Probably the red flag hung from the general's tent ; cf. c. 7. 5 n.

7   **§ 8. vatesque**] See Appendix.

    in futurum] 'into the future.' Neut. of fut. part. used as subst.

9   **pilis ante pedes positis**] Cf. 7. 16. 5 : '*aspice, imperator,*' inquit, '*quemadmodum exercitus tuus tibi promissa praestet,*' *piloque posito stricto gladio in hostem impetum fecit* ; cf. also 2. 30. 12. The *pilum* was a strong javelin, about 6 ft. 9 in. long, with barbed iron head. It was generally used for throwing, and was not suitable for a fight at close quarters.

11   **obnixos vos stabili gradu**] 'bearing up with feet firm-planted'; cf. Tyrtaeus frag. 9. 21 (Bergk) :

          ἀλλά τις εὖ διαβὰς μενέτω ποσὶν ἀμφοτέροισιν

          στηριχθεὶς ἐπὶ γῆς, χεῖλος ὀδοῦσι δακών.

In both cases the attitude of brave men fighting against odds.

12   **§ 9. vana]** Proleptic, i.e. it anticipates (προλαμβάνει) **the result of**
the action; 'when they have hurled their missiles *without effect.*'

14   **deos...deos]** In spite of the scepticism prevailing in his day, Livy
still has firm trust in the influence of the gods in human affairs, and
loves to depict his heroes as strong in faith.

The subj. of *adiuvent* and *miserint* is of course due to or. obliqua
after *veniat in mentem*; 'let each remember that it is the gods who
aid the Romans...'

Romanum] See c. 2. 12 n.

16   **§ 10. tene; at]** See Appendix.

17   **haerere iam aciem collato pede]** 'the lines fast-locked as men fight
hand to hand'; cf. Verg. *Aen.* 11. 632: *implicuere inter se acies legitque
virum vir.* Weiss. quotes *Aen.* 10. 361: *haeret pede pes, densusque viro
vir.* We can often find echoes of Virgil in Livy.

18   **alio pavore]** *Pavore* is more forcible than *labore.* 'Launch the
terror of the cavalry upon them when distracted with another fear,' i.e.
the fear inspired by the indomitable steadfastness of the Roman foot.
See Appendix.

20   **§ 11. nec dux legiones...]** 'the general did not fail the legions, nor
fortune fail the general.' Once more the Stoic *fortuna.*

CHAPTER XIII.

26   **§ 1. nulli rei...freta]** This constr. of *fretus* with the dat. instead
of the normal abl. is peculiar to Livy. For another instance, cf. c. 31. 6:
discordiae hostium fretus. Apparently the dat. after *fretus* is on the
analogy of that after *fidens*; cf. 8. 22. 7.

27   **temere...temere]** The word is connected etymologically with *tene-
brae*; 'entered upon the battle blindly, and abandoned it in blind panic.'

28   **§ 2. missilibusque telis]** Above (c. 12. 9), *missilia* is used alone.
This well illustrates the ease with which the neut. adj. became equivalent
to a subst.

29   **ferox]** 'bold.'

31   **§ 3. frons prima]** The first line, corresponding to the Roman
hastati.

suum] Emphatic: 'a terror of its own.'

p. 18.   1. **fluctuanti]** 'like a tossing sea.' Lit. 'like a thing tossing';
cf. Macaulay, *Horatius*, 50:

> 'And on the tossing sea of steel
>   To and fro the standards reel.'

Also Scott, *Marmion*, vi. 26:

> 'Then mark'd they, dashing broad and far,
> The broken billows of the war.'

3　　**cernebat]** 'As soon as each *began* to see'; cf. c. 10. 4 n.

4　　**§ 4. conferti]** From *confercio*: 'in compact order.'

6　　**equitum turmae]** Three hundred cavalry were attached to each legion, and were divided into ten *turmae* of thirty men.

7　　**signo]** This time with the trumpet, not with the flag, since the signal had to be distinguished in the confusion of battle.

9　　**§ 5. obequitando]** Not found before Livy: 'by riding close up.'

10　　**iusta caede]** 'with a thorough slaughter.' Cf. *iustus exercitus*, 'a regular army' (c. 31. 6), *iusta obsidio* (10. 45. 13), *iusta victoria*, etc.

13　　**§ 6. praeda]** The Roman general had absolute power to dispose of booty taken in war, provided that he devoted it to a purpose other than personal. Thus he could, as here, distribute it among the soldiers, or he could pay it into the *aerarium*, or else devote it to the service of some god. Note the distinction between *praeda*, the actual booty taken, and *manubiae*, the money realized by the sale of booty. Cf. Gell. 13. 24. 25: *praeda dicitur corpora ipsa rerum, quae capta sunt: manubiae vero appellatae sunt pecunia a quaestore ex venditione praedae redacta.*

15　　**§ 7. hominum]** This, the reading of the MSS., is certainly better than the proposed emendation *omnium*. We must consider that Livy has varied his constr., as he does so often. First he has used *fuit* with *ex* = 'consisted of,' and then with the gen. *hominum* with the same meaning. 'The greater part of the captives consisted of H. and L., and not (i.e. merely) of men drawn from the *plebs*.' If a change were thought necessary, *nec omnes* for *nec hominum* might be suggested. See Appendix.

　　militasse] sc. *eos. Mercede* = 'for reward,' the so-called abl. of *price*, which is really instrumental: 'had taken service by (inducement of) pay.'

16　　**fides]** 'proof.' Cf. Gk πίστις, which means either confidence in a thing or that which gives confidence—a proof.

20　　**§ 8. quisque]** Inserted in apposition to *omnes*; cf. c. 15. 3, c. 25. 9. The words *defectionem sui quisque populi* form a parenthesis, not affecting the constr. of the sentence; cf. 2. 38. 6: *domos inde digressi sunt, instigandoque suos quisque populos effecere, ut....*

CHAPTER XIV.

26   **§ 1. minime dubius**] For the constr. with acc. and inf., see
c. 12. 2 n.

27   **bellum...patres iussuros**] Once more Livy is careless as regards
constitutional details.   In c. 22. 4 he is more accurate: *ex senatus
consulto populique iussu bellum Praenestinis indictum.* The final word
as to peace and war lay with the *Comitia Centuriata.*

28   **moles**] 'trouble,' cf. c. 2. 11 n.

30   **§ 2. non enim...intuenti erant**] 'for by this time (*iam*) not merely
the speeches of M. Manlius, but his actions also, though in appearance
designed to gain popularity, seemed fraught with revolution, when their
true intent was considered.'

      Hitherto (c. 11. 7) Manlius had confined himself to speeches; he
now began to put his ideas as to the relations between creditor and
debtor into practice.   *Eadem* brings out the contrast between the
appearance and the reality.

31   **intuenti**] This dat. of the pres. part. seems to be an imitation of
the Gk constr.; cf. Thuc. 2. 49. 5: τῷ μὲν ἔξωθεν ἁπτομένῳ σῶμα οὐκ
ἄγαν θερμὸν ἦν. Lit. 'to one considering,' 'to one touching.' The
constr. becomes frequent in Livy and Tacitus; cf. 7. 10. 6: *nequaquam
visu ac specie aestimantibus pares.*   See Appendix.

32   **§ 3. nobilem**] 'renowned.'

      iudicatum pecuniae cum duci vidisset] The man had been formally
handed over to his creditor to be sold into slavery, cf. c. 11. 8 n. The
words *iudicatum pecuniae* refer to the first step in the process, that
denoted by the *rebus iure iudicatis* of the XII Tables, by which the
debtor was judicially ordered to make payment. Livy, as his wont is,
passes over the intermediate stages—the *triginta dies iusti,* the sixty
days' imprisonment, the proclamation on the three *nundinae,* and describes the moment when the debtor has been finally delivered over to
the creditor. Cf. below, § 10.

p. 19.   1. **pecuniae**] Gen. of the penalty, as after *damnare* in the
phrase *damnare capitis.* Perhaps originally the gen. depended upon
some such word as *iudicio.*

2   **manum iniecit**] Not to be confused with the *legis actio per manus
iniectionem,* by which a defaulting debtor was summarily arrested. The
meaning here is apparently as follows:—The debtor being condemned
was in the position of a slave, so Manlius came forward as *vindex,* and

laid his hand upon him in token that he claimed him as his own property (cf. the story of Verginia in 3. 44. 6): this laying of the hand upon the object to be transferred was also part of the procedure in the ceremony of *mancipatio*, or the formal conveyance of property from one party to another, cf. Gaius, 1. 119.

 patrum] Here 'patricians.'

3 **crudelitate feneratorum**] Tacitus (*Ann. 6. 16*) says: *primo duodecim tabulis sanctum ne quis unciario fenore amplius exerceret*, i.e. probably, no creditor was to charge more than 10 per cent. interest per annum. This rate of interest would be high enough to cause a considerable amount of suffering, and was very likely exceeded during these troublous times.

4 **§ 4. tum vero**] Anticipates *si*: 'in that case...if.'

5 **servaverim...videam**] *Servaverim*, the perf. subj., forms the apodosis to the hypothetical clause *si...videam*. 'I should have saved in vain...if I were to see.'

7 **§ 5. rem**] 'the money'; cf. the phrase *rem facere*, 'to make money.'

8 **palam populo**] By the strictest prose writers *palam* is always used as an adverb = 'openly.' Here it is a preposition = *coram*; cf. Hor. *Epod.* 11. 19: *te palam*, 'before thee.'

 libraque et aere liberatum emittit] Manlius first bought the rights of the creditor over the debtor, and then released the latter. This release was effected by the ceremony known as *per aes et libram*, 'by the copper and the scales.' In the presence of at least five witnesses and a man holding a pair of scales (*libripens*) the debtor pronounced a prescribed formula, at the same time striking the scales with a piece of copper. By so doing he symbolically paid his creditor and effected his own release (see Gaius 3. 173, 174). The explanation of these symbolic acts is simple. The striking of the scales with the piece of copper represented the weighing out of the *aes rude* or uncoined copper, which formed the earliest Roman currency. This ceremony was also performed at the transference of particular classes of property known as *res mancipi*, cf. Gaius 1. 119. See Maine, *Ancient Law*[15], pp. 204 ff. and 277 ff.

10 **parenti**] Cf. the analogous use of *pater* as a term of honour, Hor. *Od.* 3. 24. 27: *si quaeret 'pater urbium' | subscribi statuis*. For *parens*, cf. Cic. *ad Att.* 9. 10. 3: *quem nonnulli conservatorem istius urbis, quem parentem dixerunt*.

14 **§ 7. mergentibus semper sortem usuris**] 'with the interest ever swamping the principal.' The accumulated interest made the original

debt seem comparatively insignificant. With this sense of *sors* cf. our 'fortune.'

18   **§ 8. quodcunque sibi cum patria,** etc.] 'whatever ties had united him to his country, to his guardian deities, public or private, now united him to one man.'

penatibus publicis ac privatis] Cf. 5. 52. 3: *hos omnes deos publicos privatosque, Quirites, deserturi estis?* Besides the state worship, which was in the charge of the priestly colleges and carried out at the public expense, each *gens* and each *familia* had private rites (*sacra*) of its own; cf. 5. 52. 4, where *gentilicia sacra* are contrasted with *publica sacra* and *Romanos deos.* The *penates*, as gods of the store (*penus*), were peculiarly household deities; yet the state, as a collection of households, was also concerned in their worship. Note the alliteration.

20   **§ 9. cum iam unius hominis esset**] 'when they were now bound to one man heart and soul.' For the possessive gen., cf. c. 10. 1: *tota hostium erat.*

addita...res] 'a further step was taken, consisting of a design better calculated to throw everything into confusion.' The gen. is one of definition, and explains *res.* See Appendix.

23   **§ 10. quicquam**] *Quisquam* is properly restricted to negative sentences, but it is also used, as here, to express the barest possible amount.

24   **iudicatum addictumve**] The preliminary judgment against, and the final handing over of the debtor to the creditor, cf. c. 11. 8 n. The *-ve* seems to be only a Livian variation for *-que*, unless, as Mr Giles suggests, it is under the influence of *ne quem.*

28   **§ 11. vera an vana iaceret**] *Utrum* is omitted, as often. *Iacere* implies reckless accusation. For constr., cf. 1. 8. 6: *sine discrimine, liber an servus esset.*

thesauros Gallici auri] The gold which Camillus was said (falsely, no doubt, in order to soothe Roman vanity) to have recovered from the Gauls.

30   **avertant**] 'embezzle.'

31   **palam**] This predicative use of *palam* is common; it is found with both *esse* and *facere*, cf. Nep. *Hann.* 11. 1: *Hannibal ut palam faceret suis,* 'that he might make it plain to his men.'

32   **§ 12. enimvero**] expresses indignation, cf. Cic. *Verr.* II. 1. 26. 66: *enimvero ferendum hoc quidem non est,* 'this is *truly* intolerable.' *Videri* is a historic inf.

p. 20. 1 **tributo**] We may perhaps find in this a trace of the true

story. According to 5. 50. 7, the gold demanded by the Gauls was
supplied by the Roman matrons, not by a *tributum*, or general property
tax. That story was, no doubt, an invention. To supply the immediate
demand gold was probably borrowed from temples and individuals alike,
and was subsequently repaid by money raised by a regular *tributum*.
This version did not commend itself to the pride of the Roman historians.

2   **cessisse**] Followed by *in* and acc. = 'to become.' The phrase in
this sense is post-Ciceronian; cf. *abire in.*

§ **13. exsequebantur quaerendo**] 'they enquired pertinaciously.'
Lit. 'they followed up by asking.'

4   **differentique**] The -*i* form of the abl. of the pres. part. is common
when the part. is used as an adj., as in the often recurring *insequenti
anno*, but not otherwise. Weiss. here explains *differenti* as abl. abs.,
holding that the -*i* form has been adopted to avoid the disagreeable
sound of *differenteque*; cf. 1. 54. 6, *sequenti*, for a similar -*i* form in an
abl. abs. In the present case, however, *differenti* and *dicenti* might be
explained as free datives of the person interested. 'And when he en-
deavoured to put them off...he found,' etc. Ltb. explains them as
datives of the agent to be taken with *versae erant omnium curae.* Cf.,
for a similar constr., 23. 12. 1: *tantus acervus fuit, ut* **metientibus**
supra tres modios explesse sint quidam auctores; also § 2, above, *intuenti.*

6   **mediam**]=*mediocrem*, cf. 2. 49. 5 : *nihil medium...sed immensa
omnia volventium animo. Mediam* is to be taken with both *gratiam*
and *offensionem*, its position rendering it more emphatic.

CHAPTER XV.

11   § **1. periclitatus**] 'having tested.' Distinguish this meaning from
the intrans. use of the word, 'to be in danger,' e.g. in 40. 15. 12 : *cum
quid aliud quam ingenii fama periclitarer?*

12   **senatum**] For a similar proceeding, cf. 5. 50. 8: *in contionem
universo senatu prosequente escendit* (*Camillus*). It seems to have been
the custom on important occasions for the Senate, after meeting in the
Curia, to support the leading magistrate by forming his escort.

13   § **2. in comitio**] A space in front of the Senate House, which had
been consecrated by the augurs. Varro (*L. L.* 5. 155) says : *comitium
ab eo, quod coibant eo Comitiis Curiatis et litium causa. Contiones*
were frequently held in the Comitium, which was on higher ground than
the Forum proper. See map.

viatorem] The *viatores* were servants of the magistrates, and their
chief duty was to summon senators to the Senate, or (as in the present

case) persons before their masters. They must be distinguished from the *lictores*, since the consuls had both *lictores* and *viatores*. The tribunes of the *plebs* had *viatores*. Cf. 2. 56. 13.

16   § **3. quisque**] In apposition to *senatus* and *plebs*, denoting the individuals in the two groups. A common Livian usage. Cf. c. 13. 8.

20   § **4. quaesiturus**] With this use of *quaero*, cf. *quaestiones perpetuae*, 'standing courts.'

22   § **5. fide incolumi**] 'without any damage to credit.' Cf. c. 11. 8: *fidem moliri*. The meaning is that the debtors would be able to pay up in full.

23   **creditum**] 'the money lent,' sc. *aes*.

24   **contra**] 'on the contrary'; not to be taken with *te*.

25   **incubantes**] 'brooding over.' Cf. Cic. *pro Clu.* 27. 72: *qui illi pecuniae, quam condiderat, spe atque animo incubaret.* The Romans believed in the existence of special spirits called *incubones*, which guarded hidden treasure. Cf. Petronius, 38: *cum incuboni pilleum rapuisset, thesaurum invenit.* Cf. also our 'Incubus.'

26   **nisi facis**] Pres. used vividly for fut. For the change from *facis* to *iubebo*, cf. c. 38. 7 n.

27   § **6. in parte praedae sis**] 'may share the booty.' Cf. c. 37. 4: *in parte pari rei publicae fore*, and 4. 5. 5: *si in consortio, si in societate rei publicae esse...licet.*

29   § **7. nec**]=*ne...quidem.*

32   **adversus se**] Cf. c. 11. 9, 10, where it is said that the war against the Latins and the Hernicans was made an excuse for appointing a dictator, whose real task was to be the crushing of Manlius.

p. 21. 6. § **9. quin**] 'why (do you) not...?' *Quin* is composed of *qui* (a locative) and *ne*, and its original use was an interrogative one. Subsequently it came to be employed chiefly with subordinate clauses.

7   **intercedendo**] Here not 'by veto,' but 'by interposing your credit,' i.e. by offering bail. Cf. Cic. *ad Att.* 6. 1. 5: *ascribit...intercessisse se pro iis magnam pecuniam.*

    nervo] 'stocks.' See c. 11. 8 n.

9   **affluit**] 'that which flows away,' so 'the superfluity' of your wealth. *Affluit* is the reading of the best MSS., and is in itself perfectly intelligible. The other MSS. read *affluit*, which, as the commoner word, is far more likely to be a correction. Though no other instance of this use of *affluere* can be cited, *abundare* is analogous, if the ordinarily received derivation is correct. See Appendix.

10 § **10. impendatis, hortor]** Jussive subj. There is no need to assume an ellipse of *ut.* See c. 18. 9 n.

sortem reliquam ferte] So Madvig for the *aliquam* of the MSS., which gives no adequate meaning. Manlius, naturally enough, identifies the Senate with the rich creditors, and says : 'take the principal that remains owing, deduct from the amount what has been paid in interest'—an anticipation of the Licinio-Sextian measure for the relief of debtors (c. 35. 4). See Appendix.

12 **iam]** 'in that case.' The speaker supposes that his demands have been acceded to.

ullius] Used as subst., 'of anyone else.' Cf. 5. 23. 4 : *adventus... dictatoris...celebratior quam ullius unquam antea fuit.*

conspectior] 'more conspicuous'; cf. 45. 7. 3 *patris avique...fama conspectum eum faciebat.* Cf. also *conspiciendum* in c. 4. 12. Perhaps this use of *conspectus* is borrowed from Virgil. Cf. *Aen.* 8. 588: *chlamyde et pictis conspectus in armis.*

13 § **11. at enim]** = ἀλλὰ γάρ. The objection of opponents is anticipated. 'But,' you will say....

14 **ita solus]** 'no less single-handed.' The first *ita* means 'as I am doing,' the second is an intentional repetition with a slightly different signification.

16 § **12. nam]** implies that the answer to the question about the *aurum Gallicum* is as self-evident as the answer to the question of the saving of the Capitol. '(There is no need of argument), for....'

17 **suapte]** A slightly strengthened *sua.* The suffix *-pte* adds a certain amount of emphasis, cf. the suffixes *-met* and *-te* (in *tute*) ; *-pte,* which is very common in Plautus and is used occasionally by Cicero, seems to be a contraction for *pote* (from *potis*), the full form being seen in *utpote.*

19 **in sinu]** The fold of the toga was sometimes used as a purse. Cf. the Gk κόλπος, and the phrase ὑπὸ κόλπῳ χεῖρας ἔχων (Theocr. 16. 16), expressive of a close-fisted person. Cf. also St Luke vi. 38 : μέτρον καλὸν...δώσουσιν εἰς τὸν κόλπον ὑμῶν.

potius, quam ponatis] The fuller constr. with *ut* occurs frequently. Cf. c. 28. 8 : *potius...quam ut timorem faciat.* The first course of action is considered to be adopted with a view to the exclusion of the second ; hence the subj. is due to the notion of purpose involved. Cf. the subj. after *priusquam,* etc.

20 § **13. praestigias]** 'tricks,' properly 'juggling tricks.' Trans.: 'the more you demand that your trickery be proved, the more afraid I am that you have robbed the onlookers even of their sight.'

23   **id cogendi estis**] *Id* expresses the extent of the verb's action, and
is a kind of cognate acc. So, in the act., *cogo* is found with a double
acc., the one denoting the direct object, the other, usually a neut. pron.,
the extent of the verb's action. Cf. Verg. *Aen.* 3. 56 : quid *non mor-
talia pectora cogis | auri sacra fames?*

CHAPTER XVI.

31   **§ 1. peragere verum**] *Verum* is proleptic ; 'to make his indictment
good.' Cf. c. 12. 9 n.

32   **insimulati...senatus**] 'of false accusation against the Senate.'

p. 22.   1   **oblataeque vani furti invidiae**] 'and of bringing upon them
the odium of a baseless charge of theft.' As Weiss. points out, *vani* is
not strictly applicable to *furti*, but balances the sentence better by being
placed in agreement with it. This constr. (called by grammarians
'hypallage' or 'interchange') is fairly common in Livy. A good
instance occurs in 8. 7. 18 : **specimen** *istud virtutis* **deceptum** *vana
imagine decoris* ; we should expect *deceptae.*

3   **§ 2. viatore**] Cf. c. 15. 2 n.

Iuppiter...Iuno...Minerva] These three deities had separate *cellae*
in the temple of Jupiter on the Capitolium. Since the time of the
Tarquins they were united as the special protective deities of Rome, an
innovation probably due to the Etruscans. Cf. c. 4. 3 n.

4   **ceterique di deaeque**] Weiss. quotes Servius on Verg. *Georg.* 1. 21
(*dique deaeque omnes, studium quibus arva tueri*) : *Per pontifices in
omnibus sacris post speciales deos, quos ad ipsum sacrum, quod fiebat,
necesse erat invocari, generaliter omnia numina invocantur.* It is very
characteristic of the Roman mind that care is taken to prevent any god
being offended by chance omission. The same feeling comes out in
the common *si deus, si dea* (cf. 7. 26. 4) ; cf. also Hor. *Sat.* 2. 6. 20 :
Matutine pater, seu **Iane libentius audis.**

5   **sicine**] When *-ne* is attached to *sic*, the longer and original form of
the latter (*sice*) is used ; the same is the case with *hic*, cf. c. 17. 3 :
hocine. The change from *e* to *i* is due to shifting of accent ; cf. *légo* and
cólligo. See Giles, *Manual of Philology* §§ 161, 325 v.

7   **vinclis et catenis**] Rhetorical redundance ; no distinction in
meaning is intended.

8   **§ 3. nullius nec...nec**] The negatives do not destroy, but strengthen
one another. Distinguish between *nullus nec...nec, nullus non* = 'every
one,' and *non nullus* = 'some one.' Cf. c. 23. 9.

sed invicta sibi...fecerat] 'but the state, most submissive to lawful

authority, had made for itself certain inviolable rules.' The freedom of
the best period of the Republic was no 'Freedom free to slay herself,
and dying while they shout her name.' It is in passages like this that
the secret of Rome's greatness and of Livy's enduring worth comes out.

10   **tribuni plebis**] The tribunes of the *plebs* remained in office during
the dictatorship, but they could not hamper the dictator by interposing
their veto. Similarly there was no *provocatio* from the dictator's
sentence.

13   **§ 4. vestem mutasse**] A common sign of anxiety on behalf of a
public favourite. Here the change of dress was voluntary, but mourning
was sometimes officially ordered, a rare and high compliment. Cf. Cic.
pro Planc. 35. 87 : *at erat mecum senatus et quidem veste mutata, quod
pro me uno post hominum memoriam publico consilio susceptum est.* The
mourning of the *plebs* was probably shown by the wearing of the *toga
pulla* and the disfiguring of themselves with dust and ashes ; cf. § 8.

    capillum ac barbam promisisse] The Romans of Livy's day were
clean shaven, as may be seen from busts of the time of Augustus. This
fact, no doubt, has betrayed Livy into the present inaccuracy, for at the
time of which he is here writing beards were universal. In 5. 41. 9 he
says correctly : *barbam..., ut tum omnibus promissa erat.*

15   **§ 5. triumphavit**] At first sight another inaccuracy on Livy's part.
The *triumphator* should not, according to the general rule, have entered
the city before his triumph, whereas Livy depicts him as taking a leading
part in the proceedings against Manlius. Cf. the case of Caesar in
60 B.C., who, as he had to enter the city to stand for the consulship, was
obliged to forego a triumph. Plut. *Caes.* 13 : τοὺς μὲν μνωμένους θρίαμβον
ἔξω διατρίβειν ἔδει. But it may be that the dictator, as the embodiment
of martial law, was not bound by the rule which a consul ẃas compelled
to obey.

    invidiaeque] The *-que* is used adversatively='but.' Cf. c. 4. 10
and c. 21. 9: *arguentibusque. Invidiae* and *gloriae* are probably
'predicative' datives, though it is barely possible that they are
genitives.

21   **§ 6. Satricum**] Cf. c. 7. 1 n. Livy in c. 22. 4 calls Satricum
coloniam populi Romani, but there is no reason to believe that the
colony was other than Latin. The colonising of the place was a measure
of defence, as well as an attempt to gain popularity.

22   **iugera**] The *iugerum* was about two-thirds of an English acre; it
was originally the amount of land which could be ploughed in one day.
Cf. for the idea 2. 10. 12 : *agri quantum uno die circumaravit datum—*

the reward of Horatius, which would of course be equivalent to several *iugera*, though Macaulay's estimate would set it down at one:—

'They gave him of the corn-land
That was of public right
As much as two strong oxen
Could plough from morn till night.'

See also Frazer's note on βουλυτός in *Class. Rev.* 2, pp. 260, 261, where it is shown that in ancient times ploughing probably ceased soon after midday. The amount of land assigned seems to have varied from two *iugera* (4. 47. 6) to seven (granted at Veii, 5. 30. 8).

26   **§ 8. facie reorum**] 'by an expression such as men under accusation wear.' Both in Greece and at Rome it was the custom for the accused and his friends to try to awaken sympathy by such outward display of misery.

CHAPTER XVII.

p. 23. 4 **§ 1. itaque**] For position, see c. 4. 8 n.

7   **§ 2. Sp. Cassium**] Cf. 2. 41. 1. In 486 B.C. Spurius Cassius, when consul, concluded the treaty with the Hernici, and afterwards proposed an agrarian law, the chief feature of which was the granting of a share in the distribution to the Latins. He was suspected of aiming at regal power, and was condemned to death. As in the stories of Sp. Maelius and M. Manlius, so in the account of Cassius many features have been introduced, which properly belong to the later agrarian struggles.

8   **Sp. Maelium**] Cf. IV. 13 and 14. In 439 B.C. Sp. Maelius, a wealthy knight, sold corn to the people at a very low price. This brought upon him suspicion of aiming at a tyranny, and he was murdered by the Master of the Horse, C. Servilius Ahala. We have here, perhaps, some confusion with the story of the Gracchi.

11   **§ 3. saginare**] Properly used of fattening animals. The people 'fatten up' their leaders, only to let them be killed. Tacitus (*Hist.* 2. 88) has *gladiatoriam saginam*, a special food for gladiators.

[**populares**] **suos**] The two words together would naturally mean 'their own countrymen.' Hence Madvig bracketed *populares* as a gloss upon *suos*, 'their champions.' See Appendix.

12   **hocine**] See c. 16. 2 n. Translate: 'ought this to have been the fate of a man of consular rank for not replying at the dictator's beck?' Or. recta: *hocine patiendum fuit, si non respondit? Hoc* is used (instead of *illud*) for the sake of vividness.

18   § **4. M. Manlii**] sc. *speciem observatam.* Passages such as this show Livy's fondness for rhetoric. Cf. Introd. § 3.

20   **Iove**] In the temple of Jupiter was his terracotta image, covered with costly robes, with the face painted scarlet—the sign of a *triumphator.*

21   § **5. selibrisne farris**] Cf. 5. 47. 8. The soldiers presented Manlius with what was of the greatest value during the privations of a siege ; each gave a half-pound of meal and a *quartarius* (about ⅛ pint) of wine. Afterwards, however, the gift seemed but mean.

22   **Capitolino**] Join with *Iovi.* Cf. c. 5. 6 n. and see Appendix.

23   **pati**] This, as representing *patimini* in the or. recta, should by strict rule be *paterentur.* The rule is that questions in the 1st and 3rd persons in the or. recta, which are generally rhetorical and do not call for an answer, are put in the inf. in the or. obliqua; those in the 2nd person, in the subj. But, like most grammatical 'rules,' it is not a hard and fast one. Cf. c. 39. 10 : *aestimaturos.* The question here is essentially, though not formally, rhetorical.

24   **adeo**] For this use of *adeo* in indignant questions, cf. Iuv. 3. 84 : *usque adeo nihil est, quod nostra infantia caelum | hausit Aventini baca nutrita Sabina ?*

27   § **6. quod**] See Appendix.

28   **ex senatus consulto**] It is hardly likely that a prisoner could be set free by decree of the Senate alone. Probably Livy, as so often elsewhere, has abbreviated the procedure. The *senatus consultum* was simply advice given to the magistrate, and it was through the magistrate himself that the release was effected.

32   § **7. a Velitris**] A good instance of Livy's anxiety to secure variety. He might have used *Veliterni* for the people of Velitrae. Cf. c. 13. 8.

p. 24. 2 **cives Romani**] In spite of this assertion, there is no reason to suppose that Circeii and Velitrae were other than Latin colonies. They are included in the list of Latin cities given by Dionysius (5. 61).

3   § **8. itaque**] Note position again.

      in quo...temperaverant] 'a point in which they had at least (*tamen*) spared their allies.' The Ciceronian constr. is the dat. of the person spared. Cf. *Verr.* II. 2. 6. 17 : *si cuiquam denique ulla in re unquam temperarit.* *Tamen* implies that the answer to the Latins and Hernicans, though severe, was *nevertheless* not so severe as that given to the colonists.

4   **senatus verbis**] 'in the Senate's name.'

6   **legationis ius**]   This was part of the *ius gentium*, not part of the *ius civile,* which was applicable only to Roman citizens.   See c. 1. 6 n.

CHAPTER XVIII.

13   **§ 1. recrudescente**]   'breaking out again.'   Properly applied to half-healed wounds.   Cf. Cic. *ad Fam.* 4. 6. 2: *nunc autem hoc tam gravi vulnere etiam illa, quae consanuisse videbantur, recrudescunt.*

sub exitum]   See Appendix.

20   **§ 2. fenoris expugnandi**] ' of storming the stronghold of usury.'

23   **§ 3. iam**]   See Appendix.

24   **domum**]   The fact that this house was on the Capitol (cf. c. 19. 1 and c. 20. 13) made these meetings seem the more dangerous.   The first step of a would-be tyrant was to seize the citadel.   Cf. Kylon's attempt at Athens.   Thuc. 1. 126: κατέλαβε τὴν ἀκρόπολιν ὡς ἐπὶ τυραννίδι.   Diodorus (15. 35. 3) says: Μάρκος Μάνλιος ἐπιβαλόμενος τυραννίδι καὶ κρατηθεὶς ἀνῃρέθη.

28   **§ 4. inexperto**]   Pass. 'unused to.'   The word is not found in Cic. or Caes. : cf. the pass. sense of *expertum* § 13 below.

quod nec ausus esset] 'the *thought* that he had not ventured.' Oblique.

29   **Sp. Maelio**]   Cf. c. 17. 2 n.   Livy rather carelessly ascribes to the dictator the deed committed by his Master of the Horse.

p. **25.** 6   **§ 6. quot enim clientes...**]   The *plebs* is assumed to be made up of clients.   But this is, in all probability, only partially true. The client, who was closely attached to some patrician house, was indeed a plebeian; but besides the clients there must have been many other plebeians, e.g. Latins who had settled in Rome for trade or other purposes, and who were not bound to any patrician *gens* by the close tie of clientship.   Livy himself seems to recognize this in other passages; cf. 5. 32. 8: *clientibus, quae magna pars plebis erat.*

As for the reading, the *quot enim* of the MSS. may well be retained. Livy says: 'if you fought with equal numbers you would win; (much more will you do so now), *for* you are greatly superior in numbers.'   Cf. the elliptical use of *nam* in c. 15. 2 n.   See Appendix.

9   **§ 7. ius**]   i.e. their strict legal claims, chiefly with regard to debt; **ipsi** = *ultro*, ' of their own accord.'

13   **§ 8. nullus fui**] 'I was as good as lost.'   This use of *nullus* is common in Plautus and Terence, where *nullus sum* frequently = *perii* ; cf. Plaut. *Cas.* 305: *si id factum est, ecce me nullum senem.*

vidistis]   *Videre* here = Gk περιορᾶν, ' to allow.'

16   **§ 9. abominamini]** 'express abhorrence.' The words are half ironical. "You do well to express abhorrence (and say) 'Heaven will avert this.'" Pious wishes without works will do little.

18   **dent...oportet]** *Dent* is a jussive subj. and might well stand alone without *oportet*. It is not necessary to suppose that there is an ellipse of *ut*; *oportet* is almost parenthetical. Cf. 22. 53. 5 : *in haec verba, L. Caecili, iures postulo* ; also c. 15. 10 : *sed quid ego vos, de vestro impendatis, hortor?*

19   **armato togatoque]** 'in war and peace.'

21   **§ 10. auxilium]** refers to the *ius auxilii* of the tribunes of the *plebs*, whereby they could interfere to rescue a plebeian from arbitrary oppression on the part of a patriciah magistrate.

22   **quatenus imperari vobis sinatis]** 'how far you are to suffer yourselves to be lorded over.' Lit. 'it to be lorded over you.' The negative character of the tribunate is emphasized, see below, § 13.

24   **usu possidemini]** 'you become theirs by mere use.' The expression is a legal one. Full ownership could, by Roman law, be acquired by simple possession of the object for one or two years, cf. Ulpian 19. 8 : *usucapio est autem dominii adeptio per continuationem possessionis anni vel biennii. Possessio* denoted occupation, whether with or without legal title ; hence it is implied here that the patricians have no right to the superiority which they assume. Cf. 1. 46. 1 : *iam usu haud dubie regnum possederat*, i.e. Servius Tullius had not been formally elected king, but had secured his position by possession.

31   **§ 13. expertum]** Pass. sense, though from deponent verb, cf. § 4.

33   **resisterent]** The tribunate of the *plebs* was in origin a purely negative office. Gradually, however, the tribunes won a considerable power of initiative in legislation, when they ceased to be mere officers of the *plebs*, and became real magistrates of the people.

p. 26. 2 **§ 14. prohibete ius de pecuniis dici]** Manlius' aim is a χρεῶν ἀποκοπή, or universal repudiation of debts. This could be effected, if the tribunes of the *plebs* interfered to rescue every debtor who had been adjudged to his creditor. For the phrase, cf. 2. 27. 1 : *quam asperrime poterat ius de creditis pecuniis dicere.*

3   **patronum]** The relation between the patron and the client was of the most sacred character ; hence the pride with which Manlius claims the name. Cf. the XII Tables: *Patronus si clienti fraudem fecerit, sacer esto.* Also Verg. *Aen.* 6. 609, where *fraus innexa clienti* suffices to consign the guilty one to the nethermost hell. *Fides*, no doubt, is intended to stand in contrast to this much-detested *fraus.*

7   **§ 16. dicitur]** Livy, though he clearly has no sympathy with
Manlius, maintains his reputation for candour.   There was considerable
difference of opinion among Roman writers as to the guilt or innocence
of Manlius.   Plut. *Cam.* 36 says that he was condemned ἐπὶ τεκμηρίοις
φανεροῖς: Cicero (*Phil.* 2. 44. 114) is vague: *propter suspicionem regni
appetendi*: Servius on *Aen.* 8. 652, on the other hand, thinks the
condemnation unfair: *Manlius...inimicorum oppressus factione.* Cf. c.
20. 4.

cum quibus] Some suitable word must be supplied from *pervenerint*,
which, though only applicable to *ad finem*, is by zeugma connected with
cum quibus as well.   Livy never seems to use *quibuscum*, which is the
ordinary form in Cicero; cf. 1. 45. 2, 4. 24. 2, 38. 9. 2.   But in the
present instance we feel that *cum quibus* is more natural than *quibuscum*,
perhaps because *quibus* is interrogative, not relative.

CHAPTER XIX.

13   **§ 1. domum privatam]** See c. 18. 3 n.
15   mole] 'trouble,' 'danger,' cf. c. 2. 11 n.
    § 2. Servilio Ahala] We should say, 'of *a* Servilius Ahala.' It
was he who, as Master of the Horse, struck down Sp. Maelius in
439 B.C.: cf. c. 17. 2 n.
17   iactura] Properly used of the throwing overboard of cargo in order
to lighten a ship in distress; from this comes the general meaning
'sacrifice'; cf. 5. 39. 12: *facilem iacturam esse seniorum*, and Iuv. 3.
125: *nusquam minor est iactura clientis*, 'the throwing overboard of
a client.'
18   **§ 3. decurritur]** 'recourse was had to,' implying more or less
extreme measures.   With the whole sentence, cf. Caesar *B. C.* 1. 5
(the final breach between Caesar and the Senate): *decurritur ad illum
extremum atque ultimum senatus consultum, quo, nisi paene in ipso urbis
incendio atque in desperatione omnium salutis, latorum audacia nunquam
ante descensum est.*

vim] Exactly our 'force.'
19   ut videant magistratus, etc.] Cf. 3. 4. 9. This was the regular
formula of the *senatus consultum ultimum*, which practically amounted
to the declaration of martial law.   It is almost certain that Livy is
guilty of an anachronism in placing the *s. c. ultimum* so early as this.
The truth is that, so long as the dictatorship existed, this measure was
superfluous.   But after the Second Punic War the dictatorship died out,
and the *s. c. ultimum* took its place.   It was the weapon employed against

the Gracchi, Saturninus, and the Catilinarians, and also, as we have seen, by the Pompeians against Julius Caesar. Cf. Sallust, *Cat.* 29. 2, 3.

21 **§ 4. plebi**] Remember that there are two forms *plebs* and *plebes*, the former making gen. *plebis*, the latter *plebi* or *plebei*. The form *plebis* occurs below, § 5.

22 **et ei**] See Appendix.

potestatis...finem] Under the tyranny, which Manlius was aiming at, all would be reduced to a like level of impotence.

23 **patrum auctoritati**] Here not the sanction of the patrician members of the Senate, necessary for the confirmation of laws and elections, but the general opinion of the whole body.

26 **§ 5. ingentis dimicationis**] Defining gen.: 'that would be attended by a mighty conflict.'

29 **§ 6. quid cum plebe aggredimur eum**] 'why, in attacking him, do we attack the *plebs* as well?'

31 **ruat**] 'may perish'; cf., for the phrase, Pref. § 4: *ut iam magnitudine laboret sua*, and Hor. *Od.* 3. 4. 65: *vis consili expers mole ruit sua*.

§ 7. diem dicere] See c. 1. 6 n., and cf. c. 20. 12. It seems very unlikely that the tribunes would have conducted a prosecution involving a capital penalty at this period. It is far more likely that the trial took place before special commissioners, *duumviri perduellionis*. See Introd. § 4 c.

32 **simul**] *Viderint, facti erunt*, and *intuebuntur* are all to be taken with this word, while the main statement is given by *favebunt*. Note also that *intuebuntur* governs *accusatores, reum*, and *crimen*, the natural order being changed to bring out the verbal antithesis.

p. 27. 1 **ex advocatis**] 'instead of supporters.' The Latin word for 'advocate' in the legal sense is *patronus*. An *advocatus* is generally a friend who lends his support or advice; cf. Cic. *pro Clu.* 40. 110: *quis eum unquam non modo in patroni, sed in laudatoris aut advocati loco viderat?* In post-classical prose *advocatus* is used in the sense of *patronus*.

2 **de plebe, patricium**] Livian variation for *plebeios, patricium*: cf. c. 17. 7 n.

intuebuntur] The change from fut. perf. to fut. simple is merely due to Livy's love of variety, it has no particular force.

3 **in medio**] 'set for decision.' The *regni crimen* is the object of conflict between the accuser and the accused.

nulli] For *nemini*, as often in Livy.

CHAPTER XX.

With this chap. cf. Introd. § 4 c.

14   § **1. utique**] 'at least,' a limiting particle; cf. c. 35. 5: *consulum utique alter*, 'at least one of the consuls.' There is a different use of the word with negatives, when it serves to make the negative more emphatic; cf. 2. 59. 4: *monentes, ne utique experiri vellet imperium*, 'that he should not on any account...'

15   **sordidatum**] Cf. c. 16. 4 and 8 nn.

      § **2. non modo...**] 'and saw with him not merely no patrician, but not even relations, etc.' *Nec...patrum quemquam = et...patrum neminem*, while the neg. *ne* in *ne...quidem* is superfluous after *nec*; cf. c. 25. 10 n.

16   **cognatos**] These are blood-relations; *affines* are marriage connections. *Agnati*, on the other hand, are blood-relations traced through the male line only.

18   **venisset**] Subj. in or. obliqua, expressing the thought in the minds of the *plebs*.

19   § **3. App. Claudio**] See 3. 58. 1. Appius Claudius was the *decemvir*, infamous for his crime against Verginia; he is said to have committed suicide in prison.

22   **primus**] Cf. c. 11. 7 n.

24   § **4. fallax indicium**] The charge of embezzling the *aurum Gallicum*.

26   § **5. nec dubito**] For the constr. with the acc. and inf., cf. 12. 2 n. The remark is an excellent illustration of the way in which Livy shirks difficulties. He candidly admits there were no proofs of treason, yet feels sure Manlius must have been guilty; cf. the way in which he deals with the difficulty connected with the numbers of the Volscians in c. 12.

27   **plebi**] This must be an inaccuracy. In § 10 Livy says that the trial took place before the Comitia Centuriata in the Campus Martius, and in any case a purely plebeian assembly could not possibly have decided a charge of high treason. This is another instance of Livy's indifference to constitutional details, his main interest is in the moral to be drawn from the story (*illud notandum*, etc.).

31   § **6. expensas pecunias tulisset**] simply means 'had lent money.' Lit. 'for whom he had entered sums (into the account book) as paid out.' On the other hand, *acceptum refero* means ' I owe,' cf. Cic. *Verr.* II. 1. 39. 100 : *quod minus Dolabella Verri acceptum rettulit, quam Verres*

illi expensum tulerit, 'whereas D. credited Verres with a less sum than Verres put down as paid to him.'

32 venire] From *veneo,* 'I am sold.'

prohibuisset] Possibly by inducing the tribunes of the *plebs* to interfere in their behalf, but more probably, as in the case of the centurion (c. 14), by paying their debts for them.

§ 7. ad haec] 'in addition to this.' More usually *ad hoc,* as below.

33 decora belli] 'military distinctions.'

p. 28. 2 in quibus]=*et in eis.*

3 murales coronas] The man, who first scaled the walls of a besieged city, was granted a golden crown decorated with turrets: cf. the mural crown which appears upon the head of Cybele, e.g. upon coins of Smyrna (Hill, *Greek and Roman Coins,* Pl. VIII. 10); cf. Gell. 5. 6. 16.

civicas] The *corona civica* was presented to the Roman soldier who had preserved the life of a citizen in battle. The crown was made from leaves of different kinds of oak, and bore the words *ob civem servatum.* Augustus was granted the *corona civica* by the Senate, and upon coins of his appears the oak-crown with the words *ob cives servatos.* Cf. Pliny *N. H.* 16. 11 and Gell. 5. 6. 11.

4 § 8. [produxit] The MSS. read *produxit* and *nominatum.* The least unsatisfactory emendation is that of Madvig, viz. to strike out *produxit* and to change *nominatum* into *nominatim.* In that case *commemorasse* must be supplied from above. The insertion of *produxit* may be due to a copyist, who failed to understand the absence of a verb after *cives.*

Yet this reading is not free from difficulty. Manlius mentioned and showed the crowns he had won by saving the lives of citizens; there would not be much point in adding that he mentioned the fact that he had preserved citizens from the enemy; we should rather expect to find that he brought them forward in person. There is a further awkwardness in the necessity of supplying *commemorasse* from above, when *protulisse* has followed it. See Appendix.

inter quos]=*et inter eos.*

5 magistrum equitum] Pliny (*N. H.* 7. 103) says: *P.* (read *C.*) *Servilium magistrum equitum servaverat, ipse volneratus umerum, femur.* Livy's meaning must therefore be that Manlius had rescued Servilius some years before (perhaps in 389 B.C.), when the latter was Master of the Horse, not that Servilius was Master of the Horse at the present time (cf. c. 2. 6).

6 pro fastigio rerum] 'proportioned to the height of his exploits.'

The *fastigium* is properly the triangular gable or pediment of a building, hence 'height,' 'summit'; cf. 1. 38. 6, where *fastigium* = 'slope'; there the sloping *side* of the pediment is thought of, here the apex.   For the expression, cf. Milton, *Par. Lost* 1. 24 f. :

> 'That to the height of this great argument
> I may assert Eternal Providence.'

7   **aequando**] 'equalling.' The word is in apposition to *oratione*. This modal gerund is frequently used by Livy, and indeed by Latin writers generally. Cf. 3. 53. 9: *qui aequo iure in civitate vivit nec inferendo iniuriam nec patiendo*, where we should translate simply 'neither doing nor suffering wrong'; cf. also c. 23. 4.

11   **§ 9. Capitolinam arcem**] This seems to be a general expression for the whole Mons Capitolinus. The two summits, Capitolium (S.W.) and Arx (N.E.), are distinguished below; between these two summits was the depression known as *inter duos lucos*. See map.

15   **§ 10. in campo Martio**] The regular place of meeting for the Comitia Centuriata, which, as a military assembly, had to be convened outside the *pomerium*. The previous proceedings had taken place at a *contio*. Plutarch (*Cam.* 36) wrongly represents the trial as taking place in the Forum (ἀγορά): εἰσαγομένων δὲ τῶν κατὰ τοῦ Μαλλίου δικῶν μεγάλα τοὺς κατηγόρους ἔβλαπτεν ἡ ὄψις· ὁ γὰρ τόπος, ἐφ' οὗ βεβηκὼς ὁ Μάλλιος ἐνυκτομάχησε πρὸς τοὺς Κελτούς, ὑπερεφαίνετο τῆς ἀγορᾶς ἀπὸ τοῦ Καπιτωλίου καὶ παρεῖχεν οἶκτον τοῖς ὁρῶσιν.

20   **§ 11. prodicta die**] 'the day of trial having been adjourned.' There was no provision in law for the adjournment (*ampliatio*) of trials before the Comitia. But, as Prof. Mommsen points out, it would be easy for the presiding magistrate to break up the meeting under pretext of an unfavourable omen, and to complete the trial on another day.

in Petelinum lucum extra portam Flumentanam] The Porta Flumentana was close to the river, in the low-lying ground by the Forum Boarium, S.W. of the Capitol; cf. 35. 9. 2 and 3. The *lucus Petelinus* (also mentioned in 7. 41. 3) must therefore have been situated just outside this gate, on the river bank. But how in this case could the people have avoided seeing the Capitol, which rose just above them? The suggestion that the trees of the wood shut out the view is not very satisfactory. Prof. Mommsen therefore conjectures that either (1) the position of the Porta Flumentana has been given wrongly (by Paulus, an epitomator of Festus), or (2) the words *extra portam Flumentanam* are a late addition, and that the *lucus Petelinus* lay right the other side of Rome, perhaps on the Esquiline. See map.

22   esset] The subj. expresses purpose; the object of the change was
to avoid the sight of the Capitol.

concilium populi] The expression is inaccurate. The assemblies
of the *populus*, i.e. of the whole citizen body, patricians and plebeians
alike, were always called *comitia*, those of the *plebs* by itself *concilia*.
There can be little doubt that Livy, who, as we have seen (§ 5), attaches
small weight to accuracy in these matters, really means the *Comitia
Centuriata*.

24   § 12. sunt, qui] We do not know who these authorities were, but
in all probability they included the earlier and better annalists, such as
Fabius and Piso. This alternative account was the one given by Nepos
(ap. Gell. 17. 21. 24): *ut Cornelius Nepos scriptum reliquit verberando
necatus est*, i.e. he was put to death *more maiorum*, as the result of
condemnation by *duumviri perduellionis*.

duumviros] The more correct term was *duumviri perduellionis
iudicandae*. They were commissioners specially appointed to try men
accused of the crime of *perduellio*, or high treason. Only three cases
of trial by *duumviri perduellionis* are known, consequently details of
procedure are very uncertain. In the case of Horatius (I. 26), the
commissioners were nominated by the King; in that of Rabirius (63 B.C.),
when an obsolete form of procedure was revived, they were chosen
by lot.

25   anquirerent] Legal term, 'to hold a trial,' used of the prosecuting
magistrate in a *iudicium populi*. It is often found with *capitis* or
pecuniā, denoting the punishment demanded by the accuser.

auctores sint] 'relate.'

26   de saxo Tarpeio] Throwing from the Tarpeian rock appears to
have been the punishment specially inflicted by the tribunes of the
plebs, since they had no lictors assigned to them. See map.

28   § 13. notae] 'marks of ignominy'; cf. the well-known *nota
censoria*.

29   Monetae] The temple of Juno Moneta was vowed by L. Furius
Camillus (7. 28. 4) and dedicated on June 1st 344 B.C. The name
Moneta is probably connected with *moneo*, and is perhaps reminiscent
of the warning of the approach of the Gauls given by the sacred birds
of Juno. Part of the temple was used as a mint, with the result that
moneta subsequently came to mean 'a mint' and 'money.' Suidas
(s.v. Μονῆτα) says that this name was given to the goddess, and the
mint attached to her temple, on account of her good advice in the war
against Pyrrhus. Later on another temple was dedicated to Juno

Moneta on the Alban Mount; see 42. 7. 1, 45. 15. 10. For the destruction of Manlius' house, cf. 2. 41. 11, where the house of Sp. Cassius is said to have suffered a similar fate. It should be noted that Cicero (*de domo* 38. 101) gives a rather different version with regard to the house of Manlius: *eius domum eversam duobus lucis convestitam videtis.* See map.

31 § **14. gentis Manliae decreto**] Just as the *paterfamilias* had jurisdiction in the *familia*, so the *gentiles* had the right of issuing decrees in matters affecting the welfare of the *gens.* It is a fact that after this date we meet with no patrician Manlius bearing the *praenomen* Marcus. Cf. Cic. *Phil.* 1. 13. 32, and especially Suet. *Tib.* 1, where the *gens Claudia* is said to have issued a similar prohibition: *cum praenominibus cognominibusque variis distingueretur, Lucii praenomen consensu repudiavit, postquam e duobus gentilibus praeditis eo, alter latrocinii, caedis alter convictus est.*

33 **nisi...memorabilis**] Livy seems to mean that Manlius might have attained to the position of a Julius Caesar, had he not been born at a time when the hatred of a tyranny was still strong within the Roman breast. For the brief and pithy form of sentence, cf. Tac. *Hist.* 1. 49 (of Galba): *omnium consensu capax imperii, nisi imperasset.*

CHAPTER XXI.

p. **29.** 16 § **1. excepit**] 'followed.' See c. 3. 4 n.

20 § **2. velut sorte quadam**] Again Livy's Stoic fatalism comes out, though here he half apologizes by *velut* and *quadam.*

exercendo Romano militi datos] For this dat. of purpose with the gerundive, cf. *decemviri legibus scribendis*, and § 4, below, *quinqueviros Pomptino agro dividendo*; and, for the dat. after a participle, cf. *comitia consulibus rogandis habita.* It is closely akin to the 'predicative' dat.

22 **Lanuvini**] Lanuvium was one of the oldest of the Latin cities, situated on the S.W. spur of the Alban range. It has been suggested that its present secession was due to the occupation of the *ager Pomptinus.*

23 **quae...urbs**] Here the city is placed in appos. to the citizens, the converse of *Sutrium, socios*, c. 3. 2.

24 § **3. civibus suis**] Cf. c. 17. 7 n.

25 **primo quoque tempore**] 'at the first possible opportunity,' cf. c. 3. 2 n.

26 **ad populum**] Here Livy gives the correct procedure. The declara-

tion of war, however, lay with the *Comitia Centuriata*, not with the *Comitia Tributa*, as he states directly afterwards; cf. c. 22. 4.

27　§ **4. quinqueviros...triumviros**] The numbers of these extraordinary commissioners varied according to the extent of the land which had to be surveyed and divided; thus twenty were appointed by Caesar's agrarian law (59 B.C.). These commissioners were elected by the *Comitia*, usually as the result of a proposal by the Senate.

28　**Nepete**] Acc. of motion towards. We should say 'for founding a colony at Nepete.' The colony was no doubt the result of the events recorded in c. 10; the importance of the place as an outpost against Etruria would render the step advisable, while the colonization might give some relief to the distressed plebeians.

31　§ **5. omnes tribus**] This cannot be right, for the declaration of war was never passed in the *Comitia Tributa*. As in 5. 18. 2, the confusion between the *Comitia Tributa* and the *Comitia Centuriata* seems due to the tribal basis according to which the centuries were distributed in the later period of the Republic. The reform, by which each tribe furnished ten centuries, must have taken place between the First and the Second Punic Wars.

p. **30.**　1　§ **6. et**] 'and indeed'; cf. c. 11. 9 n.

3　§ **7. inclinabat**] The full sentence would be: 'the majority was leaning towards the sending, (and would have sent), had not, etc.' Livy is fond of this idiom, whereby the true apodosis is suppressed and its place taken by a seeming apodosis in the indic., cf. 3. 43. 7: *et Romam ferri protinus Siccium placebat*, (and he would have been carried there), *ni decemviri funus militare ei publica impensa facere maturassent.* Cf. also Verg. *Ecl.* 7. 45: *numeros memini* (a fact), *si verba tenerem* (I should remember the whole song).

5　**piacula**] 'scapegoats' to appease the anger of the Romans. The word means primarily a victim offered to appease the anger of the gods.

6　§ **8. senatu**] Notice that this refers to the colonial Senate, not to the Roman. The names of many of the political institutions of Rome are found in the Latin cities also, but we cannot be sure that the functions of the Latin Senates corresponded to those of the Roman Senate. The Latin dictators and praetors have only the name in common with the Roman magistrates bearing these titles; cf. c. 26. 4 n.

9　§ **9. Praenestinorum**] Praeneste, Tusculum, Gabii, and Labici all lay E. or S.E. of Rome. See map. The growing discontent of the oldest members of the Latin League indicates the fact that Rome was growing more oppressive in consequence of her successes against the Etruscans and Volscians. See Introd. § 4 b.

CHAPTER XXII.

23   § **1. tribunis**] See Appendix.

24   **si qui**] 'in case any,' cf. Verg. *Aen.* 1. 181: *prospectum late pelago*
petit, Anthea si quem | iactatum vento videat. The subj. is practically
one of purpose ; 'in order to check any inroad.' Note the variety of
constr.—*ad praesidium...si qui.*

27   § **2. ita, ut**] 'with the result that.'

30   § **3. et anceps erat nec...censebant**] The 'patriotic' spirit in
which the Roman annalists wrote comes out in this sentence. We may
suspect that the difficulty of the operations was chiefly responsible for
the action of the Romans. A similar spirit can be seen in the accounts
given of the defeat on the Allia. Weiss. quotes 8. 14. 5 to show how
far scruples with regard to colonies sufficed to restrain the Romans.

p. **31.**   1   § **4. ex senatus consulto populique iussu**] The correct
constitutional procedure; cf. c. 21. 3 n.

3   **coloniam populi Romani**] Cf. c. 16. 6 n.

14   § **6. extra ordinem decretum**] i.e. was assigned by the Senate
contrary to the usual procedure. The consuls or consular tribunes
usually determined their spheres of operation either by mutual agreement (*comparatio*) or by lot (*sors*); cf. c. 30. 3. Later on, indeed, the
Senate arrogated to itself the right of assigning the *provinciae* of the
magistrates, but at this period it did so, in all probability, only by
special request. Cf. 8. 16. 5: *et ne forte casu erraretur, petitum ab*
consulibus, ut extra sortem Corvi ea provincia esset; also 37. 1. 7:
(*Laelius*), *cum senatus aut sortiri aut comparare inter se provincias*
consules iussisset, elegantius facturos dixit, si iudicio patrum quam si
sorti eam rem permisissent. The present unusual mode of appointment gave Camillus a moral, if not a legal, precedence over his
colleague, whose position was the result of the lot.

16   **non tam e re publica**] 'not so much (as it proved) to the advantage
of the state.' Livy here anticipates.

18   **restituit**] The subject, which is suddenly changed, is M. Furius
Camillus. This change of subject is not uncommon in Livy; cf.
c. 40. 3.

19   § **7. exactae iam aetatis**] 'advanced in years.' A descriptive gen.
The phrase implies that a man's active career is finished.

20   **comitiisque iurare parato in verba excusandae valetudini**] 'at the
elections, when he was prepared to repeat on oath the form of words

8—2

usual in a plea of ill-health.' *Iurare in verba* is the regular phrase for swearing according to a fixed form of words; cf. Hor. *Epist.* I. I. 14: *iurare in verba magistri*, 'to take the oath imposed by the trainer on the gladiator.' *Excusandae valetudini* is dat. after *solita*.

22   **vegetum**, etc.] Notice the *v* alliteration. The Romans seem to have been very fond of it; cf. Lucr. 5. 993: *viva videns vivo sepeliri viscera busto*, and Cic. *pro Mil.* 11. 30: *vi victa vis.*

23   **civiles...excitabant**] 'wars would rouse him, though by this time he did not take much share in politics.'

24   **§ 8. quaternum millium**] Apparently only in round numbers; there were usually 4200 men in a legion.

25   **ad portam Esquilinam**] This was E. of the city, and from it branched the roads to Tibur (E.) and Praeneste (S.E.). As Satricum lay S. of the city, in the Pomptine district, the Porta Capena would have been, one would think, a more natural place of meeting. See maps.

28   **§ 9. praestabant**] *Praestare*, meaning 'to excel,' is derived from *prae* and *stare*; it is a different word from *praestare*, meaning 'to make good,' which comes from *praes stare*, 'to stand as surety'; cf. Prof. Conway's edition of Bk II, c. 18. II n.

30   **dilaturi**] This use of the fut. part. to express intention is rare in strictly classical prose, but becomes common in Livy; cf. 8. 29. 12: *ut...refugerent hostes,...situ urbium moenibusque se defensuri.* Perhaps it is an imitation of the Greek use of the fut. part. Trans. 'resolved to make no delay in putting their all to the hazard.'

CHAPTER XXIII.

p. **32.** 1 **§ 1. praesentis dimicationis fortunam**] 'the hazard attending an immediate combat'; cf. 22. 12. 10 (of Fabius Cunctator): *neque universo periculo summa rerum committebatur.* The characters of M. Furius and L. Furius are very like those of Fabius and Minucius respectively, though in a speech Minucius is made to contrast the apathy of Fabius—*hic novus Camillus*—with the energy displayed by Camillus against the Gauls (22. 14. 9).

3   **qui occasionem...quaerebat**] 'who was seeking an opportunity of assisting his resources by strategy in prolonging the war.'

6   **§ 2. explicare**] 'deploy.'

10   **§ 3. ex incertissimo**] 'from the most unreliable sources.' For the superlative of the adj. used as subst., cf. I. 9. 3: *ex infimo nasci.*

12   § **4.** **elevando…collegae]** 'seeking to impair the influence of his
colleague in the only way he could—on the ground of age.' For the abl.
of the gerund=pres. part., cf. c. 20. 8: *aequando.*

14   § **5.** **cunctatorem]** again reminds us of Fabius, *unus qui nobis
cunctando restituis rem* (*Aen.* 6. 846, modelled on a line of Ennius).
      ex] See c. 4. 5 n.

16   **rapere]** 'to capture swiftly,' 'to seize.' There is no necessity to
adopt *capere*, the reading of the inferior MSS. *Rapere*, usually simply
'to plunder,' here implies swift assault and capture; it is a much more
graphic word than *capere*, though perhaps no precise parallel to its
present sense can be cited; cf., however, Lucan 6. 14: *praeceps rapiendas
tendit ad arces.* See Appendix.

      residem] 'remaining idly.' The word is not found in Cicero or
Caesar. In 2. 32. 5: *residem in urbe plebem*, it is used in the simple
sense of 'remaining,' from which the further idea of sluggishness is
easily developed.

18   § **6.** **tempus]** 'favourable moment'; cf. the common *in tempore=*
'at the right time.'

19   **instruendis]** See Appendix.

      § **7.** **frigere ac torpere]** The qualities properly belonging to the
old man's body are transferred to his mind. Cf. Scott, *Lay of the Last
Minstrel*, 2. 30:

> 'My hairs are grey, my limbs are old,
> My heart is dead, my veins are cold.'

Also Byron, *Childe Harold* 3. 8:

> 'Years steal | Fire from the mind as vigour from the limb.'

20   **quid attinere…pati]** 'what point was there in allowing?' The
question is rhetorical, and really=a neg. statement, *non attinere.*

29   § **9.** **negare…neque…neque]** cf. c. 16. 3 n. The negatives are not
mutually destructive, when, as here, 'the first neg. is general and is
followed by several subordinate members each with a neg.' See Roby,
Syntax, § 2246.

33   § **10.** **collegae imperium se non posse impedire]** It was with a
view to avoiding the collision of the equal *imperia* of the consuls that
a dictator was appointed at times of national danger. In 217 B.C. the
nomination of Minucius to act as dictator as well as Fabius completely
frustrated the purpose of the office, which lapsed after the Second Punic
War. The *imperium* was always regarded as one and indivisible, a view
based upon the character of the kingly *imperium*. When both consuls
were in the city, they arranged that the initiative in public business

should be assumed by each alternately for the period of a month, the senior consul being said *fasces habere* (cf. 2. 1. 8 and 3. 36. 4); each, however, could check the other by *intercessio*. When they both took the field together, this right of *intercessio* ceased, so that a consul had no legal check whatsoever upon his colleague (*non posse impedire*). As a matter of fact some agreement was usually arrived at, whereby the one consul voluntarily placed himself in a subordinate position (cf. c. 6. 16 and esp. 3. 70. 1), or else each assumed command on alternate days. Of course what has been said of the consuls applies equally to the consular tribunes.

p. 33. 1 **e re publica**] Cf. c. 22. 6.

2 **§ 11. eam**] See Appendix.

3 **esset...sint**] See c. 39. 11 n.

munia] In origin the same word as *moenia*; cf. Paulus: *moenia praeter aedificia significant et munia, hoc est officia.*

8 **§ 12. opponit**] sc. *hostibus.*

CHAPTER XXIV.

12 **§ 1. simul**]=*simul ac*; cf. c. 1. 6 n.

13 **§ 2. ab tergo**] The hill, rising up behind the main force of the enemy, concealed their reserves; the Romans pursued their seemingly routed foes, and were thus drawn into a trap. Cf. the tactics of William at the battle of Hastings.

14 **multitudo suppeditabat**] 'their numbers were sufficient,' i.e. for the purpose; cf. 1. 55. 7: *manubiae...vix in fundamenta suppeditavere.* Distinguish between this neuter use of *suppeditare* and its trans. meaning 'to supply'; the latter is frequent in Cicero.

15 **cohortes**] Used here generally for 'troops,' not in the later technical sense; cf. 30. 4 n.

reliquerant] but *rettulit* above. A *constructio ad sensum.*

16 **inter commissum iam certamen**] For the constr., cf. c. 1. 1: *ad captam eandem urbem.*

appropinquasset] Oblique, expressing the thought of the enemy: *ubi appropinquaverit.*

18 **§ 3. opportunus**] 'readily exposed.'

19 **versus...aciem**] We cannot translate very literally. 'Thus the victors in turn were plunged into alarm; the unexpected appearance of the enemy and the slope of the valley caused the Roman line to give way.' *Novo hoste* and *supina valle* are really ablatives of attendant circumstances, or abl. abs.

23   **§ 4. recipiebat se]** 'was retiring'; the expression implies retreat
in good order.

24   **ferociae]** 'boldness,' not 'ferocity.'

25   **§ 5. cum]** The so-called 'inverted' use of *cum* to mark a sudden
event. 'When' is used in a precisely similar way in English.

   subiectus] 'lifted' on horseback, probably because of his advanced
age, which had impaired his activity. As parallels are quoted 31. 37. 10:
saluti fuit eques, qui raptim desiluit pavidumque regem in equum subiecit,
and *Aen.* 12. 288: *corpora saltu | subiciunt in equos.*

26   **oppositis]** i.e. to bar the flight of the Romans, not to check the
on-coming Volscians.

32   **§ 7. tenuit effusos]** 'checked their disorder.'

p. **34.** 1   **circumagi signa]** Cf. c. 8. 1 n.

   obverti] Cf. c. 7. 3 n.

2   **praeterquam quod]** Where no finite verb follows, *praeterquam*
generally stands alone without *quod*. Weiss. compares 29. 18. 13.

3   **inter prima signa]** Cf. c. 7. 3 n. This cannot be regarded as
evidence that the standards were carried in the front line in battle,
since here the front ranks are in flight, and the *signa* are in disorder.

5   **in vicem]** Equivalent to an adj. 'mutual'; cf. 9. 3. 4: *his in vicem
sermonibus,* and 3. 6. 3: *ministeria in vicem.*

7   **§ 8. non castigando...versus]** Cf. c. 20. 8 n.

10   **reum fortunae eius diei]** 'responsible for that day's fortune.'

14   **§ 9. quod miserrimum est]** These words are of course to be taken
with what follows.

15   **§ 10. optimum visum est...equos]** The MSS. give *fluctuantem
aciem,* but the change to *fluctuante acie* is very slight, final *m* being
a constant source of corruption. If the reading given in the text be
retained, we must translate: 'it seemed best, considering the wavering
of the line, that the horses should be handed over (to the grooms).'
But it is almost impossible to extract all this from *tradi.* Something
like *optimum visum est ex fluctuante acie extrahi equos* might be
suggested: 'that the horses should be withdrawn from the wavering
line.' See Appendix.

16   **invadere]** The sudden change from passive to act. inf. is quite in
Livy's manner; cf. 5. 39. 11: *placuit...Vestales sacra publica...auferre,
nec...deseri cultum deorum.*

19   **certamine animi]** 'zeal,' cf. Verg. *Aen.* 5. 197: *olli certamine
summo | procumbunt* (of the rowers).

20   **§ 11. enixae]** 'strenuous.' The adj. is rare, but the adv. *enixe*

is found both in Cicero and Caesar. 'The issue of the day felt the might of their strenuous valour' is Livy's poetical way of expressing 'their valour turned the fortune of the day.'

Volsci...magna pars] Apposition, instead of partitive gen.; cf. 24. 7. 6: *interfectores pars in forum...pars Syracusas pergunt.* This constr., known as partitive apposition, is used more freely by Livy than by previous writers; it is, however, generally confined to a limited number of words, such as *pars...pars, alius...alius, alter...alter, quisque, uterque,* etc. Cf. c. 34. 5 n.

CHAPTER XXV.

29 **§ 1. ubi]** =*et ibi.*

30 **secreti]** Here used in its primary meaning of 'separated.' We can easily see how it gets the secondary one of 'secret.'

aliis] =*ceteris,* as often. Greek, οἱ ἄλλοι.

31 **publico consilio]** 'with authority from the state'; cf. c. 13. 7: *publica ope.*

p. 35. 2 **§ 2. si videatur]** Livy puts this in to show the courtesy of Camillus to his beaten colleague; it prepares us for the general's subsequent act of magnanimity.

3 **§ 3. documento...fuerat]** 'had served as a warning.' Predicative dat.

4 **tamen]** The connection of thought is: L. Furius had shown himself completely humbled, *yet,* in spite of that, he could not expect Camillus to overlook his rashness.

9 **§ 4. in...penes]** Note the variety.

12 **§ 5. censuissent]** Once more Livy omits the constitutional steps necessary to a declaration of war; cf. c. 14. 1 n.

13 **permisso]** This use of the abl. abs. of the past part. without apparent subject, but with dependent clause following, is found far more frequently in Livy than in previous prose writers. The dependent clause must be regarded as the subject. One or two instances of the constr. are cited from Cicero, but none from Caesar; on the other hand, Tacitus uses it frequently; cf. *Ann.* 11. 38. 2: *nuntiatum Claudio epulanti perisse Messalinam,* non distincto *sua an aliena manu.* Cf., for other instances from Livy, 5. 19. 9: *edicto, ne*; 9. 16. 5: *impetrato, ut.*

14 **spem]** 'expectation,' a common neutral meaning of *spes.*

15 **§ 6. moderatione animi]** 'piece of fairness'; cf. a common meaning of the Gk μέτριος. Camillus did not allow personal feelings to influence him with regard to L. Furius.

19   § **7. itineri**]   See Appendix.

20   **togati**]   'in everyday garb,' i.e. unarmed.

25   § **9. ianuas**]   House doors as opposed to *portae*, the city gates.

   tabernis apertis proposita omnia in medio]   'the shops open and
all the wares exposed to view.'

27   **suo quemque operi**]   Cf. c. 13. 8 n.

   ludos litterarum]   *Ludus* means 'a place of exercise,' hence, as
here, 'a school'; cf. German 'Gymnasium,' which is not what we
understand by a gymnasium, but a grammar school; cf. also Plaut.
Rud. 43: *e ludo fidicinio*, 'from the music school.'

   strepere]   A strong instance of zeugma; *audivit* must be supplied
from *vidit*. The variety of constr. in this sentence is noteworthy.

   discentium]   'scholars'; cf. c. 2. 13 n.

28   **repletas...puerorum**]   The only passage in which *replere* is found
with the gen.; the usual constr. is the abl. *Implere*, on the other hand,
is frequently used with a gen. in Livy.

   vulgus aliud]   'the general throng.'

29   **qua quemque suorum**]   The position of *quemque* before *suorum* is
unusual, but, beyond Livy's love of variety, there does not seem to be
any particular reason for it; cf. 5. 20. 8.

30   **ferrent**]   Subj. of frequent occurrence; cf. c. 8. 6 n. *Usuum causae*
simply means 'particular business.'

   § **10. nihil usquam...simile**]   'nowhere any sign of persons in
astonishment, still less in alarm.' Literally, 'nothing anywhere like
not only to persons in alarm, but (not) even to persons in astonishment.'
For the superfluous *ne*, cf. c. 20. 2 n.

32   § **11. rei...oblatae ad tempus**]   'feint,' or 'trickery.' Literally,
'anything brought forward for the occasion.'

p. 36. 1 **tranquilla**]   Nom. neut. plur.

CHAPTER XXVI.

6   § **1. patientia**]   'submissiveness'; cf. Tac. *Hist.* 2. 29: *silentio,
patientia, postremo precibus ac lacrimis veniam quaerebant.*

   senatum]   Cf. c. 21. 8 n.

11   § **2. non praecipiam gratiam publici beneficii**]   'I will not seize
in advance the popularity to be gained from an act of clemency which
belongs to the state.'

12   **habueritis**]   The fut. perf. in Latin is sometimes used as an emphatic
fut. (cf. *sed de te tu videris*, 'but you must see to yourself') and it may be

so used here 'you shall have.' It is, however, possible to give the tense its usual force, 'you will have had from me the power of pleading,' whatever the issue may be.

13   quem] sc. *dare.*

17   § **4. dictator**] The dictators of the Latin cities are to be distinguished from the Roman dictators. We find them at Alba, Lanuvium, Tusculum, Nomentum, and elsewhere; cf. Cic. *pro Mil.* 10. 27. Sometimes, as at Alba, the annual dictator was a purely religious functionary, somewhat resembling the *rex sacrorum* at Rome; but more often he was a civil magistrate, and the office a survival of an original Latin kingship. The commoner name for the chief Latin magistrates was *praetores* or *duumviri.* The Roman dictator, on the other hand, was a quite extraordinary magistrate, and had nothing in common (except the name) with the annual dictators of the Latin cities. It seems probable that Julius Caesar, in accepting the dictatorship for life, had the Latin, rather than the Roman, magistracy in mind. Cf. 3. 18. 2, and see Mommsen, *Hist. of Rome* (Eng. Trans.) I. p. 442 n.

quibus] 'we, against whom.'

21   § **5. plebis**] We must remember that Rome was originally only one among many Latin townships, all pretty well on a level with regard to power. It is not therefore surprising to find many of the familiar institutions of Rome existing elsewhere in Latium.

22   **nisi si quando**] 'unless some day.'

24   **auribus**] i.e. the false rumours of Tusculan disaffection.

26   § **6. praestitimus**] Cf. c. 22. 9 n.

sicubi]=*si-(c)ubi,* 'if anywhere,' 'wherever'; cf. *necubi, sicunde, necunde.*

29   **di immortales faciant, tam felix, quam pia**] 'may the gods make it as happy in its issue, as it is right.' The expression=*ut tam felix sit quam pia est.*

§ **7. quod ad crimina...censemus**] The sentence as it stands is hardly intelligible. We must conclude that Livy forgot the drift of the first half of the sentence, and wrote down what he imagined to be a contrast to it; or, if a — were put after *tamen,* it might be supposed that the speaker broke off suddenly at that point. 'With regard to the charges against us, which induced you to declare war, although there is no point in disproving by words what is refuted by facts, yet—(sc. I will not refuse to do so); even if the charges were true, etc.'

The simplest course, however, is to regard *etsi* as an interpolation (it might easily have come in from *etiamsi* following), and to place a semi-colon after *attinet.* The sense is then plain: 'there is no need to disprove what is evidently false; yet, even supposing the charge were true, it would be safe to admit it.'

p. **37.** 1 **peccetur...satisfiat**] 'let men offend against you, so long as you are worthy to receive a satisfaction of this kind.' A rather obscure way of expressing 'offences against you give you an opportunity of showing your clemency.'

2   § **8. fere**] It was, of course, well understood that these speeches were the invention of the historian, and merely served to sum up the situation.

3   **civitatem**] It is probable that Livy is wrong in saying that the Tusculans received the full citizenship shortly after this date, in spite of passages such as 8. 14. 4 and c. 33. 6. In 8. 7. 2 they are found joining with the Latins against Rome, while Festus includes them among the towns which were first granted only *half-citizen* rights; it seems likely, therefore, that it is the *civitas sine suffragio* which is referred to in the present passage. Tusculum, however, is called by Cicero (*pro Planc.* 8. 19) *municipium antiquissimum*, and must in any case have been one of the earliest Latin towns to receive the full citizenship: some indeed hold that it already possessed the half-citizenship, and now received full citizen rights. Cf. Greenidge, *Roman Public Life*, p. 298 n.

CHAPTER XXVII.

16   § **3. incertam famam aeris alieni**] 'the uncertain reports which prevailed with regard to debt.' Since four new tribes were created in 387 B.C. from citizens newly enrolled the year before (c. 4. 4 and c. 5. 8), there must have been censors in 388 B.C., though Livy does not give their names. It was very important that the amount of land owned by a debtor should be ascertained, and that the property should be duly valued, since otherwise the creditors might easily take an unfair advantage of their position, and force the debtors to sell their land at a low price. Livy also implies that the censors recorded the amount of debts, but such a record is unlikely.

17   **invidiosius**] See Appendix.

18   **elevaretur**] 'was being minimised'; cf. c. 23. 4.

    quibus fide...expediebat] 'to whose advantage it was that credit should appear to be endangered by lack of faith rather than lack of fortune on the part of the debtors.' The context makes it clear how *fides* and *fortuna* are to be understood. The creditors wished it to be believed that the debtors could pay, but would not.

22   **§ 4. religio erat]** 'was a matter of religious scruple.' The origin of this curious superstition is given in 5. 31. 6: *C. Iulius censor decessit ; in eius locum M. Cornelius suffectus, quae res postea religioni fuit, quia eo lustro Roma est capta*; cf. also 9. 34. 20.

23   **§ 5. vitio creati]** Some ceremonial flaw had invalidated their election; cf. c. 1. 5 n. A good instance of the nature of such flaws is found in 4. 7. 3: *tertio mense quam inierunt* (sc. *tribuni militum*) *augurum decreto perinde ac vitio creati honore abiere, quod C. Curtius, qui comitiis eorum praefuerat, parum recte tabernaculum cepisset.* It was important to choose the right spot for taking the auspices prior to holding the elections.

27   **§ 6. tabulas publicas]** The *Tabulae Censoriae,* in which were recorded the amount of property belonging to individuals. It does not seem probable, however, that debts were registered in them at this period.

30   **obiectari]** For the inf. after *cum interim*, cf. c. 11. 4 n. *Cum interim* practically = *tamen*, and does not affect the constr. ; cf. 4. 51. 4 : *iacere tam diu irritas actiones quae de suis commodis ferrentur,* cum interim *de sanguine ac supplicio suo latam legem confestim* **exerceri.**

31   **§ 7. ab Antio...ab Satrico]** Cf. c. 3. 5 n.

p. 38.   3 **consistere in contione]** 'to take their stand in a mass meeting.' The expression shows the informal character of such assemblies.

5   **§ 8. quod si]** 'but if.' *Quod* is here simply a connecting particle, probably parallel to the Gk use of ὅ in Thuc. 2. 40. 3: ὅ τοῖς ἄλλοις ἀμαθία μὲν θράσος, λογισμὸς δὲ ὄκνον φέρει. For another view, cf. Munro on Lucr. 1. 82 ; he adopts the explanation that *quod* is an old abl. = *qua re*, 'therefore.' Cf. *quod ubi* in c. 7. 2 and c. 8. 2.

6   **addici]** The judicial handing over of the debtor to the creditor. See c. 11. 8 and c. 18. 14 nn.

9   **sui]** Partitive gen., 'what of his own.' This departure from the normal *suum* seems due to Livy's fondness for variety of construction ; so *alieni* for *alienum.*

10   **supersit]** *Utrum* is omitted, as often. Cf. c. 14. 11 n.

     nervo] See c. 11. 8 n. The state of affairs prevailing at Rome at this time should be compared with the similar distress at Athens in the time of Solon; cf. Solon Fr. 2. 33 ff. :

> ταῦτα μὲν ἐν δήμῳ στρέφεται κακά· τῶν δὲ πενιχρῶν
> ἱκνοῦνται πολλοὶ γαῖαν ἐς ἀλλοδαπὴν
> πραθέντες δεσμοῖσί τ' ἀεικελίοισι δεθέντες.

The cause of distress was similar in both cases, viz. the misfortunes to which the small landowner was constantly exposed, and which drove him to borrow at exorbitant rates of interest from the larger proprietors.

16 **§ 10. iuniores]** See c. 2. 6 n.

17 **in]** See Appendix.

cura...exsequendi] 'the anxiety to claim their rights in the matter of debt.' Note the accumulation of genitives, which is not infrequent in Livy.

19 **in agro Gabino]** Gabii lay about half-way on the road between Rome and Praeneste. See map.

CHAPTER XXVIII.

29 **§ 1. certum]** There is no occasion to adopt the conjecture *creatum*. The meaning clearly is that the Romans no longer had a 'definite' leader in the person of Camillus, and were therefore likely to be without any concerted plan of defence; cf. 3. 50. 16: *nullodum certo duce*, and 9. 45. 10: *sine ducibus certis*. See Appendix.

31 **§ 2. acto]** 'set in motion.' The better MSS. read *facto*, which might be right, the meaning in that case being, 'an army having been hurriedly got together.'

protinus] 'continuously.' The word stands for *pro-tenus*, 'right forward,' the *e* being changed to *i* through the shifting of accent (cf. c. 16. 2 n. on *sicine*). The meaning 'continuously' is therefore more in accordance with the etymology of the word than is the more common 'forthwith.' Cf. *quatenus*.

32 **ad portam Collinam]** The *porta Esquilina* was the gate through which the *via Praenestina* entered Rome. The Praenestines therefore extended their ravages farther N. to the *via Nomentana*, which led up to the *porta Collina*. See map.

p. 39. 3 **§ 3. creavere]** A decree of the Senate was followed by the nomination of a dictator by one of the consular tribunes; cf. c. 2. 5 n.

4 **§ 4. quod ubi]** 'and when this....' Different from *quod ubi* in c. 7. 2 and c. 8. 2.

11 **§ 6. ac...ac]** We should have expected Livy to avoid using *ac* meaning 'and' immediately before *ac* used in the comparative sense of 'as.' The Romans could not have been so sensitive upon such a point as we are; cf. c. 30. 8: *inde...inde*.

12 **contactum religione]** Cf. c. 1. 11 n.

20 **§ 7. obnoxia]** 'servile'; cf. Ovid *Met.* 5. 235: *summissaeque manus faciesque obnoxia mansit*. The primary meaning of the word is 'liable to punishment.'

21　§ **8. potius quam ut**] See c. 15. 12 n. We find there *potius quam* with the subj. without *ut*.

22　**nefasta**] Just as a *dies nefastus* prevented legal business, so a *terra nefasta* might be considered as a bar to victory.

23　§ **9. quin**] 'nay more.' Introduces a climax.

24　**ut Romae pugnaverint**, etc.] Cf. 5. 49. 5 and 6: *iustiore altero deinde proelio ad octavum lapidem Gabina via, quo se ex fuga contulerant* (sc. *Galli*), *eiusdem ductu auspicioque Camilli vincuntur. Ibi caedes omnia obtinuit ; castra capiuntur, et ne nuntius quidem cladis relictus.*

CHAPTER XXIX.

p. **40.**　1　§ **1. intentique**] 'eager for the fray'; a stronger expression than the usual *parati*. The word expresses the confidence felt by the enemy in the advantage derived from the place of battle.

2　**nec...dederint**] 'nor (as the issue will prove) will the gods have given them....' *Dederint* is probably fut. perf. ind., perhaps with pure fut. sense as in c. 26. 2. It would be possible to take it as subj. expressing a wish, for *nec* is found for *neve* even in the strictest prose writers. The fut. perf. sense, however, better suits the tone of confidence assumed by the dictator.

6　§ **2. di testes foederis**] See c. 1. 10 n. Treaties were reckoned under the head of *religiones*, as receiving the direct witness of the gods. The Fetiales, through whom treaties were made, were under the protection of Iuppiter Feretrius, from whose temple were taken the *lapis silex* and the *sceptrum*, part of the special *apparatus* of the college. Other deities, such as Dius Fidius, were also closely concerned with the making and observance of treaties. Cf. the Gk Ζεὺς Ὅρκιος, and, generally, ὅρκιοι θεοί.

7　**per vestrum numen**] refers to the oath taken by the *numen* or 'power' of the gods. *Numen* is connected with *nuere*, 'to give assent by nodding.' Cf. the description of Zeus in *Il*. 1. 528: ἦ καὶ κυανέῃσιν ἐπ' ὀφρύσι νεῦσε Κρονίων.

10　§ **3. constabat**] See c. 10. 4 n.

12　**praelati**]=*praeterlati*; cf. 1. 45. 6: *praefluit* for *praeterfluit*. Several instances of this usage occur in Livy.

13　§ **4. dissipati**] This, the reading of the MSS., is probably correct. Translate: 'there, scattered as they were in consequence of flight, they occupied a spot...,' i.e. though disorganized, they temporarily collected themselves for a stand. Weiss. compares 8. 24. 10: *ex fuga palatos.*

For the meaning of *ex*, cf. 7. 39. 10: *ex iniuria insanientis.* See Appendix.

14   **tumultuario**] 'hasty.' Cf. 5. 37. 7: *tumultuario exercitu,* 'a hastily levied army.' See Appendix.

15   **recepissent**] The subj. is due to the thought implied in *ne*. The direct would be: *si intra moenia nos receperimus, extemplo uretur ager.*

depopulatis] Perf. part. of deponent verb used passively. With *depopulor* this use of the perf. part. is common in all writers; cf. Caesar *B. G.* 1. 11. 3: *depopulatis agris.*

18   **§ 5. oppido...Praeneste**] Instrumental abl. after *includunt*.

19   **§ 6. oppida**] Cf. c. 4. 8 n. Similarly we find smaller townships dependent upon Tibur (7. 19. 1).

26   **§ 8. signum**] This custom of removing the gods of a conquered city to Rome was a common one; cf. 5. 22. 3 ff., where, after the capture of Veii, the statue of Iuno Regina is carried to Rome with elaborate ceremonial.

Cicero (*Verr.* 2. 4. 129) says that T. Quinctius Flamininus removed a statue of Iuppiter Imperator (?=Ζεὺς Στρατηγὸς or Στράτιος) from Macedonia, and placed it on the Capitol. Cicero clearly knows of no other statue of Iuppiter Imperator at Rome, and we can hardly help concluding that Livy has made the serious mistake of confounding T. Quinctius Cincinnatus with T. Quinctius Flamininus, the conqueror of Macedonia.

27   **Iovis Imperatoris**] Probably the Latin equivalent of the Roman Iuppiter Optimus Maximus, the ruling and presiding deity among the gods.

§ 9. inter cellam Iovis ac Minervae] See c. 4. 3 n. There must have been a doorway leading from the one *cella* to the other, and the statue would be placed in a niche made in one of the sideposts.

28   **tabula**] That there was some confusion regarding the nature of the offering dedicated by T. Quinctius Cincinnatus is shown by a passage from Festus (p. 363): *trientem tertium pondo* coronam auream *dedisse se Iovi donum scripsit T. Quinctius, cum per novem dies totidem urbes et decimam Praeneste cepisset.* Here mention is made of a golden crown of 2½ pounds, but not of a statue.

29   **fuit**] implies that the inscription had disappeared in Livy's day; the *ferme* shows that his knowledge of it was not at first hand. Perhaps *fuit* also indicates a state (*remained* inscribed) in contrast to the single act of dedication (*dedicatum* est); cf. c. 3. 8 n.

These inscriptions were written in Saturnian verse, as we learn from Atilius Fortunatianus (1. 8. 2 Gaisford), a late writer on metre: *apud nostros autem in tabulis antiquis, quas triumphaturi duces in Capitolio figebant, victoriaeque suae titulum Saturniis versibus prosequebantur, talia repperi exempla*; cf. also 40. 52. 5 ff. and 41. 28. 8 ff.

31   **§ 10. die vicesimo**] The abdication of the dictator after such a short period of office is an illustration of the fact that he was appointed for a particular work and was expected, in normal circumstances, to lay down office immediately after that work was completed; cf. c. 1. 4 n.; also 3. 29. 7: *Quinctius sexto decimo die dictatura in sex menses accepta se abdicavit.*

CHAPTER XXX.

p. 41. 7 § 1. aequatus...numerus] This shows that there was a temporary revival of plebeian influence, since for several years previously the patricians had carried all before them at the elections.

10   **§ 3. gratia**] 'in popularity.'

11   **sine sorte...data**] These expressions have been explained in c. 22. 6 n.

12   **patres**] Here=the Senate. *Ex patribus*, above (§ 2), is 'from the patricians.'

13   **§ 4. cohortes**] A general expression for 'troops.' The *cohors* proper, which formed the tenth part of a legion and contained three *manipuli*, was not created till about the time of the Second Punic War.

14   **velut circumventis**] 'under the impression that they had been surrounded'; dat. after *praesidio essent*. It will be best to split up the sentence in translating: 'under the impression that these had been surrounded (for a false report to that effect had been brought), they hurried to their protection. They did not, however, even secure the author of the report—it was a Latin foe who had deceived them, under pretence of being a Roman soldier,—but themselves plunged headlong into an ambuscade.'

17   **praecipitavere**] Used intransitively; in the later books the passive is generally found in this sense of falling into a danger. *Se praecipitare* implies voluntary, *praecipitare* alone rather involuntary or unconscious action.

18   **§ 5. restantes**] Cf. c. 32. 7. Livy several times uses *resto* in the sense of *resisto*. The usage appears to be archaic and poetical; cf. Lucr.

2. 450: *aeraque quae claustris restantia vociferantur,* 'the bolts which cry out as they chafe against the staples.' Cf. also Tac. *Ann.* 3. 46. 6: *paulum morae attulere ferrati restantibus lamminis adversum pila et gladios.*

caedunt caedunturque] Perhaps modelled on Verg. *Aen.* 10. 756: *caedebant pariter pariterque ruebant | victores victique.* It seems certain that Livy was well acquainted with the *Aeneid* before its actual publication in 19 B.C. See Introd. § 3.

21 § **6.** fortunae] It is impossible to decide dogmatically whether this is gen. or dat. Either 'what little of the Roman people's good fortune yet remained' or 'whatsoever was yet left to the fortune of the Roman people' makes good sense.

24 § **7.** postquam...afferebantur et apparuit] 'when reports as to the tranquillity of affairs among the Volsci *kept coming in* and it *became* evident.' Note the change of tense, and cf. c. 10. 4 n. and 2. 6. 3.

26 § **8.** inde...inde] The repetition seems awkward to us, but cf. c. 28. 6 n. The first *inde* probably refers to place, the second to time; if both are taken as referring to place, the repetition is less tolerable.

27 quantum a Volscis] 'as far as could be expected from the Volscians.' This seems preferable to the translation 'as far as the Volscians were concerned,' in which case the Volscians are contrasted with the Latins. The point is that the Volscians henceforth ceased to be dangerous, but did not altogether cease from making their accustomed inroads ; we find them renewing their attacks next year (c. 31. 3).

28 tumultuatum] sc. *est.* *Tumultuari* is a deponent vb, meaning 'to make a disturbance.' The passive sense is only found impersonally ; cf. Caes. *B. G.* 7. 61: *hostibus nuntiatur in castris Romanorum praeter consuetudinem tumultuari,* 'that there was an unusual disturbance.'

29 § **9.** Setiam] A Latin colony, situated on the flank of the Volscian hills just above the Pomptine marshes. See map. Ceaseless struggles with the Volscians had no doubt depleted its population since the time it was founded, about 382 B.C. ; cf. Vell. Pat. 1. 14: *post septem annos quam Galli urbem ceperunt, Sutrium deducta colonia est ; et post annum Setina* (i.e. *Setia*); *novemque interiectis annis Nepe.*

ipsis] Cf. c. 3. 2 n.

31 tribunorum militum ex plebe] To be taken closely together : 'of the plebeian military tribunes.'

CHAPTER XXXI.

p. 42. 12 **§ 2. cuius noscendi causa**] Cf. c. 27. 3: *censoribus quoque eguit annus, maxime* **propter incertam famam** *aeris alieni.*

14   **bello impediti sunt**] Each *paterfamilias* and each person *sui iuris* was required to make a personal statement as to the amount of his property before the censors in the Campus Martius. It is obvious that war would keep many from attending, and so render a postponement of the census necessary.

   § 3. fuga]=*fugientes* in sense. For the personification of the abstract noun, cf. c. 32. 10: *plus tamen timor quam ira celeritatis habuit.* Cf. also 8. 19. 9: *turba extremae fugae.*

18   **§ 4. contra**] 'on the contrary,' as often.

20   **debellatum**] See Appendix.

   tributum] This was a special war tax, the proceeds of which could be devoted to any military purpose (cf. c. 32. 1); it was imposed upon each Roman citizen, and was proportioned to the amount of property possessed by any individual and registered in the *tabulae censoriae.* The actual sum raised varied according to the needs of the treasury. Theoretically the tax was regarded as a loan, to be repaid at the earliest opportunity; but it appears to have been levied annually from the time that regular pay was given to the Roman soldier (406 B.C.) up to 167 B.C., when the wealth which flowed in from the provinces enabled the state to take the burden of the *tributum* off Roman citizens.

21   **diceret**] Madvig's alteration to *diceretur* is unnecessary. Strictly speaking, no doubt, *quis* should apply to the same person in both parts of the sentence; but surely this is a case in which the reader's intelligence could not fail to supply the right meaning. See Appendix.

24   **§ 5. dextrorsus**] 'towards the right': compounded of *dexter* and *vorsus.*

   in] See Appendix.

26   **Ecetram**] Acc. of motion to a town, here without the *ad* which Livy often inserts. The place was situated E. among the Volscian mountains. See map.

28   **§ 6. discordiae**] For the dat. after *fretus*, see c. 13. 1 n.

29   **iusto...iusta**] The first means 'regular' (cf. c. 13. 5 n.), the second probably combines the ideas of 'thorough' and 'righteous.'

30   **§ 7. quippe**] Explanatory: 'the fact was that.'

32   **in extrema finium]** Neut. adj. used as subst. with gen. depending
on it. Livy is fond of this constr., which is rarely found in prose before
him; cf. c. 32. 5: *subita belli*; 5. 29. 4: *per aversa urbis*; 9. 35. 7:
per obliqua campi, etc. Lucretius uses this constr. with great freedom;
cf., e.g., 1. 315: *detrita viarum | saxea*, and see Munro's note; cf. also
Verg. *Aen.* 1. 422: *strata viarum.* This is one of the cases where Livy
shows a liking for poetic diction.

Romano] Contrast with *Volscis* above, and see c. 2. 12 n.

p. 43. 1 **hostico]** Another adj. used as subst.; cf. the frequent
publicum for *publicum aerarium.* The word *hosticus* is not found in
Cicero or Caesar, who use *hostilis.*

2   **§ 8. tectis agrorum]** 'country houses,' i.e. scattered villas as
opposed to villages.

3   **satis]** From *sero*: 'crops.'

5   **praeda]** Is connected with *prehendo*, and means anything captured.
In ancient warfare *homines* were as much part of the booty as anything
else; they were sold into slavery, and the price formed part of the
manubiae.

CHAPTER XXXII.

7   **§ 1. postquam...erant]** 'as soon as things *began to be* quiet.'

8   **celebrari]** 'became frequent.'

9   **tantum abesse spes..., ut]** This constr. is a simple variation of the
usual *tantum abesse ut spes esset, ut.*

10   **tributo]** Cf. c. 31. 4 n.

fenus] We might rather have expected *aes alienum.* The interest
on the debt is put instead of the debt itself.

in murum] This is generally taken to refer to the Servian wall,
which may have suffered from the Gallic invasion. But it is strange
that the wall should have been allowed to remain unrepaired for such a
long time; its restoration would surely have been a matter of greater
importance than the facing of the Capitol with hewn stone (c. 4. 12 n.).
Livy's language is vague, but seems rather to imply that the wall was an
entirely new one.

11   **locatum]** 'let out to contract.' The opposite is *conducere*, 'to take
a contract.'

20   **§ 8. coacta]** sc. *plebs.* The plebeians were so deep in debt that
their only hope of getting mercy from their patrician creditors lay in
propitiating them by such a concession as this. Note the repetition

9—2

(from § 2) of *coacta*, which is probably intentional, and emphasizes the complete humiliation of the *plebs*.

25   § **4.** **sacramento adactis**] 'bound by oath.' *Sacramento* is an instrumental abl.; cf. *sacramento dicere*, 'to take the oath of obedience,' and *sacramento rogare*, 'to invite (men) to take the oath.'

27   § **5.** **ad subita belli**] See c. 31. 7 n.

29   § **6.** **ubi cum**] 'and there, when'; cf. c. 25. 1 n.

30   **ut...sic**] 'if...yet.' For the whole sentence, cf. 8. 7 n.
       satis certam] See Appendix.

p. **44.** 2 § **7.** **militiam Romanam edoctae**] In the case of vbs. which take a double acc., the acc. of the thing can remain after the passive. So after *rogatus*, etc. The English idiom is the same.

3   **restabant**]=*resistebant*. See c. 30. 5 n.

5   § **8.** **gradu demoti**] Here we must translate 'forced from their position.' But it can be seen how insensibly *gradus* passes from the meaning 'step' to that of 'position' by comparing c. 12. 8 with the present passage. Weiss. cites 7. 8. 3: *primum gradu moverunt hostem, deinde pepulerunt.*

     ut semel] Exactly our 'when once' meaning 'as soon as ever'; *iam* is used vividly for *tum*.
       inclinavit] See c. 8. 6 n.

9   § **10.** **proxima fuit**] 'followed.'

10   **prope vestigiis**] Beware of thinking that *prope* governs *vestigiis*; of course as prep. it is always followed by the acc. It is here an adv., and *vestigiis* is a local abl. 'on their tracks.' *Cum* is concessive, 'although.'

11   **plus tamen...habuit**] Simply means 'the pursued were swifter than the pursuers.' Another instance of Livy's favourite personification of abstract nouns.

12   § **11.** **extrema agminis**] Cf. *subita belli* in § 5, and see c. 31. 7 n.

13   **carpere**] 'to harass,' a frequent meaning in Livy; cf. Caes. *B. C.* 1. 78: *equitatu praemisso, qui novissimum agmen carperet*, and Tac. *Ann.* 12. 32. 2: *si ex occulto carpere agmen temptarent.*

15   **apparatu bellico**] Further defined in c. 9. 2, where Antium could not be captured for lack of *tormenta* and *machinae*. For these military operations, which are repeated with such remarkable regularity, cf. Introd. § 4 b.

Chapter XXXIII.

22 **§ 1. seditio]** 'dissensions.' The word regularly used of the struggles between patricians and plebeians at Rome is here applied to the quarrel between allies.

23 **in quo...consenuerant]** This piece of rhetorical exaggeration seems to apply to the Volscians rather than the Antiates; cf. c. 2. 13 and c. 12 *passim.* For the Antiate war, see c. 6. 4 ff.

24 **spectarent]** 'were contemplating.'

27 **§ 2. utrisque...alteros]** The plur. is regular, when two sets of persons are referred to, as, in this case, the *Latini* and the *Antiates*; cf. 36. 16. 5: *Aetolorum utraeque manus Heracleam sese incluserunt.*

    per...quo minus] Translate: 'that the others in no way prevented them from....' In 2. 31. 11 we find *quin* after the phrase, but *quominus* is usual; *ne* is also found occasionally.

28 **§ 3. a]** To be taken with *sese vindicaverunt*: 'by departing...freed themselves from.'

29 **Antiates...dedunt]** 'the Antiates, as soon as these inconvenient witnesses of their salutary decision were removed, surrendered their city and lands to the Romans.' Weiss. says that *urbem* refers to Satricum, not Antium, but this does not seem probable. The sense is simply that the *Antiates* were afraid to surrender so long as the Latins were with them, but, as soon as they were gone, adopted the wise plan of a voluntary submission. The problem raised by the calm retreat of the Latins under the eyes of the Romans was not one likely to disturb Livy.

32 **§ 4. Volscos]** It will be observed that here Livy identifies the *Antiates* with the *Volsci*; cf. § 1.

p. 45. 4 **matris Matutae templum]** *Mater Matuta* was a very ancient Italian goddess, whose worship must have been widely spread. We find evidence of her cult at Rome, where her temple was restored and re-dedicated in 396 B.C. (cf. 5. 19. 6 and 5. 23. 7), and where she was annually worshipped at the festival of the *Matralia* on June 11th; she was also worshipped at Pisaurum in Umbria, and at Praeneste.

    With regard to the character of the goddess, it is clear that she was an ancient deity of matrons, and it is likely that her aid was invoked at child-birth. She may also have been a goddess of the dawn (cf. *mane*, *matutinus*), and hence it has been plausibly conjectured that she was specially concerned with births that took place in the morning. Prof.

Mommsen (*Hist. of Rome* 1. p. 209 n.) has pointed out that the names Lucius and Manius indicate a belief that the morning hour was a lucky one for birth. *Mater Matuta* subsequently, under Greek influence, became identified with Leucothea, a sea-goddess. See Warde Fowler, *The Roman Festivals*, pp. 154–156.

5   § 5.   sua religio] 'religious feelings of their own': *sua* is emphatic.

6   vox horrenda] These mysterious warnings played a great part in Roman religious belief (cf. 5. 32. 6 and 5. 50. 5, the warning given to M. Caedicius of the approach of the Gauls, and the temple subsequently founded in honour of *Aius Locutius*). They accorded well with the vagueness which characterised the Roman conception of deities.

7   ni...amovissent] Oblique: or. recta, *ni...amoveritis.* Notice that the apodosis has to be supplied from *minis.*

8   § 6.   impetus] Nom., 'an impulse.'

10   in civitatem] Cf. c. 26. 8 n.

17   § 9.   Tusculi] For reading, see Appendix. The situation was as follows : the Tusculans had fled into the fortified acropolis (*arx*), which was a conspicuous hill rising from the plain. The Latins, who had captured the walled town (*oppidum*), which lay on the level ground around the *arx*, were now at one and the same time besieging the Tusculans and being themselves besieged by the newly arrived Roman army. Cf. Caesar's position during his siege of the Gallic fortress of Alesia (*B.G.* VII. 68 ff.).

simul...atque...una ac] Livian variety of expression.

23   § 10.   potirentur] Oblique, expressing the thought in the mind of the Latins.

24   § 11.   excipit] 'follows'; cf. c. 3. 4 n.

27   molientesque] 'and attacking,' exactly as in c. 11. 8: *moliri fidem*; cf. c. 2. 14 n.

28   § 12.   effracta] 'broken off' (from within).

31   ad unum omnes] 'to a man.'

CHAPTER XXXIV.

For the Licinio-Sextian laws, cf. Introd. § 4 c.

p. 46.   4   § 1.   tranquilla] goes closely with *quanto magis*. Translate: 'the more calmness prevailed everywhere abroad owing to the success of that year's wars, so much the more, etc.'

5   tantum] The MSS. read *tanto*, but Madvig's change to *tantum* is very likely right. *tanto* would require us to understand *magis* from

crescebant, a rather doubtful constr.   A copyist would be tempted to write *tanto* after *quanto*.   See Appendix.

6   **cum…impediretur**] 'since ability to pay was being hampered by the very fact that payment was a necessity.'   There is a strong emphasis on *necesse erat*, which implies that immediate payment was required.   Many would be unable to pay at once owing to depreciation in the value of land or from other temporary causes, whereas they could have managed to do so, had time been allowed them.

7   **§ 2.   ex re**] 'from their property,' in contrast to their person.

8   **fama et corpore**] Cf. c. 11. 8 n.   They suffered the degradation of slavery and sometimes personal violence as well.

9   **poenaque in vicem fidei cesserat**] 'punishment suddenly took the place of credit,' i.e. instead of being trusted for the repayment of the loan, they were made to work it off by personal labour.   Notice the plup. tense, which, though very nearly equivalent in sense to an aorist, probably gives the idea of suddenness.   *Summiserant* has the usual plup. sense.

10   **§ 3.   obnoxios**] is proleptic, the effect of *summittere* being anticipated: 'they had been brought to such a pitch of humiliation'; cf. c. 28. 7 : *pax obnoxia*.

11   **non modo**] = *non modo non*, as it does regularly before *ne…quidem*, when the two clauses have a common predicate, and if a neg. does not precede *non modo* (cf. c. 20. 2 n.).   The neg. wanted after *non modo* must be supplied from that in *ne…quidem*.

For the fact, cf. 32. 3 : *tribunos etiam militares patricios omnes coacta principum opibus fecit.*   Livy does not give the consular tribunes for the year 376–5 B.C., but four names are given by Diodorus (15. 71. 1).

14   **§ 4.   acri experientique**] 'of energy and enterprise'; cf. Cic. *pro Clu.* 8. 23: *vir fortis et experiens.*   Note that *experientia* = 'experience' is post-Augustan; its classical meaning is rather 'experiment.'

15   **usurpati modo**] 'merely assumed.'

17   **§ 5.   id**] 'this state of affairs'; it refers to the gist of the whole of the last sentence.

18   **moliundi**] 'of effecting'; cf. c. 2. 14 n.

19   **sui corporis**] 'of his standing,' i.e. patricians.   So in the *Digest* we find *corpus fabrorum*, meaning 'a guild of workmen.'

20   **inter id genus**] 'among that class' (the plebeians).

21   **filiae…erat**] 'of the two married daughters the elder was, etc.'   Partitive apposition.   The plur. is split up into its component parts and the vb. is in the singular in agreement with each of the latter; cf.

41. 18. (15): *quando duo ordinarii consules eius anni, alter morbo, alter ferro periisset.*

23   **affinitas**] 'marriage connection'; cf. c. 20. 2 n.

25   **§ 6. cum...tererent**] Cf. Cic. *pro Mil.* 10. 28: *paulisper, dum se uxor, ut fit, comparat, commoratus est.* The '*ut fit*' is gently ironical.

29   **risui sorori fuit**] *Risui* is a predicative dat.: 'she brought a smile upon her sister's face.'

This story is evidently a pure invention, for, as has been often pointed out, the younger Fabia could not have been ignorant of the custom, seeing that her father had been consular tribune (c. 22. 5). Weiss. cites, in illustration of the practice, Plin. *N. H.* 7. 112: *Cn. Pompeius...intraturus Posidonii domum...fores percuti de more vetuit.*

32   **§ 7. num quid vellet**] Here in the straightforward sense: 'if he had any commands to give.' But like our 'good bye,' originally = 'God be with you,' *numquid vis* came to be used without any thought of the real meaning, simply as a formula of leave-taking.

p. 47. 1. **malo arbitrio**] An instance of Livy's tendency to moralise.

2   **§ 8. confusam**] Cf. c. 6. 7, where, however, the cause of confusion is different.

3   **morsu animi**] 'annoyance.'

satin' salve] 'is anything amiss?'; cf. 1. 58. 7, where Lucretia's husband greets her with these words. The expression is colloquial, and, with the spelling *salve*, may be explained as = *satin' salve agis?*, *salve* being an adv. This seems the correct spelling, not *salvae*, though with the latter the phrase can be easily explained as = *satin' salvae res se habent?*

4   **piam**] 'kind.' *Pietas* often means the 'right feeling' which should subsist between members of a family.

6   **§ 9. elicuit...ut**] 'induced her to.'

7   **impari**] Through lack of the *genus patricium.*

8   **honos**] = 'the consulship.' See c. 37. 5 n.

12   **§ 11. cuius spei...deesset**] The phrase is equivalent to an adj. balancing *strenuo*; cf. c. 35. 5: *cuncta ingentia et quae sine certamine maximo obtineri non possent.*

CHAPTER XXXV.

21   **§ 1. nisi...locatis**] 'unless their representatives were placed.' This constr. of *nisi* with an abl. abs. is a favourite one with Livy; cf. c. 37. 4: *nisi imperio communicato.*

22   **§ 2. accingendum**] 'they must gird themselves.' The Latin passive
not infrequently has a reflexive or middle signification; indeed it is
probable that it was a middle in origin. Cf. the Greek, where certain
forms serve for both middle and passive. Cf. 26. 7. 6: *una ea cura
angebat, ne, ubi abscessisset, extemplo* dederentur, where *dederentur*
means 'should surrender themselves.' So we find *appelli,* 'to push
oneself in'; *pasci,* 'to feed oneself,' etc.

26   **§ 3. fieri**] sc. *eos.*

29   **§ 4. leges**] 'bills'; they had not yet become laws. The purpose
of these proposals was evidently (1) to give the richer plebeians access
to an office which brought with it so much social distinction and influence, and (2) to relieve the poorer plebeians from the pressure of
debt, and to give them a new start in life by supplying them with land.

30   **unam de aere alieno**] This is identical with the proposal of Manlius
(c. 15. 10). The measure amounted to an abolition of interest on loans
previously contracted; it was not so sweeping a remedy as that of
Solon, which was, according to the best authorities (Plut. *Sol.* 15,
Arist. 'Aθ. Πολ. 10), a χρεῶν ἀποκοπή, or *novae tabulae,* to use the
Roman expression.

32   **pensionibus**] 'instalments.' It is the usual word in this connection
(cf. 7. 27. 3), but *portionibus* of the MSS. might be correct. *Pensionibus*
is hardly a sufficiently out-of-the-way word to need a gloss, as *portionibus* is supposed to be.

        § 5. de modo agrorum] Suspicion has not altogether unjustifiably
arisen with regard to this law, which, in the extent of land implied,
does not well accord with a time previous to the subjugation of Italy.
It is probably another instance of the tendency to read into early history
situations which occur in later times, but it does not follow that no bill
to limit the amount of land which could be occupied was introduced at
this period. See Introd. p. XXIX.

p. 48. **2. consulumque**] An *ut* must be supplied from the preceding *ne,* unless it has fallen out before *utique.*

        utique] 'at least'; cf. c. 40. 16, where Appius Claudius inveighs
against this condition. The experience of the plebeians at the elections
of consular tribunes had convinced them of the necessity of the proviso;
at this period there was little danger of both consuls being plebeians; cf.
c. 37. 4: *nisi alterum consulem utique ex plebe fieri necesse sit, neminem
fore.*

6   **§ 6. agri, pecuniae, honorum**] Cf. Macaulay, *Jacobite's Epitaph* :
        For him I threw lands, honours, wealth away,
        And one dear hope, that was more prized than they.

7 **publicis privatisque consiliis**] i.e. in the Senate and at informal meetings.

9 **rogationes**] Cf. *leges*, above, in § 4. Both terms are used for 'bills,' but *rogatio* accurately describes the procedure. The magistrate *asked* the people for their assent to the proposal (*velitis iubeatis, Quirites?*), which only became law after that assent had been given.

10 **§ 7. tribus**] The assembly was the exclusively plebeian *concilium plebis*, which voted by tribes. The reason why the patricians did not rely upon defeating the bill by the withholding of the *senatus auctoritas* was clearly that they preferred to use the plebeian weapon against the *plebs*. This would serve at once to draw off part of the odium from themselves, and to sow dissensions among their opponents.

12 **recitari**] Interesting as showing the practical application of the *veto*. The tribune who interposed his *veto* forbade the clerk to read out the contents of the bill; disobedience to this order would be regarded as an offence against the tribunician *sacrosanctitas*; cf. Ascon. *in Cornel.* p. 58: *P. Servilius Globulus tribunus plebis...ubi legis ferundae dies venit et praeco subiciente scriba verba legis recitare populo coepit, et scribam subicere et praeconem pronuntiare passus non est.*

sollemne] e.g. *mittere tribus in suffragium.*

13 **ad sciscendum plebi**] *Plebi* is probably dat. after *solemne*, 'usual for the *plebs* in passing resolutions.' Weiss., however, takes *ad sc. pl.* together, 'usual for the passing of a resolution by the *plebs*.'

14 **§ 8. pro antiquatis**] 'virtually rejected,' because the *plebs* never had a chance of accepting the proposals. *Antiquare rogationem* is the opposite of *iubere rog.* On the voting tablets V. R. (=*uti rogas*) indicated approbation of a measure, A. (=*antiquo*) rejection. The word is explained as =*antiqua probo*, 'I prefer the old state of things.'

15 **bene habet**] Colloquial: 'very good,' implying a threat.

17 **§ 9. agite dum**] *Dum* is here an enclitic; cf. the Gk. δή in φέρε δή, ἄγε δή. This use is very frequent in Plautus and Terence; *dum* is probably an acc. of time. Somewhat parallel is our 'wait a while,' 'wait a bit.'

18 **faxo**] Another form frequent in the comic poets, and used here colloquially. It is explained as =*fecero* in sense, though in formation it is an old aor. subj. Here it is simply=an emphatic future; cf. c. 41. 12: *faxitis.*

veto] The technical word is *intercedo*; cf. c. 38. 5. Livy is notoriously inaccurate in such matters, and though we find a similar meaning of *vetare* in 3. 13. 6, the modern use of the word '*veto*' has a very slender foundation to rest upon.

qua...auditis] 'wherein you so gladly hear our colleagues agreeing.' So we must translate, if the *qua* of the MSS. is retained. For this absolute use of *concinere*='to agree,' cf. Cic. *N. D.* I. 7. 16 : *Stoici cum Peripateticis re concinere videntur, verbis discrepare.* See Appendix.

28   § **10. per quinquennium]** This period of five years without curule magistrates is generally regarded as an impossibly long one. It is true that it is supported by the *Fasti consulares*, but on the other hand, Zonaras (i.e. Dio Cassius) gives the time as four years, Diodorus (15. 75. 1), as only one. The truth seems to be that the *solitudo magis-tratuum* was a device to set the *Fasti* straight.

CHAPTER XXXVI.

30   § **1. esset]** Oblique, expressing the thought of the colonists.

32   § **2. novis civibus]** Cf. c. 26. 8 n.

p. 49.   1. **verecundia]** Abl.: 'with a feeling of shame.'

5   § **3. per interregem]** Because, owing to the *solitudo magistra-tuum*, there was no consul or consular tribune to hold the elections; cf. c. 1. 5 n.

14   § **5. expugnari]** It is significant of the unreality of these wars and sieges that Livy forgets to tell us what happened to Velitrae. Plutarch (*Cam.* 42) says that it surrendered to Camillus during his last campaign: τὴν γὰρ Οὐελιτρανῶν πόλιν εἷλεν ἐν παρέργῳ ταύτης τῆς στρατείας ἀμαχεὶ προσχωρήσασαν αὐτῷ. It is very probable, as Weiss. suggests, that this war against Velitrae was an invention to account for the delay in passing the Licinio-Sextian proposals.

27   § **7. auctor]** 'prompter.' He had suggested the course adopted by Licinius and Sextius; *suasorem*='advocate.'

28   **se...ferebat]** 'declared himself'; cf. *prae se ferre*, which means 'to assert.'

§ **8. cum]** 'whereas'; concessive.

30   **ut ferme solent qui a suis desciscunt]** This dictum of Livy's is hardly borne out by history. Renegades have usually proved the most active and bitter opponents of the cause they have deserted; cf., e.g., Labienus against Caesar.

capti et stupentes animi] 'weakened and dazed in mind.' *Animi* is really a locative, as in *pendere animi*. We find *captus animi* in Tac. *Hist.* 3. 73, but the more usual expression is *captus mente.* For *capio* in this sense, cf. the common *captus oculis*, 'blind.'

31   **vocibus alienis]** 'with words borrowed from others.' Madvig's

emendation *capti et stupentes, animis a voce alienis,* 'with minds at variance with their words,' is specious, but unnecessary. See Appendix.

domi] i.e. by the patricians. They had been carefully schooled in private.

p. **50.** 3 **§ 9. universa]** Emphatic: 'the *plebs* in undivided body.'

6 **§ 10. tractandi]** Best taken with *artifices*: 'experts at managing.'

8 **§ 11. bina iugera]** This argument which Livy puts into the mouths of the tribunes and Fabius is quite sophistical, inasmuch as no real comparison could be instituted between the small allotments of arable land and the large tracts of *ager occupatorius,* which were as a rule only suitable for pasturage; cf. c. 16. 6 n. Moreover, whereas the allotments granted to colonists were held in full ownership, the pasture lands always belonged, in theory at least, to the State.

9 **quingenta]** We might have expected the distributive *quingena* corresponding to *bina.* But as in c. 37. 6 (see n. there) Livy prefers to vary his expressions.

12 **locum sepulturae]** The rich had private tombs either within the precincts of their villas or along the sides of the highways. Artisans, slaves, and the poorer classes generally were buried in public cemeteries, such as the notorious one on the Esquiline, which was obliterated by Maecenas. The horrors of these public cemeteries, as described by Prof. Lanciani (*Ancient Rome in the light of recent discoveries,* pp. 64 ff.), lend special point to this passage.

§ 12. an placeret] This represents *an placet (vobis)?* of the recta. It is virtually a rhetorical question, but being equivalent to a question put in the 2nd person, is represented by the subj. in the oblique. For the use of *an* in questions where a neg. answer is expected, see c. 7. 5 n.; *an placeret* = 'could it be that they thought it right?' i.e. 'surely they did not think it right.'

13 **potius quam]** See c. 15. 12 n.

sorte] i.e. the principal *alone,* without addition of interest.

CHAPTER XXXVII.

18 **§ 1. maiore...quam sua]** This implies that Licinius and Sextius, belonging as they did to the wealthy portion of the plebeians, had no real interest in assisting the debtors, nay, they might even be acting against their own interests in so doing. But they could not afford to dispense with the aid of the poorer plebeians in their efforts to obtain the consulship, and thus were forced to make this concession to them.

19   **§ 2. atqui**] This use of *atqui*, a more emphatic *at*, with the acc.
and inf. after *adfirmabant*, is strange.   We must suppose that Livy had
the original words of the speakers vividly in his mind : 'after uttering
these indignant complaints...they declared, "Well, anyhow, there will
never be any limit...unless etc."' Instead, however, of putting them in
direct speech he wrote them in or. obliqua.

22   **plebes fecisset**] See Appendix.

24   **§ 4. imperium...auxilium**] Again indicates that the tribunes were
not magistrates in the strict sense of the term.   Their original business
was to rescue those who suffered from the undue exercise of the consular
imperium.

25   **nisi imperio communicato**] Cf. c. 35. 1 n.

26   **in parte pari...fore**] For the phrase, cf. c. 15. 6 n.

27   **ratio**] The magistrate who presided at the elections had the power
of rejecting candidates, if he thought they were not properly qualified.
Thus *rationem habere alicuius* means 'to admit as a candidate.'

29   **necesse**] Note the stress on this word.

       § 5. an] 'could it be that?' cf. c. 7. 5 and 36. 12 nn.

31   **summus honos**] A regular phrase for the consulship ; cf. Juv. 1.
117 : *sed cum summus honor finito computet anno*, etc., where it is used
instead of *consul*.

32   **quattuor et quadraginta annos**] 444–401 B.C. inclusive.

33   **§ 6. quid crederent**] Represents a question in the 2nd person in
the or. recta, and is therefore in the subj., not in the inf., in the obliqua.
See Appendix.

p. 51. 1 **octona loca**] Livy once (5. 1. 2) gives eight consular tribunes,
but he is there clearly in error, and includes the two censors in their
number.   In this passage it adds point to the argument to place the
number of consular tribunes as high as possible, and it looks as though
Livy were relying on his former error for proof.   The military tribunes
with consular power were originally three in number (5. 2. 10), later
six.   Note once more Livy's love of variety—*duobus* (cardinal) and
octona (distributive) used side by side, where two distributives might
have been expected.   See Appendix.

2   **occupare**] Rather implies unfair methods.

9 ·   **§ 8. curules magistratus**] At this period the Consular Tribunate
(or Consulship), Dictatorship, and Censorship.

10   **post P. Licinii Calvi tribunatum**] 400 B.C.   See 5. 12. 9.

13   **§ 9. quin contra**] 'nay, on the contrary.'

15   **paucis ante annis**] In B.C. 409.   See 4. 54. 2, 3.

18   **§ 10. columen**] Cf. our expression 'a pillar of the state.'

21   **§ 11. imperium...nobilitatem**] This is a good summary of the changes actually brought about by the opening of the consulship to the plebeians. A nobility of birth gave way to a nobility of office, since the *ius imaginum*, i.e. the right to have their waxen portraits set up in the family *atrium*, was now opened to plebeians : the presence of these portraits was the outward and visible sign of the nobility of a family.

22   **magna ipsis fruenda, maiora liberis relinquenda**] Literally : 'great things to be enjoyed by themselves, greater to be left to their children,' i.e. 'things great as sources of personal enjoyment, but greater as bequests to hand on to their children.' The supine in *-u* would have been the natural constr., as Ltb. says, but the form is not found with these verbs.

24   **§ 12. accipi**] 'were well received' : in colloquial language, 'went down.'

    pro duumviris sacris faciundis decemviri] See c. 5. 8 n. where the MSS. have the form *faciendis*. Matters were not yet ripe for a plebeian assault upon the genuinely Roman priesthoods. The keepers of the Sibylline Books were priests of Apollo, a purely Greek deity, and as such had nothing to do with the *auspicia*, which the patricians regarded as belonging peculiarly to themselves.

25   **pars**] 'half,' as explained by c. 42. 2.

CHAPTER XXXVIII.

33   **§ 1. circumactus est annus**] The magisterial year ; cf. c. 1. 4 n. : *anno circumacto.*

p. 52.   2 **nam**] The connection with what goes before is not at first sight apparent. *Nam* explains *suspensa* and *dilata* : 'undecided and postponed (but not abandoned), for the plebs kept re-electing....' Livy does not imply that the elections of the military tribunes and of the tribunes of the *plebs* were simultaneous ; he merely gives the reason for the delay in getting the measures passed.

3   **qui**] See Appendix.

7   **§ 3. tribus**] The *concilium plebis* voting by tribes ; cf. § 4.

9   **ad...decurrunt**] 'have recourse to.' For the phrase, cf. c. 19. 3 n. See Appendix.

11   **§ 4. cooptat**] Usually *creat* or *dicit* ; *cooptare* is generally used of a body of men which itself elects its new members, e.g. a priestly *collegium.*

17   **§ 5. quanto...vinceretur**] 'the *veto*, though more powerful in law,
was yet being overcome.' This picture of the unconstitutional disregard
of the *intercessio* is probably taken from the events of the last few years
of the life of the Republic.

19   **uti rogas**] See c. 35. 8 n.   At this period, when the voting was by
word of mouth, the words were a direct answer to the magistrate's
question '*velitis iubeatis, Quirites?*'   In later times, when voting was
by tablet, V.R. became merely a conventional sign.

24   **§ 6. intercessioni ... auxilium**]   We can easily see how the
original *ius auxilii* of the tribunes developed into a general power of
veto, which in the end proved fatal to the working of the Republican
Constitution.

26   **§ 7. nihil**] Adverbial: 'in no way.'

27   **inseram**] From *insero*, pf. *inserui*. No patrician magistrate could
preside in a *concilium plebis*.

28   **tendent**] The fut. following on the pres. *cedunt* is quite in Livy's
manner, and has no special significance. *Tendo* with inf. does not occur
in strict prose writers, and may be due to the influence of Virgil; cf.
Aen. 2. 220: *ille simul manibus tendit divellere nodos.*

32   **§ 8. emoverent**] Another poetical word, used frequently by Livy.
Virgil has it; cf. *Aen.* 2. 493: *emoti procumbunt cardine postes.* The
usual word for the moving on of a crowd by a lictor is *summovere*;
cf. 3. 48. 3: *lictor summove turbam.*

33   **sacramento...adacturum**] For the phrase, see c. 32. 4 n.

p. 53. 1 **§ 9. incusserat**] Another plup. where we should expect a
perf. Perhaps it gives the idea of suddenness, as in c. 34. 2; or possibly
completion may be indicated: 'the effect of this was to inspire great
terror.'

4   **vitio creatus**] See c. 1. 5 and c. 27. 5 nn.

5   **scivit**] The regular word for a resolution of the *plebs*; cf. c. 35. 7.
In the case of the *Comitia* the expression is *populus iussit.*

6   **pro dictatore**] 'as dictator.' Distinguish from the later use of *pro*
in *pro consule, pro praetore*, etc., where the meaning is rather 'in place
of a consul' than 'in the capacity of a consul.'

     quid egisset] i.e. did anything against the constitution, such as
interfering with the *concilium plebis*. Even a dictator was bound to
obey the fundamental laws of the constitution, as appears from other
passages; cf. 7. 3. 9 (very parallel to this), 7. 21. 1, 2. No doubt, in
spite of what Livy says in § 13, the threat of fine can only refer to a
prosecution to be instituted against Camillus after resignation of the

dictatorship; cf. 9. 26. 12: *ipsos adeo dictatorem magistratumque equitum reos magis quam quaesitores eius criminis esse, intellecturosque id esse,* simul magistratu abissent.

quingentum milium] i.e. 500,000 pounds of uncoined copper (*aes rude*). The amount is absurdly large, and Livy implies his disbelief in this version of the story. Probably the heavy bronze coinage (*aes grave*) was not yet in existence, it being now supposed that it only dates from the middle of the 4th century B.C. See Hill, *Greek and Roman Coins*, p. 45. Before that time the copper was simply weighed out as occasion required, as in the ceremony *per aes et libram*. The point, however, must not here be pressed, since the question as to whether coined money existed at this time or not was not likely to occur to Livy's mind.

7 **§ 10. auspiciis**] Livy is inclined to believe the first version of the story, viz. that there had been some flaw in Camillus' appointment. Plutarch, however (*Cam.* 39) says that Camillus resigned from fear of the threats, though feigning ill health: ταῖς δ' ἐξῆς ἡμέραις σκηψάμενος ἀρρωστεῖν ἐξωμόσατο τὴν ἀρχήν. This would be unworthy of Livy's hero.

12 **§ 11. haud sine pudore...repetiturum**] 'since he would have been ashamed to resume....'

15 **§ 12. in ordinem cogi**] 'humiliated'; cf. our 'to reduce to the ranks.' In 3. 35. 6 the phrase is used of self-abasement. Plin. *Ep.* 1. 23 uses *in ordinem cogi* in reference to the tribuneship 'being brought into contempt.'

§ 13. The general sense is: If Camillus (as some asserted) had been driven by the tribunes to resign, the latter would certainly have been strong enough to carry through their proposals at once; this was contrary to known facts.

19 **dictaturae...fuit**] 'the dignity of the dictatorship was always the higher one.' Yet the passages quoted above (§ 9 n.) show that Livy gives other instances of collisions between tribunes and dictator. The present meaning of *fastigium* should be compared with that in c. 20. 8.

CHAPTER XXXIX.

29 **§ 1. dictaturam abdicatam**] The constr. *abdicare magistratum* is occasionally used by Livy, as here and in c. 18. 4. The Ciceronian constr. is always *abdicare se magistratu*, and this is also more usual in Livy.

30 **velut per interregnum**] The consular tribunes were nonentities.

31 **latoribus**] Cf. c. 37. 1 n. It is there implied that the tribunes' interest in the relief of the plebeian debtor's distress was merely feigned.

33 **§ 2. iubebant...antiquabant**] It is very important to express the force of the imperf. rightly. We must say 'they were proceeding to pass,' or something equivalent. The absence of a conjunction (*asyndeton*) serves to bring out a contrast, as often.

p. **54.** 1 **in omnia simul**] i.e. they were putting the question with a view to forcing through all the measures together. *In* here expresses purpose, as in 21. 43. 7: *in hanc tam opimam mercedem agite*; cf. the common *in spem* (c. 11. 5).

A law which embraced several proposals of distinct character was known as a *lex satura*; cf. Festus *s.v. satura: satura et cibi genus dicitur ex variis rebus conditum, et lex multis aliis conferta legibus, et genus carminis ubi de multis rebus disputatur.* It can easily be understood that such laws might be very dangerous, inasmuch as the bad could be forced through with the good.

3 **§ 3. C. Licinio**] This cannot be the tribune of the *plebs*, but was no doubt some near relation. The prominence of the *Licinii* in these chapters makes it probable that Livy is here following the annalist Licinius Macer (1st cent. B.C.), who wrote with a strong democratic bias.

7 **§ 4. tribuni consularis**] Refers back to the statement that Licinius had been *tribunus militum* (*consulari potestate*). Manlius pleaded that, in appointing Licinius his Master-of-Horse, he was showing no more favour to the *plebs* than the whole people had shown in electing the same man consular tribune; cf. 23. 11. 10: *magistrum equitum, quae consularis potestas sit, fusum fugatum.* As a matter of fact the Magister Equitum, being entirely subordinate to the dictator, had not as much influence as a consular tribune.

12 **§ 6. privatim...publice**] A striking example of the use of adverbs in an adjectival sense. Note that this is helped out by their position between the adj. and the subst.; cf. c. 4. 1 n.

13 **consenuisse**] 'had lost their natural force.' For this sense of *consenescere*, cf. Cic. *ad Att.* 2. 13. 2: *quanto in odio noster amicus Magnus! cuius cognomen una cum Crassi Divitis cognomine consenescit*; Pompey's title of Magnus had lost its force.

16 **§ 7. ablegatione**] A rare word used instead of the commoner *relegatio*. The war had been made a pretext for sending the plebeian voters into an honourable banishment.

17 **fulmen]** Equivalent to 'overpowering might.' Livy had probably taken the expression from the poets; cf. Lucr. 3. 1034: *Scipiadas, belli fulmen, Carthaginis horror*, and Verg. *Aen.* 6. 842: *duo fulmina belli, Scipiadas*. Cicero (*pro Balbo* 34) has a similar expression.

21 **§ 9. forum]** The spot where many distressing scenes would occur as the result of the harsh law of debt; cf. c. 14. 3. It was in the *forum* that the debtor was finally handed over to the mercy of his creditor.

23 **§ 10. aestimaturos]** The or. recta would be *quando...aestimabitis?* We should therefore expect a subj. in the or. obliqua according to strict rule. But the question is virtually rhetorical and equal to a neg. statement, *nunquam aestimaturos*; cf. c. 17. 5 n.

25 **incidant]** Note the quantity, *incīdere*, 'to cut away.' For the gerundive with *inter*, cf. c. 11. 5 n.

27 **per quos]** Again the absence of a connecting particle serves to bring out the contrast forcibly.

senes] No doubt with reference to *consenuisse* in § 6.

29 **relinquat]** *Relinquere*, parallel to *postulare*, might have been expected. As it is, we must supply another *ut*, dependent upon *postulare*.

§ 11. statuerent] Many instances of the varying use of primary and secondary tenses of the subj. in or. obliqua have occurred before; cf. c. 6. 8 ff.: *creasset...possit*, etc., c. 17. 3: *iugulentur... fingerent...responderet*, c. 23. 10, 11, etc. The present passage, however, shows the variation so strikingly, that it seemed best to reserve discussion of the constr. for this place. In an Appendix to his edition of Bk. II, Prof. Conway has examined Livy's use of primary and secondary tenses of the subj. in or. obliqua after a past vb. of saying or thinking. He shows that, with a few exceptions, Livy is in the habit of keeping the tense of the or. recta, wherever practicable. But since this is impossible in the case of the Imperative, Fut., and Fut. Perf. Ind., he usually converts these into secondary tenses of the subj. Thus in § 10 *relinquat* repeats the pres. subj. of the recta, but *statuerent* represents the imperat. *statuite*. In the next sentence, *vellent* and *reficerent* are not in accordance with Prof. Conway's rule, but seem, as he says, to be under the influence of the secondary tenses immediately preceding; a return is made to the primary tenses with *opus sit* and *velint* (§ 12). For further information on this point Prof. Conway's Appendix should be consulted.

Exceptions to the canon appear to occur in c. 6. 8: *creasset* for *creaverit* (cf., however, Prof. Conway's foot-note, p. 192), c. 17. 4: *vidissent* for *viderint*, and c. 23. 9: *gesta essent* for *gesta sint*.

31   coniuncte] i.e. in the form of a *lex satura*.

p. 55. 1 **§ 12. nihil**] Adverbial: 'in no way.'

CHAPTER XL.

The speech of Appius Claudius is an interesting example of the way in which Livy seeks to give vividness to a situation by bringing forward a person to express the feelings of a whole class of men concerned in it. The speech may be regarded as summing up the objections to the compulsory election of one plebeian consul, and the grounds upon which the patricians rested their claims to exclusive possession of the chief magistracy. The following is a brief analysis: *C.* 40. I deny that our clan has always opposed the interests of the *plebs*; it has only done so when they were detrimental to the interests of the state as a whole (§§ 3–7). On the present occasion the proposals of Licinius and Sextius simply amount to a plot to deprive the people of their right to choose the chief magistrates from whomsoever they will (§§ 8–20). *C.* 41. The basest plebeian will be able to force himself into the consulship (§§ 1–3).

But all this concerns human equity merely; I now come to the offence in the sight of heaven. Patricians only are qualified to consult the gods by the auspices, and therefore patricians only can be elected consuls without impiety against the gods. Remember, it is only by our careful observance of religion that we have grown great (§§ 4–12).

5   **§ 1. prae**] The strictest prose writers employ *prae*, in causal sense, only after a neg. Livy does not always observe this rule; cf. 5. 13. 13: *prae metu...obiectis foribus extremos suorum exclusere.*

    stupor silentiumque inde] 'amazement and then (i.e. in consequence) silence.'

6   **defixisset**] The whole phrase has a poetical ring about it. Perhaps Livy is again indebted to Virgil; cf. *Aen.* 1. 495: *dum stupet obtutuque haeret defixus in uno.*

    § 2. App. Claudius Crassus] Prof. Mommsen (*Hist. of Rome*, vol. I. App.) has shown that there is reason to believe that the character of the Claudii has been consistently misrepresented by Livy, who perhaps follows the annalist Licinius Macer. Examination of the political actions of members of the clan does not reveal a bitter hostility to the *plebs*. For the force of *ob*, cf. *obnuntiatis*.

13 **§ 3. adversatos esse**] Note the sudden change of subject, not uncommon in Livy.

14 **§ 4. inftias eo**] *Infitias* is an acc. of motion towards. Literally, 'I proceed to a denial'; cf. *exsequias ire*, 'to attend a funeral.' This is an instance in which later Latin reverts to a constr. common in ante-classical Latin. Livy uses the phrase several times.

adsciti sumus] For the migration of Attus or Attius Clausus, afterwards called App. Claudius, from Sabine territory to Rome, and his subsequent enrolment among the *patres*, see 2. 16. **4, 5.**

15 **enixe**] Cf. c. 24. 11 n.: *virtutis enixae*.

18 **§ 5. ausim**]=*ausus sim*, a subj. of mild assertion; the form is an archaic one. It is remarked that this is the only occasion on which Livy uses *ausim* in a positive sentence.

19 **aliam incolenti urbem**] The phrase vividly describes the real position of the *plebs* at the earliest period of the struggle. Patricians and plebeians were as two peoples within one city, each with its own magistrates and assembly.

20 **quis**] Construe closely with *nisi*.

24 **§ 6. Claudiae familiae**] Probably here not used loosely for *Claudiae gentis*, but = 'of a branch of the Claudian clan.' Each *gens* was divided into a number of *familiae*, usually distinguished by a special *cognomen*. In § 3, above, *gens* and *familia* are apparently synonymous.

26 **duobus ingenuis**] If the father or mother had been servile, the son would have ranked as a *libertinus*.

28 **§ 7. si dis placet**] Ironical.

29 **negent...non...non**] Cf. c. 16. 3 and c. 23. 9 nn. The repetition strengthens the negation.

32 **§ 8. quid est aliud dicere ?**] 'that is the same as saying.'

p. 56. 4 **§ 9. coniunctim**] Cf. c. 39. 11: *coniuncte*. Another instance of Livy's love of variety.

5 **§ 10. Tarquinii**] The noun in apposition takes an adjectival meaning, 'tyrannous.' For a similarly free use of a proper name, cf. *sullaturire*, 'to play the Sulla,' a word coined by Cicero (*ad Att*. 9. 10. 6).

6 **succlamare**] A word of which Livy is fond, but which does not occur in Cicero or Caesar. It generally expresses a reply or objection, as here.

bona venia vestra] Again has an ironical ring: 'be so good as to.'

8 **§ 11. 'non' inquit 'licebit, ut...'**] For the reading and punctuation, see Appendix. Translate: 'You will not be allowed,' says he,

'to pass the bills relating to usury and land (a matter which touches you all so closely), without this portent taking place in the city of Rome—the appearance of L. Sextius and C. Licinius here as consuls, the thought of which you detest and abhor.' Appius, of course, puts into the mouth of the tribune words he would never have uttered, mingling his own views with the imaginary demands of the speaker.

14   **§ 12. mortiferum vitali]** 'The death-dealing with the life-giving'; neut. adjj. used as substantives.

19   **§ 13. volunt]** 'make out,' 'represent.'

23   **§ 14. quo]** From the enclitic *quis*: Gk. τις unaccented.

24   **§ 15. sermo]** Note the emphasis on this word which is contrasted with *rogatio*, also put first for the sake of emphasis.

       civilis] means 'becoming to a citizen.'

29   **§ 17. sint...peteret]** The tenses probably express more and less likely contingency respectively.

30   **Porsinna]** The spelling of this name varies; we find also Porsenna; e.g. in *Aen.* 8. 646, and Porsĕna (Hor. *Epod.* 16. 4); cf. Macaulay's *Horatius*, Introduction, where the use of Porsĕna is defended.

33   **L. ille Sextius]** The interposition of *ille* is contemptuous. Note the ease with which the Roman *praenomen* and *nomen* could be separated from each other.

p. 57. 1   **esse]** = *haberi*, 'to be accounted.' For the reading *consule*, see Appendix.

       de repulsa dimicare] 'should run the risk of a defeat.'

2   **§ 18. in commune...vocare]** 'to open to all alike'; cf. *rem in medium vocare.*

4   **necesse sit...liceat]** These are both emphatic.

5   **societas...consortio]** 'partnership...fellowship.' Weiss. compares 4. 5. 5: *si in consortio, si in societate reipublicae esse...licet.* Consors denotes closer relationship than *socius*, but probably Livy had no very clear distinction of meaning in his mind.

9   **§ 19. aliud]** The unusual position is due to Livy's love of variety. The normal order occurs above (§ 8).

CHAPTER XLI.

14   **§ 1. et ita maxima...debeant]** The desire to secure verbal antithesis seems to have led Livy into obscurity. Translate: ' They intend to win the greatest honours in such a way as to owe no gratitude, not even as much as is due for the very smallest favour.' The general

meaning is: 'the plebeians, if this law is passed, are sure of the highest office in the state; consequently they will not feel as much gratitude for this greatest of gifts, as they would for the smallest, if they were compelled to sue for it.' The sentence is an amplification of c. 40. 20. *Pro* means 'in proportion to,' as in such phrases as 21. 29. 2: *proelium atrocius quam pro numero pugnantium editur.* For another passage, where a fondness for verbal contrast has resulted in obscurity, see 22. 38. 11: *se, quae consilia magis res dent hominibus* quam homines rebus, *ea ante tempus immatura non praecepturum.* The words *quam homines rebus,* if taken strictly, have no meaning.

16 occasionibus] 'by watching their opportunities,' i.e. by waiting till no other plebeian candidate comes forward, and so securing their election without contest.

17 § 2. est aliquis] 'there is sure to be someone.'

22 § 3. tanquam regum in Capitolio] Cf. c. 40. 10, above: *Tarquinii tribuni plebis,* and § 10, below. References are found elsewhere to these statues of the Kings set up on the Capitol; cf. Appian *B. C.* 1. 16 (of the death of Tib. Gracchus): Γράκχος αὐτός, εἰλούμενος περὶ τὸ ἱερόν (i.e. the temple of Jupiter), ἀνῃρέθη κατὰ τὰς θύρας, παρὰ τοὺς τῶν βασιλέων ἀνδριάντας. The reference, however, to these statues as existing at this period is an anachronism.

26 erit] See Appendix.

27 § 4. etenim] This, the reading of the MSS., may well be retained. Appius apologizes for dwelling so long on points which merely affect the dignity of a class of men. *Etenim* explains *satis*: 'I have said enough and to spare on this point, for it is one concerning mere human dignity.' Madvig's alteration to *at enim* gives, of course, good sense, but does not seem necessary.

30 auspiciis...ignoret?] Cf. c. 2. 5 n. and Val. Max. 2. 1. 1: *apud antiquos non solum publice sed etiam privatim nihil gerebatur nisi auspicio primo sumpto;* also Cic. *in Vat.* 6. 14: *auspicia, quibus haec urbs condita est, quibus omnis res publica atque imperium continetur.*

33 § 5. patres] Here unmistakably means 'patricians.'

plebeius...magistratus] The tribunes of the *plebs* and the plebeian aediles, being without the right of taking the auspices, were not elected under the presidency of a magistrate empowered to take the auspices; cf. 5. 14. 4: *comitiis,* auspicato quae fierent, *indignum dis visum honores vulgari discriminaque gentium confundi;* cf. also 4. 6. 2.

p. 58. 2 § 6. populus] The whole people in the *comitia* as contrasted with the *plebs* in its *concilia*.

3   **ipsi**]   Explained by *privati*.   Though they held no magistracy, the patrician members of the Senate (*patres* in the restricted sense) had the *auspicia* in their keeping, whenever the chief magistrates resigned without holding the elections of their successors (*interregnum*).

4   **interregem prodamus**]   See c. 1. 5 n.

    privati]   See Appendix.

6   **§ 7. plebeios consules**]   Livy, in putting this argument into the mouth of Appius, appears to have overlooked the fact that the plebeian consular tribunes must have had the power of taking the auspices.

8   **§ 8. esse...pascantur**]   See Appendix.   The words are in or. obliqua, and represent the arguments used by the scoffers: 'what does it matter, if the sacred chickens refuse to feed?'   The pres. subj. indicates several indefinite occasions, the perf. one particular.

9   **pulli**]   This method of augury was known as *auspicia ex tripudiis*; it was especially resorted to upon military expeditions owing to its conveniènce.   The birds, generally chickens, were carried about in cages, and the omen was drawn from the manner in which they fed.   If they fed so eagerly that some of the food fell from their mouths, then the omen was favourable (*tripudium solistimum*); if they refused to feed, it was unfavourable : cf. 10. 40. 4 : *nam cum pulli non pascerentur, pullarius auspicium mentiri ausus tripudium solistimum consuli nuntiavit*; also 9. 14. 4.   It is evident from the present passage that reluctance to come from the cage was also considered an evil omen.

The various methods of augury in vogue among the Romans may be briefly mentioned.   They are given by Festus, pp. 260, 261; *quinque genera signorum observant augures publici, ex caelo, ex avibus, ex tripudiis, ex quadrupedibus, ex diris*.   They included therefore the observation of (1) signs from the sky, particularly thunder and lightning.   (2) The flight and cries of birds.   (3) The behaviour of sacred chickens.   (4) The movements of animals.   (5) Miscellaneous warnings.   The first four were known as *auguria impetrativa*, i.e. signs specially asked for, the last as *auguria oblativa*, i.e. signs sent from heaven unasked for.

si occecinerit avis]   'if a bird has uttered an ill-omened cry.'   This is probably to be referred to (2) in the note above.   The observation of the flight and cries of various birds was the oldest means of augury employed at Rome (as we might infer from the word *auspicium*), though later it fell into disuse.   The present omen might, however, come under (5).

The use of the word *occinere* is another of Livy's archaisms; cf. c. 5. 7 n.   For the force of *ob*, cf. *obnuntiatio*.

11   **nostri]** See Appendix.

rem] 'state.'

12   **§ 9. pace deorum]** 'the favour of heaven'; cf. c. 1. 12.

13   **pontifices, augures, sacrificuli reges]** Religious offices at this time
strictly confined to patricians. The *rex sacrificulus* is better known as
rex sacrorum. He was theoretically the inheritor of the old religious
functions of the Kings, but was, in reality, of little importance, being
quite subordinate to the *Pontifex Maximus*. He announced the coming
festivals of the month upon the Nones; he was also regarded as the
representative head of Roman family life (cf. the βασιλεύς at Athens).
The small amount of influence attaching to this office is indicated by
the fact that, even to the latest times, the *rex sacrorum* was selected
from the patricians only, whose monopoly in this point the *plebs* did
not think it worth while to contest. On the other hand, the colleges
of pontifices and augurs, who had real political importance, were thrown
open to the plebs by the *lex Ogulnia* of 300 B.C.

14   **apicem Dialem]** i.e. the special hat worn by the *Flamen Dialis*
or priest of Jupiter; it was also known as *albogalerus* from its whiteness.
Apex is here put instead of *flamen*, the wearing of the *albogalerus* being
characteristic of the priest, who was not allowed to appear in the open
air without his special hat.   An *albogalerus* is figured in Ramsay,
Antiqs.[15] p. 381; see p. 382 for the *apex* and *ancilia*.

The *apex*, which was worn by the *Salii* and all the *flamines*, was
essentially a pointed piece of olive wood, surrounded with wool; the
cap, to which this was attached, was usually, though not invariably,
conical in shape. Here *apex* is used for the cap and piece of wood
combined. The *Flamen Dialis*, together with the *Flamen Martialis*
and *Flamen Quirinalis*, was known as a *Flamen maior*, and was chosen
to the end from the ranks of the patricians.

15   **ancilia]** The shields in the custody of the *Salii* or priests of Mars,
and carried annually in procession by them during the month of March.
According to legend the original shield fell from heaven, and the remaining eleven were copies of it. The *ancile* closely resembled in shape
the figure 8; the word is perhaps derived from *an* (=*amb*, as in *anceps*)
and *caedo*, i.e. cut in on both sides.

The *Salii* were divided into two colleges, each consisting of
12 members. The *Salii Palatini* owed their institution, as it was said,
to Numa, while the younger *Salii Collini* were created by Tullus Hostilius.
The *Salii* were to the last chosen from patricians only.

penetralia] No doubt the reference is to the Temple of Vesta and

and the Vestal Virgins, who were necessarily patrician maidens and whose purity was regarded as of supreme importance. But there is also a more particular allusion to the *penetralia* or shrine within the *atrium* of the Vestals, in which were stored the most holy pledges of Rome's existence, among them the *Palladium*: cf. 5. 52. 7. None might enter here except the Pontifices and the Vestals, whereas the Temple of Vesta with the perpetual fire was accessible to the general public. See especially Lanciani, *Ancient Rome in the light of recent discoveries*, pp. 134 ff.

16   § **10.** **auspicato**] Cf. § 6, above.

18   **patres auctores**] The precise meaning of *patrum auctoritas* has been the subject of much dispute. The most probable view is that it was the final act of sanction given by the patrician members of the Senate to laws and elections made in the *comitia*; cf. c. 42. 10: *patricii se auctores futuros negabant*. In connection with this chapter may be quoted a passage from (Cicero) *de domo sua* 14. 38 (cf. Seeley, *Livy* I³, Introd. p. 63); it describes the effect of the disappearance of the patriciate: *ita populus Romanus brevi tempore neque regem sacrorum, neque flamines, nec salios habebit, nec ex parte dimidia reliquos sacerdotes, neque auctores centuriatorum et curiatorum comitiorum; auspiciaque populi Romani, si magistratus patricii creati non sint, intereant necesse est, cum interrex nullus sit, quod et ipsum patricium esse et a patriciis prodi necesse est.* It almost looks as though Livy had had this passage before him, when writing the present chapter.

25   § **12.** **faxitis**]=*feceritis*; cf. c. 35. 9 n.

CHAPTER XLII.

28   § **2.** **decemviris sacrorum**]=*dec. sacris faciundis*; cf. c. 5. 8 and c. 37. 12 nn.

ex parte] Half from the patricians and half from the *plebs*, as is explained in the next sentence.

p. **59.**   8.   § **4.** **Velitrarum obsidionem**] For this siege and its issue, see c. 36. 5 n.

10   **belli Gallici**] Cf. Plut. *Cam.* cc. 40, 41. The most interesting feature of Plutarch's account is the alteration in the Roman equipment, said to have been introduced by Camillus at this time to repel the onslaught of the Gauls. The latter were chiefly formidable on account of the terrible blows which they inflicted with their long swords. To meet this danger, Camillus made the Roman soldiers wear smooth

helmets of iron (ἐχαλκεύσατο μὲν κράνη τοῖς πλείστοις ὁλοσίδηρα καὶ λεῖα ταῖς περιφερείαις, ὡς ἀπολισθαίνειν ἢ κατάγνυσθαι τὰς μαχαίρας), and carry brazen shields, and taught them to use the *pilum* as a weapon of defence, as well as of offence (αὐτοὺς δὲ τοὺς στρατιώτας ἐδίδαξε τοῖς ὑσσοῖς μακροῖς διὰ χειρὸς χρῆσθαι καὶ τοῖς ξίφεσι τῶν πολεμίων ὑποβάλλοντας ἐκδέχεσθαι τὰς καταφοράς).

13 § 5. Claudius] Q. Claudius Quadrigarius, an annalist of the Sullan age. He recorded the history of Rome from the capture of the city by the Gauls to his own times. Livy always calls this annalist Claudius simply, but there is no reason to doubt his identity with the Q. Claudius Quadrigarius mentioned by Velleius Paterculus and Aulus Gellius. Claudius, who appears to have been rather more trustworthy than the majority of the later annalists, is largely used by Livy in the 4th decade.

14 in ponte pugnam] Cf. vii. 9 and 10; under the year 361 B.C. Livy there relates the battle between the Romans and Gauls on the river Anio. Little reliance can be placed on the historical accuracy of these fights with the Gauls. It is highly probable that in the present instance the victory of M. Furius Camillus is simply taken from the later victory of L. Furius Camillus in 349 B.C. See vii. 26.

17 § 6. decem haud minus post annos] A careless statement in view of Livy's own account in vii. 9. With this use of *minus*, inserted as it were parenthetically without affecting the constr. of the sentence, cf. that of *plus* and *amplius*, e.g. *amplius duo milia,* 'two miles and more.'

18 in Albano agro] See map.

22 § 8. palati alii...tutati sunt], 'the rest (*alii=ceteri*, as often) roamed about, the majority making for Apulia, and protected themselves from their enemy both (*cum*) by their distant flight and also (*tum*) by their wide dispersion, which fear and panic alike had produced.'

24 terrorque] See Appendix.

25 consensu patrum plebisque] This does not give the strict constitutional practice with regard to the granting of a triumph. Livy wishes to depict the unanimity with which Camillus' triumph was welcomed. The granting of a triumph lay with the Senate alone, and in 7. 17. 9 we find that a triumph *populi iussu* was regarded as unconstitutional. See also 3. 63. 9.

28 § 9. dictator senatusque victus] The dictator did not interfere as in c. 38. 6 ff. The senate authorised the election of consuls instead of consular tribunes; unless, indeed, *senatus* is used loosely for *patres,*

and the meaning is that the *patrum auctoritas* made the resolutions law.

30 **adversa nobilitate**] 'in the face of patrician opposition.'

32 **§ 10. patricii**] The consent of the patrician portion of the senate was required for the confirmation of elections as well as for laws passed in the *Comitia*. For the phrase *patricii auctores* instead of *patres auctores*, see c. 41. 10 n.

p. 60. 2. **§ 11. tandem**] See Appendix.

4 **praetore**] Later known as the *praetor urbanus* in contrast to the *praetor peregrinus*. The full significance of this concession on the part of the *plebs* can only be grasped by remembering that *praetores* was the early name of the highest magistrates of the state; cf. 3. 55. 12, and Cic. *Leg.* 3. 3. 8 : *regio imperio duo sunto ; iique praeeundo, iudicando, consulendo, praetores, iudices, consules appellamino* (so MSS. ; some edd. *appellantor*). Now that the sacred consulship had been thrown open to the *plebs*, the patricians wished to retain for themselves an office which would at once deprive the consulship of a part of its powers and soothe their wounded vanity by its name ; cf. 7. 1. 6. But there was also a more practical reason for the creation of the new magistracy. The consuls now had their time so fully occupied with the conduct of military affairs, that it was impossible that they could adequately superintend the administration of justice. The praetorship was thrown open to the plebeians in 337 B.C. Cf. Greenidge, *Roman Public Life*, pp. 120 ff.

6 **§ 12. concordiam**] Plutarch (*Cam.* 42) records the vowing of a temple to Concord by Camillus on this occasion, and its confirmation by the people : συνελθόντες ἐψηφίσαντο τῆς μὲν Ὁμονοίας ἱερόν, ὥσπερ εὔξατο Κάμιλλος, εἰς τὴν ἀγορὰν καὶ τὴν ἐκκλησίαν ἄποπτον ἐπὶ τοῖς γεγενημένοις ἱδρύσασθαι. This was the temple facing the Forum below the *Mons Capitolinus*. See map.

7 **merito...deum immortalium fore**] 'would be in accordance with the merit of the immortal gods'; cf. Cic. *ad Att.* 5. 11. 6 : *et hercule merito tuo feci*, 'I acted in accordance with your desert.' Weiss. quotes 28. 9. 8 : *se...decernere patres merito deorum primum, dein, secundum deos, consulum responderunt*. See Appendix.

si quando unquam alias] The redundancy of the phrase is noteworthy. This characteristic of Livy makes it necessary to employ caution in bracketing seemingly unnecessary words.

8 **ut...adiiceretur**] Depends at once on *dignam* and *id*, being explanatory of both : 'that the occasion was worthy (of the celebration)

and that it would be in accordance with the merit of the immortal gods that *ludi maximi* should take place,' etc.

ludi maximi] These were the games which became known as the *ludi Romani*. Their foundation is attributed by Livy to Tarquinius Priscus, in celebration of a victory over the Latins; cf. 1. 35. 10: *sollemnes deinde annui mansere ludi, Romani magnique varie appellati.* Prof. Mommsen, however, has shown (*Röm. Forsch.* 2. pp. 42 ff.) that in all probability the games were originally held merely from time to time as the result of vows made by successful generals (*ludi votivi*, cf., e.g., 4. 27. 1), and that subsequently, very possibly on the present occasion, they became the annual *ludi Romani*, which by Cicero's time lasted from the 5th to the 19th of September. These games were closely bound up with the worship of Jupiter, the central point of the festival being formed by the *epulum Iovis* on the 13th (the ides). September was the natural month for celebrating successes gained in war, for, as a rule, it marked the close of the summer campaigns. Cf. Warde Fowler, *The Roman Festivals*, pp. 215 ff.

9 **§ 13. recusantibus**] This explanation of the origin of the curule aedileship can scarcely be correct, since the cost of the games would at this time be practically covered by the state allowance, extravagant expenditure on the part of the aediles being characteristic of later Republican times only. The patricians seem to have seized the opportunity of gaining two more magistracies for themselves in return for the plebeian consulship.

12 **ut**] To be taken closely with *id*: 'they would gladly become aediles for the sake of honouring the immortal gods.' Weiss. takes *id* as referring to *munus* and *ut* as = ' on condition that.'

13 **§ 14. senatus consultum**] Livy's language might lead us to suppose that the curule aedileship was founded by decree of the senate; this is unlikely. Probably a resolution of the people was passed creating the magistracy, and then the senate directed the dictator to hold the elections.

14 **dictator populum rogaret**] i.e. he held the elections in his capacity of supreme magistrate. The Curule Aediles were elected by the *Comitia Tributa*. The next year (cf. 7. 1. 6) it was agreed that they should be chosen from patricians and plebeians in alternate years, and this custom continued for a considerable time. The work of the new aediles was much the same as that of the plebeian aediles; besides the *cura ludorum*, they had charge of the police of the city and of the corn supply.

APPENDIX ON THE TEXT OF BOOK VI.

All the existing MSS. of the first decade of Livy are, with one exception, founded on a recension of the text made by one Victorianus towards the end of the fourth century. In this recension the sixth book, together with the seventh and eighth, was revised by Nicomachus Flavianus; the third, fourth, and fifth books were allotted to his son Nicomachus Dexter. Of the MSS. the most important are the Medicean (M) in Florence, of the eleventh century, and the Parisian (P), of the tenth century. Besides these there exists a much earlier MS., the codex Veronensis of the fourth century. It contains the greater part of the third, fourth, and fifth books, and parts of the early chapters of the sixth, viz. of cc. 1. 3 to 4. 9 and cc. 6. 4 to 7. 1. The opinion of Prof. Mommsen, who published this MS. in the Commentationes of the Berlin Academy of 1868, is that it goes back to an archetype anterior to the Nicomachean recension; hence its importance. The MS. (known as V) is, however, inferior as a whole to the Nicomachean archetype, though it has, as will be seen, in some cases preserved the true reading.

> M = Codex Mediceus.
> P = Codex Parisiensis.
> V = Codex Veronensis.

Mdg. = Madvig, *Emendationes Livianae* (Ed. 2).

Weiss. = W. Weissenborn's annotated edition of Livy (5th ed.), revised by H. J. Müller (H. J. M.).

Ltb. = F. Luterbacher's ed. of Livy, Book VI.

Zingerle = A. Zingerle's edition of the text, 1890.

C. 1 § 6. **legatus**] Bracketed by Cobet.

§ 8. After *Camillus* the MSS. read *iterum*. This was removed by Baumgarten-Crusius. Weiss. remarks that it is not usual to insert the number of times a man has held the office of *interrex*. Ltb. reads *proditus,* comparing, among other passages, 4. 43. 9: *postremo L. Papirius Mugilanus proditus interrex. Iterum,* as Weiss. says, probably came in from the following line.

§ 11. **rei nulli**] The reading of P, adopted by Mdg. VM read *rei nullius,* which Weiss. followed, interpreting thus: *rei nullius agendae* is explanatory of *insignem,* 'they made the day distinct, i.e. a day of doing nothing.' H. J. M. and Ltb. adopt Freudenberg's conj. *religione rei ullius,* 'they distinguished the day by religious scruple against doing anything.' Ltb., however, (after T. Faber) suggests that *re nulla... agenda* may be the true reading.

2 § 3. **defectionis**] From V, which has *adedefectionis.* The other MSS. (according to H. J. M.) read *defectioni.* Ltb. and Zingerle, however, say they read *defectione,* and adopt this in their text.

§ 8. **Mecium**] VP. M *mestium.* Another MS. *metium.*

§ 11. **militibus munitum**] Supplied by V only, and generally adopted by edd. It might, however, very well be a scribe's insertion to bring out the point of the sentence more clearly.

3 § 5. **ante moenia, patentes portas**] Ltb. reads *ante patentes portas* after V.

§ 7. **portas**] Mdg. would omit the second *portas.*

4 § 8. **relinquerent**] The MSS.; except V, which has *relinqueretur.* The latter reading is adopted by H. J. M., Ltb., and Zingerle.

5 § 3. **habuerint**] Mdg. MSS. *habuerunt.*

§ 5. **moverunt**] Mdg. M¹ *moverent,* M² *moverant,* P *moverat.*

eodem] MSS. Ascensius, followed by H. J. M., would read *eandem.* Ltb. after Wesenberg omits *eodem.* Can *tempore* have fallen out?

6 § 5. **voluntarios**] Bracketed by Mdg. as a gloss.

§ 7. **in animo**] MSS.; except V, which has *id animo.* Wölfflin *animo.*

§ 8. **dictatorem**] MSS. Bracketed by Mdg. Weiss. suggested *imperatorem.*

honorato] V. Other MSS. *honoratum.* Aldus *honoratorum.*

§ 13. **ad urbem**] V. Other MSS. *in urbe.*

§ 14. **alia belli**] V. P *belli alia,* M *belli atia.*

§ 16. **in partem**] V. Other MSS. *in partes,* which might be right.

7 § 2. **restitantes**] Gronovius. MSS. *resistentes,* which is by no means impossible.

§ 4. **et Aequis**] MSS. Heusinger, followed by Ltb., *ex Aequis.* It is true that the reading of the MSS. would, taken strictly, imply that the victory had been gained over a united force of Volscians and Aequians.

But Livy was so accustomed to the collocation *Volsci et Aequi*, that he probably wrote it down here without thinking.

8　§ 7. **fugam impediebat**] Edd. generally for *fuga impediebat* of the best MSS. Some MSS. have *fuga impediebatur*, which might be the true reading.

9　§ 6. **in Volscos**] A. Perizonius. MSS. *in Volscis*.

§ 9. **tanta**] MSS.; except M which has *montana*. Heerwagen *non tam a*, adopted by Weiss., Ltb., and Zingerle.

10　§ 8. **iis**] Wesenberg. MSS. *his*. Livy sometimes retains *hic* in or. obliqua, but in the present instance *his* would be especially awkward, coming as it does immediately after *eos*.

11　§ 3. **esse**] Mdg. omits *esse* and reads *apud exercitus tantum...*

§ 7. **primus**] T. Faber. MSS. *primum*.

12　§ 8. **vatesque**] The reading of the inferior MSS. The better MSS. have *vatesve*, which Weiss. retained, comparing c. 14. 10 : *iudicatum addictumve*.

§ 10. **tene ; at**] Wesenberg. MSS. *teneas*, which Weiss. retained, comparing 3. 48. 4 : *ignosce...sinas*.

pavore] MSS. Mdg. *labore* on slight MS. authority.

13　§ 7. **hominum**] MSS. Siesbye *omnium*, which, as Ltb. says, gives no intelligible constr. Wesenberg suggested *nec hominum solum*. *nec omnes* would give a good sense, but would leave the origin of the corruption unexplained.

14　§ 2. **intuenti**] Gronovius. MSS. *intuenda*, which might after all be right.

§ 9. **commodioris**] Aldus. MSS. *commotiores*, which Weiss. thought might bear an active meaning 'more violent.' Wesenberg *accommodatioris*.

15　§ 9. **afluit**] For the existence of this form, see Dombart in *Neue Jahrbücher für Philologie*, 1877, pp. 341 ff. No other example of the meaning 'to flow away from' is adduced from classical Latinity ; cf. Gellius 5. 16. 3 : *Epicurus autem afluere semper ex omnibus corporibus simulacra quaedam corporum ipsorum...putat*. For the meaning 'to be present in abundance,' several examples are cited, though there is usually a discrepancy between the MSS. Cf. Livy 3. 26. 7 : *neque honori magno locum neque virtuti putant esse, nisi ubi effusae afluant opes* (so M. P¹ has *afluent*, other MSS. *affluent*) ; also 23. 4. 4 : *afluenti copia voluptatium*. See Fügner, *Lex. Liv.*, *s.v.*

§ 10. **reliquam**] Mdg. MSS. *aliquam*. Of other conjectures Huschke's *at aequam* and Morstadt's *antiquam* may be mentioned.

17   § 3.   **populares suos**] MSS. Mdg. bracketed *populares*, Duker *suos*. The former is more likely to have been a gloss. Kraffert *viros* for *suos* (so H. J. M. and Zingerle). Weiss. *patronos*, and Ltb. *patronos suos*.

§ 5.   **Capitolino**] MSS. Bracketed by Kiehl. Mdg.'s later conjecture *Capitolini* is not improbable in view of such passages as 7. 4. 3 and 7. 32. 15. It is adopted by Zingerle.

§ 6.   **quod**] Mdg. after Doujat. MSS. *id quod*. H. J. M. *eo quod*.

18   § 1.   **sub exitum**] Mdg.; MSS. *sub exitu*.

§ 3.   **iam**] Gronovius. M *iam in*, other MSS. *in*. H. J. M. thinks *in propinquum* arose from *in propinquo* a gloss on *aderat*.

§ 6.   **quot enim**] MSS.; Mdg. *quoteni* (cf. Cic. *ad Att.* 12. 33).

§ 12.   **[et]iam**] Gronovius. MSS. *etiam*.

19   § 4.   **et ei**] Mdg. after Stroth (Cic. *de fin.* Excursus I); MSS. *et*, which A. Perizonius removed as corrupt.

20   § 8.   **produxit**] MSS. Bracketed by Mdg. Ltb. adopts Rhenanus' conjecture *produxisse*, and alters *nominatum* into *nominavisse*; he further changes *inter quos* into *interque eos*. This gives a good sense, but fails to account for the corruption. Zing. follows Ltb., but keeps *nominatum*.

nominatim] Mdg. for *nominatum* of MSS.; Mommsen, *Röm. Forsch.* 2. pp. 185, 186 n., thinks that if Mdg.'s reading is adopted, *absentem*, which is pointless, must be struck out as well as *produxit*.

22   § 1.   **tribunis**] Several Edd. bracket this word after Muret.

23   § 5.   **rapere**] So the better MSS. *Capere*, the reading of the inferior MSS., is adopted by Ltb. and Zingerle, and recommended by H. J. M.

§ 6.   **instruendis**] Gronovius. MSS. *instruentem*.

§ 11.   **eam**] T. Faber. MSS. *etiam*.

24   § 10.   **fluctuante acie**] Heerwagen. MSS. *fluctuantem aciem*, except M[1], which has *fluctuantem acie*. Mdg. suggested (*non*) *in fluctuantem aciem* **trudi** *equos*. Would not **trahi** be less of a change and give a better sense? Possibly *ex fluctuante acie extrahi* might be right, the corruption having arisen from the alteration of *trahi* into *tradi*.

25   § 7.   **itineri**] So Edd. generally for *itineris* of the MSS., which is, however, possible.

27   § 3.   **invidiosius**] Mdg.; MSS. *invidiae eius*. Duker *invidiose*.

§ 10.   **in**] Wanting in MSS.; inserted by Stroth.

28   § 1.   **certum**] MSS. Kraffert suggested *creatum*, which is adopted, yet hesitatingly, by H. J. M.

§ 2.   **acto**] So inferior MSS. Better MSS. *facto*.

29   § 4.   **dissipati**] MSS.; Mdg. reads *dissipata*, comparing 28. 20.

8 and 29. 33. 6. In both these cases and also in 38. 27. 8 the order is *ex dissipata…fuga.* Judging from the last passage, Ltb. thinks that some such word as *congregati* may have fallen out here.

31 § 4. **debellatum]** Morstadt. MSS. *bellatum.*

diceret] MSS.; Mdg. reads *diceretur*, but see note. Ltb. adds that, if *diceretur* were the true reading, we should expect *neve*, not *aut.*

§ 5. **in]** Mdg.; wanting in MSS.

32 § 6. **certam]** Mdg.; MSS. *claram.* The latter might, after all, be right.

33 § 9. **Tusculi]** Mdg. brackets the first *Tusculi*, but this does not seem necessary.

34 § 1. **tantum]** Mdg., who compares c. 38. 5. MSS. *tanto.*

35 § 4. **pensionibus]** Cuiacius. MSS. *portionibus.*

§ 9. **qua]** So better MSS. Inferior MSS. *quam*, which many adopt, translating ' which you hear our colleagues chanting in accord.'

36 § 8. **animi, vocibus alienis]** After MP, which have *vocalienis.* Other MSS. *vocum alienis* and *vocem alienis.* Mdg. reads *animis a voce alienis.*

37 § 2. **plebes fecisset]** So inferior MSS. M *plebi fecissent*, which Harant would read.

§ 6. **quid]** Doujat. MSS. *qui.*

octona loca] For the question as to the number of the consular tribunes, cf. Greenidge, *Roman Public Life*, p. 112 n. It should be mentioned that a fragment of the *fasti consulares* recently found gives the names of *nine* consular tribunes for the year 380 B.C., under which year Livy (c. 27) gives six and Diodorus eight names (15. 50). See Mommsen in *Hermes* 1903, pp. 116 ff., where it is shown that the nine names are probably due to the blending together of various sources.

38 § 1. **qui]** So inferior MSS. MP *quia*, which might be right.

§ 3. **ad civem]** MSS. Mdg. brackets *ad.* H. J. M. takes *ad* from before *civem* and places it before *summum imperium*, while Ltb. inserts an additional *ad* before the latter words.

40 § 11. **non…licebit, ut]** Mdg.; MSS. ' *non* ' inquit ' *licebit; tu…*'. The latter might be right: ' you will not be allowed to do so,' says he ; ' you would pass the bills…and this portent would not take place.'

§ 17. **consule]** Mdg.; MSS. *consulem*, which would make *haud pro dubio* an adverbial expression.

41 § 3. **erit]** Wesenberg. MSS. *sit.*

§ 4. **etenim]** MSS.; Mdg. *at enim.*

§ 6. **privati]** Crévier. MSS. *privatim.*

§ 8. **esse...pascantur**] Mdg.; MSS. *est...pascentur.* Mdg. ob-
serves that, putting aside the awkwardness of the direct speech, we
should expect *erit*, not *est*, and that the use of the fut. and fut. perf. is
unintelligible, for the remark is a general one, and has no special
reference to the future.

nostri] Mdg.; MSS. *vestri*, which is not impossible.

42 § 8. **terrorque**] MSS. Harant *errorque*; Zingerle adopts this.

sese] Bracketed after Crévier. Others bracket *se* after *fuga.*

§ 11. **tandem**] A. Perizonius. But the *tamen* of the MSS. gives
fair sense.

§ 12. **immortalium**] After this word the MSS. have *causa libenter
facturos,* which Mdg. removed; the words were clearly interpolated
from § 13.

EDITIONS AND EDITORS.

The following is a list of the more important editions of Livy[1]; the date, the editor's name, and the place of publication are given. Editions of special note are marked thus*.

1469. Editio Princeps (without Bks. 33 and 41—45), *cura* Jo. Aleriensis. Rome.

1518. Asulanus (Aldine Edition). Venice.

1518. Preface by Hutten and D. Erasmus. Mainz.

1531. S. Grynaeus. Basel.

1535. B. Rhenanus and S. Gelenius. Basel*.

1555. C. Sigonius. Venice.

1608 and 1628. J. Gruter. Frankfurt-am-Main.

1645 and 1665. J. F. Gronovius. Leyden*.

1679—82. J. Doujatius. Paris.

1738—46. A. Drakenborch (*cum notis* C. A. Dukeri *et variorum*). Leyden and Amsterdam*.

1823—27. J. Th. Kreyssig. Leipzig.

1841—46. (Up to Book 23 only.) C. F. S. Alschefski. Berlin.

1853 ff. W. Weissenborn. Berlin*. (Subsequently revised by H. J. Müller.)

1857—64. (Text only.) M. Hertz. Leipzig.

1861—65. (Text only.) J. N. Madvig and J. L. Ussing. Copenhagen. Second Edn of Vols. I. and II., 1872—75.

A brief account of certain scholars who have contributed to the emendation of the text or to the interpretation of the language of Livy

---

[1] In preparing this list of editions and scholars I have derived my information chiefly from Emil Hübner's *Grundriss zu Vorlesungen über die Römische Litteraturgeschichte*, W. Pökel's *Philologisches Schriftsteller-Lexikon*, and various articles in the *Encyclopaedia Britannica*.

may perhaps be of interest. The list is of course by no means a complete one, but will be found to contain the names of a large number of the scholars mentioned in the above Appendix on the Text.

ASCENSIUS (1462—1535). So called from his birth-place, Asche near Brussels; his real name was Badius. Printer and scholar. Edition of Livy, 1513, Paris.

BAUMGARTEN-CRUSIUS, D. C. W. (1786—1845). Born at Dresden. Edition of Livy, 1825—26.

COBET, C. G. (1813—1889). Born at Paris and educated in Holland. Professor at Leyden, 1846. His critical notes and emendations are collected under the titles *Novae Lectiones, Variae Lectiones, Miscellanea Critica,* and *Collectanea Critica.*

CRÉVIER, J. B. L. (1693—1765). Born at Paris. Professor of Rhetoric at the College of Beauvais. Published two editions of Livy with notes.

CUIACIUS, Jacques (1522—1590). He is generally called by the Latinized form of his name Cujas. Born at Toulouse. Professor of Law at Bourges and other places. Chiefly worked at Roman Law, but his emendations, published under the title *Observationes et emendationes,* extend to many of the Greek and Latin Classics.

DRAKENBORCH, Arnold von (1684—1748). Born at Utrecht, at which place he held a Professorship from 1716. His edition of Livy with life of the historian is of very great importance.

DUKER, C. A. (1670—1752). Born at Unna in Westphalia. Professor at Utrecht. His notes to Livy, published in 1738, are incorporated in Drakenborch's edition.

FABER, T. (1615—1672). Born at Caen. Master at Saumur.

GRONOVIUS, J. F. (1611—1671). Born at Hamburg. Appointed Professor of Rhetoric and History at Deventer in 1643 and in 1658 to the Greek Chair at Leyden. His important edition of Livy appeared in 1645.

GRONOVIUS, Jakob (1645—1716). Son of the above. Professor at Leyden and Pisa. Made additions to his father's edition of Livy.

HEERWAGEN, H. W. Born at Bayreuth 1811. Worked at Nürnberg. Died 1888.

HEUSINGER, Conrad (1752—1820). Born at Wolfenbüttel. Author of an important translation of Livy with critical and explanatory notes, Braunschweig, 1821.

KIEHL, E. J. (1827—1873). Born at the Hague. Professor at Deventer, 1855.

MADVIG, J. N. (1804—1886). Born at Bornholm. Appointed Professor of Latin at Copenhagen 1829. Subsequently Minister of Education, Director of Public Instruction, and President of the Danish Parliament. His *Emendationes Livianae* appeared in 1860 (2nd edn 1877). Published an edition of the text of Livy in conjunction with Ussing.

MORSTADT, R. A. Born at Carlsruhe in 1803. Worked at Schaffhausen.

MURETUS (Muret), M. A. (1526—1585). Born at Muret near Limoges. Lectured first at Paris, but settled at Rome in 1559.

PERIZONIUS, J. (1652—1715). His real name was Voorbroek. Professor at Leyden. His notes on Livy were incorporated by Drakenborch in his edition.

STROTH, F. A. (1750—1785). An edition of Livy by F. A. Stroth and F. W. Döring was published in 7 vols., 1796—1813.

WEISSENBORN, W. (1803—1878). Professor at Eisenach. For his edition of Livy, see above.

WESENBERG, A. S. (Born 1804.) Professor at Viborg. Published a number of emendations of the Latin Classics, and a text of Cicero's letters.

164

INDEX I.

ENGLISH.

[The references are to the notes. The numbers indicate the chapter and section.]

Ablative, absolute with clause as subject **25** 5
  of attendant circumstance **24** 3
  instrumental **12** 1, **29** 5
  local **32** 10
  of participle ending in *-i* **14** 13
  of price **13** 7
  of quality **2** 3
Abstract nouns personified **3** 8, **6** 11, **31** 3, **32** 10
Accent, shifting of **16** 2, **28** 2
Accusative, after passive verb **32** 7
  expressing extent of verb's action **15** 13
Adjectives, neuter used as substantives **6** 18, **23** 3, **40** 12; with genitive depending **31** 7, **32** 5, 11
Adverbs, used for adjectives **4** 1, **24** 7, **39** 6
Aedileship, curule **42** 13, 14
Alliteration **3** 4, **14** 8, **22** 7
Allotment of land, **16** 6, **36** 11, *Introd.* pp. xxiii, xxiv
Apodosis suppressed **21** 7
Apposition **3** 2, **21** 2
  partitive **24** 11, **34** 5
Archaeology, Livy's attitude towards **1** 2, *Introd.* p. x
Archaisms **5** 7, **35** 9, **40** 5, **41** 8
Armour, change of introduced by Camillus **42** 4
Asyndeton **39** 2, 10

Augury, methods of **41** 8
Authorities, Livy's use of **12** 2, **20** 12, *Introd.* pp. ix ff.

Beards, wearing of **16** 4
Booty, disposal of **13** 6
Buildings at Rome **4** 12
Burial at Rome **36** 11

Candour of Livy **18** 16, *Introd.* p. xii
Capitoline temple of Jupiter **4** 3, **29** 9
  triad of deities **16** 2
Carelessness of style **6** 2, **28** 6, **30** 8
Censor and debt **27** 3, **31** 2
  proceedings at death of **27** 4
Census **31** 2
Change of constr., sudden:
  Active to passive **24** 10
  Subject of sentence **22** 6, **31** 4, **40** 3
  Tenses in or. obliqua **39** 11
Characters, parallel **23** 1
Clan, decrees passed by **20** 14
Claudii, political attitude of **40** 2
Claudius (the annalist) **42** 5
Clients **18** 6
Coinage, early Roman **38** 9
Commissioners, extraordinary **21** 4
Concord, temple of **42** 12
Consular *imperium* **23** 10

Consulship, its importance to plebeians 37 11

Contrast, by asyndeton 39 2, 10

Criticism, Livy's methods of 12 2, 20 5, *Introd.* pp. xi f.

Dative, of interest 14 2, 13
predicative 6 14, 9 3, 16 5, 25 3, 34 6
of purpose (gerundival) 21 2

Debt, repudiation of 18 14, 35 4
richer plebeians and 37 1
Roman law of 11 8

Decemvirate 1 1

Declaration of war 14 1, 21 3, 22 4, 25 5

Deities, public and private 14 8
Roman mode of addressing 16 2

Dictatorship, duration of 1 4, 29 10
in Latin towns 26 4
limitations of 38 9
mode of appointment to 2 5, 6 8, 28 3

Fulness of expression 1 6, 6 5, 16 2, 42 12, *Introd.* p. xv

Future, interchanged with fut. perf. 19 7

Future perfect = fut. simple 26 2, 29 1

Genitive, of definition 2 1, 14 9, 19 5
partitive 27 8
of penalty 14 3
possessive 10 1, 3, 14 9
of quality (or description) 8 10, 11 7, 22 7

Genitives, accumulation of 27 10

Gerund, modal 20 8, 23 4, 24 8

Gerundive for supine 37 11

Graecisms 22 9

Hendiadys 9 4

Hypallage 16 1

Inaccuracies (anachronisms) 16 4, 19 3
(confusion of names) 29 8

(constitutional points) 20 5, 11, 21 5, 37 6, 42 14
(slips) 6 12, 9 5

Infinitive, in rhetorical questions in or. obliqua 23 7

Inscription, archaic from Forum 1 10

Juno Moneta, temple of 20 13

Jupiter (Capitolinus), image of 17 4
(Imperator) 29 8

Legion, divisions of 7 3
number of men in 22 8

Licinio-Sextian laws c. 35, *Introd.* pp. xxviii ff.

Magistracies, collegiate character of 11 3
curule 37 8
date of entry upon 1 9
extraordinary 5 8, 21 4

Military reforms (by Camillus) 42 4

Mint 20 13

Moral earnestness of Livy 16 3, 20 5, 34 7, *Introd.* p. xiii

Negatives, strengthened by one another 16 3, 23 9, 40 7

Obscurity (of writing) 10 9, 26 7, 41 1

Oratio obliqua (virtual), 11 8

Order of words, unusual 7 3, 25 9, 40 19

Participle, *Future*, expressing intention 22 9
Past, of deponents with pass. meaning 29 4, with substantive = subst. with dependent gen. 1 1, 2 9, 24 2
Present, used as substantive 2 13, 9 11, 13 3, 25 9

Passive, with middle meaning 35 2

Patriotic colouring 22 3

Patron and client 18 14

Phrase in place of adj. 34 11

Plebeian magistrates (no right to take auspices) **41** 5

Plebs, origin of **18** 6

Pluperfect, expressing sudden action **34** 2, **38** 9

Plural used for singular **8** 7

Poetical words and phrases **7** 3, **24** 11, **38** 7, 8, **39** 7, **40** 1, *Introd.* pp. xvi f.

Praetorship, creation of **42** 11

Prepositions, inserted before names of towns etc. **3** 5, **9** 3, **27** 7

variation of **9** 11

Present, used vividly for fut. **15** 5

Prolepsis **12** 9, **16** 1, **34** 3

Proper name used as attribute **40** 10

Religion, Livy's attitude towards **12** 9, *Introd.* p. xiv

Removal to Rome of conquered deities **29** 8

Repetition of wars **32** 11, *Introd.* pp. xix f.

Rhetoric, Livy's fondness for **17** 4, **33** 1, *Introd.* pp. xv f.

Rhetorical questions **17** 5, **23** 7, **39** 10

Senate, magistrate escorted by **15** 1

Sense, construction according to **3** 2, **24** 2, **30** 9

Sibylline Books **5** 8

Silver Latinity *Introd.* p. xiv

Singular, used in collective sense **2** 12, **12** 9, **31** 7

Slave-gangs **12** 5

Solon and debt **35** 4

Speeches, Livy's use of **26** 8, c. **40**, *Introd.* pp. xxviii, xxix

Statues of Kings on Capitol **41** 3

Stoicism, Livy and **9** 3, **12** 11, **21** 2

Subjunctive, after *potius quam* **15** 12

expressing frequency of action **8** 6, **9** 4, **25** 9

illogically used **2** 9

in questions in or. obliqua **17** 5

jussive **15** 10, **18** 9

potential **12** 6

Substantives = attributes in sense **2** 12, **40** 10

Tables, Twelve **1** 10

Tablets, votive **29** 9

Tenses, Livy's use of in or. obliqua **39** 11

Title of Livy's history **1** 1

Treaties, deities concerned with **29** 2

religious ceremonies accompanying **1** 10

Tribes **5** 8

Tribunes, consular **1** 1, **39** 4

number of **37** 6

their entry upon office **1** 9 (cf. **38** 1)

Tribunes, plebeian

authority originally negative **18** 13

powers of prosecution **19** 7

,, of punishing **20** 12

relations to dictator **16** 3

Triumph **16** 5, **42** 8

Tyranny **18** 3

Variety of expression **9** 11, **11** 5, **17** 7, **19** 7, **25** 4, **27** 8, **33** 9, **36** 11, **37** 6, **40** 9, 19

of tense **15** 6, **38** 7

Vesta, worship of **41** 9

Veto, correctness of term **35** 9

mode of employment **35** 7

unconstitutional disregard of **38** 5

Virgil, imitations of **12** 10, **30** 5, *Introd.* pp. xvi, xvii

Volscian war, duration of **2** 13

Wall, building of **32** 1

Warning voices **33** 5

Zeugma **18** 16, **25** 9

INDEX II.

LATIN.

ab, expressing motive **2** 9, **3** 8, **4** 8
  ,,   source **10** 8
abdicare magistratum **39** 1
ablegatio **39** 7
abominari **18** 9
ac (repeated with different meaning) **28** 6
accipi **37** 12
ad (with name of town) **3** 5
  =*apud* **9** 2
  =in addition to **11** 6, **20** 7
addictus **11** 8, **14** 10
adeo **17** 5
adhaerere **10** 8
adminiculum **1** 4
advocatus **19** 7
affinitas **34** 5
affluere **15** 9 (with Appendix)
agere agmen **28** 2
    cum aliquo **9** 5
agger **2** 9, **8** 9
Albanus ager **42** 6
albogalerus **41** 9
alii (=*ceteri*) **11** 3, **25** 1
Allia **1** 11
an **7** 5, **36** 12, **37** 5
anceps **9** 10
ancilia **41** 9
annus (=magisterial year) **1** 4, **38** 1
anquirere **20** 12
ante signa **7** 3
antesignani **8** 3
antiquare **35** 8
Antium **6** 4
apex **41** 9
apud (=*penes*) **11** 5
Arniensis tribus **5** 8
Arx **20** 9
at enim **15** 11
atqui **37** 2
auctoritas patrum **19** 4, **41** 10
augures **41** 9

augurium **41** 8
aura (=popularity) **11** 7
ausim **40** 5
auspicato **12** 7
auspicia **2** 5, **11** 3, **41** 4
auspicia renovare **5** 6
auxilium **18** 10, **37** 4, **38** 6
avertere **14** 11

bene habet **35** 8

Campus Martius **20** 10
Capena porta **22** 8
capitalis poena **4** 5
Capitolinus **5** 6, **17** 5
Capitolium **4** 3, 12, **20** 9
captus animi **36** 8
carpere (=to harass) **32** 11
Sp. *Cassius* **17** 2
causarii **6** 14
cedere in **14** 12
cellae (of Capitoline temple) **4** 3, **29** 9
centuriare **2** 6
certamen animi **24** 10
certus dux **28** 1
Circeii **12** 6
civitas (=full or half-citizenship?) **26** 8
App. *Claudius* (the decemvir) **20** 3
App. *Claudius Crassus* **40** 2
Q. *Claudius Quadrigarius* **42** 5, *Introd*. p. xi
cliens **18** 6, 14
coepi (constr. after) **6** 6
cognatus **20** 2
cognomen **4** 7, **5** 6
cohors **24** 2, **30** 4
Collina porta **28** 2
Comitia Centuriata **20** 10, **21** 5, **41** 10
    Curiata **41** 10
    Tributa **21** 5, **42** 14

Comitium 15 2
commentarii pontificum 1 2
comparatio 22 6, 30 3
concilium plebis 35 7, 38 3
    populi 20 11
concinere 35 9
confusus 6 7, 34 8
consenescere 39 6
conspectus (=conspicuous) 15 10
contio 5 1, 27 7
contra 15 5, 31 4
cooptare 38 4
cordi esse 9 3
corona civica 20 7
    muralis 20 7
corpus (=body of men) 34 5
creare 1 8
Cremera 1 11
cum interim 11 4, 27 6
cum ('inverted') 24 5
cunctator 23 5

decemviri sacris faciundis 37 12, 42 2
decurrere ad 19 3, 38 3
desinere (constr. after) 6 6
destinare in animo 6 7
dextrorsus 31 5
Dialis flamen 41 9
dictator (Latin) 26 4
diem dicere 1 6, 19 7
non dubito (constr. after) 12 2, 14 1, 20 5
dum (enclitic) 35 9
duumviri aedi dedicandae 5 8
    perduellionis 20 12
    sacris faciundis 5 8, 37 12

Ecetra 31 5
edoctus militiam 32 7
elevare 23 4, 27 3
elogium Introd. p. x
emittere signum 8 3
emovere 38 8
enim (used elliptically) 18 6
enimvero 14 12
enixus 24 11
Esquilina porta 22 8
et (emphatic) 11 9, 21 6

etiam (omitted) 7 1
ex (=in consequence of) 29 4
    (=instead of) 4 5, 23 5
    (=to the interest of) 22 6, 23 10
exactae aetatis 22 7
excipere (=to follow) 3 4, 21 1, 33 11
exigere 4 6
expensum ferre 20 6
experiens 34 4
expertus (in passive sense) 18 13
extra ordinem 22 6, 30 3

Fabius Pictor 12 2, *Introd.* p. xi
facies reorum 16 8
familia 40 6
fastigium 20 8, 38 13
faxitis 41 12
faxo 35 9
fenus 14 3
ferre (=to declare) 36 7
fides (=credit) 11 8, 15 5, 34 2
    (=proof) 13 7
flamines 41 9
Flumentana porta 20 11
foedus (sacred character of) 1 10, 29 2
forem virga percutere 34 6
fretus (with dative) 13 1, 31 6
frumentum 6 14
fui, fuerat, Livy's use of 3 8, 29 9
fulmen dictatorium 39 7

Gabii 21 9, 27 10
Gallicum aurum 14 11
gens (=a clan) 20 14
    (=a people) 12 4
gradus 12 8, 32 8
grassari in 5 4

haerere 12 10
hasta (at sale of property) 4 2
hastati 7 3, 8 3, 13 3
Hernici 2 3
hocine 17 3
honoratus 6 8

-*i* form of abl. of pres. part. 14 13

iactura **19** 2
igitur (position in sentence) **9** 5
imminere **9** 1
impotens **11** 6
in with acc. (=with a view to)
  39 2
in orbem **4** 10
in ordinem cogere **38** 12
in parte esse **15** 6, **37** 4
in ponte pugna **42** 5
incidere **39** 10
inclinare **8** 6
incubare **15** 5
inde...inde **30** 8
inexpertus **18** 4
infestus **5** 3
infitias ire **40** 4
ingruere **3** 1
insignis (constr. after) **1** 11
instruere (=to stock) **5** 5
inter (with gerundive) **11** 5
intercedere (=to go surety) **15** 9
intercessio **38** 6
interregnum **1** 5, **36** 3, **41** 6
itaque (position in sentence) **17**
  1
iudicatus **14** 3, 10
iugerum **16** 6
iuniores **2** 6
iurare in verba **2** 6, **22** 7
ius civile **17** 8
  gentium **1** 6, **17** 8
  imaginum **37** 11
iustitium **2** 6
iustus **13** 5, **31** 6

Labici **21** 9
Lanuvium **21** 2
Latini **2** 3
leges agrariae **5** 1, **11** 8
  regiae **1** 10
lex satura **39** 2, 11
libra et aere **14** 5
Licinius Macer **39** 3, *Introd.*
  p. xi
litare **1** 12
locare **32** 1
Lucumones **2** 2
ludi maximi or *Romani* **42** 12
ludus **25** 9

machinae **9** 2
Sp. Maelius **17** 2, **18** 4
magister equitum **39** 4
manubiae **13** 6
manus iniectio **14** 3
Martis aedes **5** 8
Mater Matuta **33** 4
Mecium, ad **2** 8
medius (=*mediocris*) **14** 13
mercatores **2** 2
minus (used parenthetically) **42** 6
missilia **13** 2
moderatio animi **25** 6
moles **2** 11, **14** 1, **19** 1
moliri **2** 14, **9** 4, **11** 8, **33** 11,
  34 5
Moneta **20** 13
movere (intransitive) **8** 5
munia **23** 11

nam (used elliptically) **15** 12, **38** 1
namque (position in sentence)
  4 8, **8** 8
nec (=*ne...quidem*) **15** 7
nedum **7** 2
nefastus **28** 8
Nepete **21** 4
neque (=*et non*) **1** 12
nervus **11** 8, **27** 8
nimius animi **11** 3
nisi (with abl. abs.) **35** 1, **37** 4
nobilis (=renowned) **14** 3
non modo...ne...quidem **20** 2,
  25 10, **34** 3
novus (=revolutionary) **11** 10
nullus **18** 8, **19** 7
numen **29** 2
numquid vis **34** 7

obequitare **13** 5
obnixus stabili gradu **12** 8
obnoxius **28** 7, **34** 3
obvertere **7** 3, **24** 7
occinere **41** 8
occipere **5** 7
opus est (constr. after) **12** 1
orator (=envoy) **1** 6

palam (predicate) **14** 11
  (preposition) **14** 5

parens **14** 5
parma **8** 6
patientia **26** 1
patres **11** 6, **41** 10
patricii auctores **42** 10
patronus **18** 14
pax (=favour) **1** 12, **12** 7, **41** 9
penates **14** 8
penetralia **41** 9
pensiones **35** 4
per aliquem stare quominus **33** 2
periclitari **15** 1
Petelinus lucus **20** 11
piaculum **21** 7
pilum **12** 8
pius **34** 8
plebi ⎫
plebis ⎬ **19** 4, 5
plebs (in Latin towns) **26** 5
Pomptinus ager **5** 2
pontifices **41** 9
popularis **17** 3
populi (=cities) **2** 2, **12** 4
Porsinna **40** 17
postquam (with imperf. ind.) **10** 4, **13** 3, **29** 3, **30** 7, **32** 1
postridiani dies **1** 12
postridie (constr. after) **1** 12
potius quam **15** 12, **28** 8, **36** 12
potuit (for *potuisset*) **11** 4
prae **40** 1
praecipitare **30** 4
praeda **13** 6, **31** 8
praelati (=*praeterlati*) **29** 3
Praeneste **21** 9
praeses publici consilii **6** 15
praestare **22** 9, **26** 6
praestigiae **15** 13
praeterquam quod **24** 7
praetor **42** 11
primus quisque **3** 2
princeps **1** 4, **2** 2
procellae **8** 7
prodicta die **20** 11
pro dictatore **38** 9
promittere barbam **16** 4
protinus **28** 2
provinciae (how assigned to magistrates) **22** 6
pte (suffix) **15** 12

pulli **41** 8

quaerere (judicial) **15** 4
quanquam (with subjunctive) **9** 6
quartarius **17** 5
-que (used adversatively) **4** 10, **16** 5
quicquam **14** 10
quin **7** 2, **15** 9, **28** 9
Quintilis **1** 12
quippe **6** 6, **31** 7
quisque (inserted in apposition) **13** 8, **15** 3, **25** 9
(unusual position of) **25** 9
quod (connective) **7** 2, **8** 2, **27** 8

rapere **23** 5
rationem habere **37** 4
recrudescere **18** 1
religiones **5** 6
religiosi dies **1** 11
repletus (with genitive) **25** 9
res (=money) **14** 5
res repetere **10** 6
reses **23** 5
restare **30** 5, **32** 7
restitare **7** 2
rex sacrificulus **41** 9
rogatio **35** 6
ruere **19** 6

Sabatina tribus **5** 8
sacramento adigere **32** 4, **38** 8
saginare **17** 3
Salii **41** 9
sata **31** 8
satin' salve **34** 8
Satricum **7** 1, **16** 6
sciscere **35** 7, **38** 9
scutum **8** 6
secretus **25** 1
seditio **33** 1
selibrae farris **17** 5
seminarium **12** 5
senatus (in Latin towns) **21** 8, **26** 1
senatus consultum **17** 6
sen. cons. ultimum **19** 3
senecta **8** 2
seniores **2** 6
Servilius Ahala **19** 2

servitia **12** 5
Setia **30** 9
Sextilis **1** 11, 12
si (with subj., expressing purpose)
  3 7, **22** 1
sicine **16** 2
sicubi **26** 6
signum (flag) **7** 5, **12** 7
    (trumpet) **7** 5, **13** 4
    (standard) **7** 3, **8** 1, 3,
    24 7
simul (=*simul ac*) **1** 6, **7** 6, **24** 1
sinus **15** 12
solitudo magistratuum **35** 10
sordidatus **20** 1
sors (=principal) **14** 7, **15** 10
spes (=expectation) **25** 5
Stellatina tribus **5** 8
subicere **24** 5
suboles **7** 1, **12** 4
subsidiarii **8** 4
succlamare **40** 10
summus honos **37** 5
suppeditare **24** 2
Sutrium **3** 2, **9** 4

tabula (votive) **29** 9
tabulae censoriae **27** 6
tacitus **12** 3
tandem **12** 3
Tarpeium saxum **20** 12
Tarquinii (place) **4** 8
    (=tyrannous) **40** 10
temere **13** 1
temperare **17** 8
tempus (=favourable opportunity)
  10 9, **23** 6

tendere (with inf.) **38** 7
togatus **25** 7
tormenta **9** 2
tribus **5** 8
tributum **14** 12, **31** 4, **32** 1
trifariam **2** 7
triumviri coloniae deducendae **21** 4
Tromentina tribus **5** 8
tumultuari **30** 8
tumultuarius **29** 4
turma **13** 4
Tusculum **21** 9, **26** 8

ubi (=*et ibi*) **25** 1, **32** 6
ullus **6** 6, **15** 10
unde (=*a quibus*) **10** 3
usu possideri **18** 10
ut fit **3** 5
utique **20** 1, **35** 5
uti rogas **38** 5
utrique **33** 2
utrum (omitted) **14** 11, **27** 8

vallum **2** 9, **8** 9
vapor **2** 11
-ve (=*-que*) **14** 10
Velitrae **12** 6, **36** 5
vestem mutare **16** 4
veto **35** 7, 9
viator **15** 2, **16** 2
videre (=περιορᾶν) **18** 8
vires (=*copiae*) **5** 5
virilis pars **11** 5
vitio creatus **1** 5, **27** 5, **38** 9
Volsci **2** 2, *Introd.* pp. xx, xxi
Volsinii **2** 2
Voltumna **2** 2